THE POLITICS OF RELIGION
IN NAPOLEONIC ITALY

The Politics of Religion in Napoleonic Italy explores the intense cultural conflict created by French rule in Italy at the start of the nineteenth century. Napoleon's desire for cultural conformity struck at the heart of Italian religious life. Yet the reforms imposed by French rule created resentment and resistance across Italy, finally leading to Napoleon's famous quarrel with Pope Pius VII.

In this fascinating study, Michael Broers traces the events leading up to the excommunication of Napoleon and the Pope's arrest and exile from Rome. In particular, attention is given to the impact these reforms had on the Italian masses and popular piety. Using previously neglected French and Italian archival sources, *The Politics of Religion in Napoleonic Italy* reveals how the alliance between Church and people grew in the face of alien, imperial rule. It exposes the vital role this union played in preventing Italy from being totally assimilated into the French empire.

Highlighting concepts of cultural imperialism more usually associated with the non-European world, this incisive piece of scholarship reveals much about the prejudices driving French imperial policy. *The Politics of Religion in Napoleonic Italy* will appeal to historians of modern France and Italy alike.

Michael Broers is Reader in the Department of History at the University of Aberdeen. He is the author of several books, including *Europe Under Napoleon, 1799–1815* (1996) and *Europe After Napoleon: Revolution, Reaction and Romanticism, 1814–1848* (1996).

THE POLITICS OF RELIGION IN NAPOLEONIC ITALY

The war against God, 1801–1814

Michael Broers

London and New York

First published 2002
by Routledge
11 New Fetter Lane, London EC4P 4EE

Simultaneously published in the USA and Canada
by Routledge
29 West 35th Street, New York, NY 10001

Routledge is an imprint of the Taylor & Francis Group

© 2002 Michael Broers

Typeset in Times by Taylor & Francis Books Ltd
Printed and bound in Great Britain by Biddles Ltd, Guildford and King's Lynn

British Library Cataloguing in Publication Data
A catalogue record for this book is available from the British Library

Library of Congress Cataloging in Publication Data
Broers, Michael.
The politics of religion in Napoleonic Italy : the war against God, 1801-1814 /
Michael Broers.
p. cm.
Includes bibliographical references and index.
1. Catholic Church–Italy–History–19th century. 2. Christianity and
politics–Italy–History–19th century. 3. Christianity and politics–Catholic
Church–History–19th century. 4. Italy–Church history–19th century.
5. Italy–Politics and government–1789-1815. I. Title
BX1545 .B76 2001
322'.1'094509034–21
2001041600

ISBN 0–415–26670–X

The eagle of empire cannot lie down with the lamb of God.
                                                    Nietzsche

CONTENTS

PREFACE

The eagle of empire and the lamb of God

All our books are personal to us, or we could not live with them. This book is no exception. I began thinking about it in 1983 and, whatever else I was involved with, it always stayed very close to me. Along the way, there was much encouragement and quite a lot of criticism, most of it constructive, some of it shocking in its incoherent displeasure, all of it revealing. For several very different reasons, I decided to stick to my guns and, for better and for worse, this is the result.

First, I felt that the simple idea behind the project was sound: The Catholic religion is a – arguably the – central cultural and social element in Italian life, and to tangle with it would be a considerable undertaking. The French did so, under Napoleon, introducing the wholesale changes of the Concordats. To my knowledge, there is no study of the period that examines this on a wide canvas or at the grassroots, so I began. It was encouraging to do so during a period when the issue of religion was at last finding its place in the history of the revolutionary period. The series of lectures given by Colin Lucas at Oxford in the early 1980s awakened me to much. The work of Donald Sutherland, Timothy Tackett, in particular and of T.C.W. Blanning beyond France, showed me what might be possible.[1] In the course of this research, there has been a flowering of fine literature, mainly by Anglo-Saxon scholars, on the mid-century Catholic revival, and this gave me an exciting historical context to which I could attempt to connect my own work on the earlier period.[2] This was also the moment when Edward Said's formulation of cultural imperialism started to make an impact, and I could see much in common with my own work.[3] There has been much hostility to this proposition but it still seems valid, if fraught with complications. If there could be cultural imperialism in one country, as foreshadowed in the works of Linda Colley and much earlier – and prophetically – in those of Eugene Weber,[4] then there was a fighting chance that it was also there in the largest, most heterogeneous empire the continent of Europe had known in modern times. I believe it was there, and that the concept is present in the archival sources *avant la lettre*. In the last stages of my work I was given timely encouragement that the concept has a place in the specific historiography of Italy by the appearance in 1998 of the volume of essays edited by Jane Schneider, *Italy's 'Southern Question'. Orientalism in One Country*.[5] It is probably an intellectual failing – nay, one of sheer lack of intelligence – that I am rooted in archival empiricism, but that approach does yield as much objectivity as can be expected in a post-modern world. The evidence came first, the interest in other frameworks came later.

There is a very odd, nervous view of Napoleonic Europe that pervades its study: Within France, it represents repression, the death of the dream; yet beyond its borders, it is a beacon of Enlightened reform in a sea of reaction. I do not dispute this, but I feel there are uncomfortable ramifications involved that must be faced. They involve a serious questioning of the character – but not necessarily the intrinsic worth – of the 'Enlightenment project'. I start from the opinion, derived from the words and deeds of his servants 'on the ground' – and from his own diktats – that Napoleon deserves to be seen as the last of the Enlightened absolutists, at least in the areas I have studied; this also admits a belief in the term 'Enlightened absolutist'. If no one else was an Enlightened absolutist – and I am not qualified to say – Napoleon was, at least in his Italian possessions. The struggle for reform here was marked and it meant confrontation with the culture embodied by the Tridentine Church. It was fundamental to the history of the Napoleonic period, and to the history of modern Italy, and it was a struggle Napoleon lost. He was neither the first nor the last to do so, but there is discomfort about bringing this to the centre of events. Should it be accorded such importance? Was the struggle not self-evident and so hardly worthy of detailed study? I do not think so and the stridency of those who told me 'We knew that anyway' made me all the more distrustful. There was a subject there if it made some people so upset. To delve into the war between the Church and the Napoleonic regimes reveals a bourgeoisie – and the term is valid, if broad – that was not entirely at ease with the new regime; a peasantry perhaps more politicized than might be comfortable to admit because it was not 'progressive' in character. To admit the power and presence of the Church in Italian society is one thing; to examine the well-springs of that power – to examine the proposition that it was all about power and superstition and find that it was not quite so – is rather different. It is important ground, however, and not to be ignored by the historian or anyone else. Beside the Enlightened reforms effected by the French was a trauma that went beyond the demands of conscription and bit deep into the life of many communities and individuals. Above all, the Church and the laity fought back, not once but many times and in many different ways. The Napoleonic response was brutal, thus raising the uncomforting spectacle of the harshness of the Enlightenment project. It was the work of a generation of men – for men they were – fed on Voltaire and Diderot, who often showed a surprising degree of 'dechristianization' for those so recently escaped from the *ancien régime*. They certainly regarded what they found in

Italy as different from their own perceptions and experience. I find it difficult to hide behind the conceit that the Enlightenment according to Voltaire
was not the Enlightenment according to Napoleon; I find it impossible to
believe that the Napoleonic empire was not the Enlightenment 'on horseback'. Above all – and this seems to be the most disconcerting point – the
Enlightenment had to be on horseback because it was embattled. Precious
few people wanted what it had to offer.

There is more to this, I think. To admit a veritable *Kulturkampf* between
the Napoleonic regime and the Tridentine Church, and to link it to comparable, if hardly identical, later struggles, casts the history of modern Europe
in a light most unflattering to liberal reformers of all stamps. These views
have been expressed in a German context and, much more guardedly, in that
of France. It is time to do so in the light of Italian evidence, too. Cultural
struggle – an internalized, inter-European model of cultural imperialism – is
a dark spectre, but it is real. I am struck by the thoughts of Allan Bloom in
that most controversial of books *The Closing of the American Mind*, when
he says, following Nietzsche,

> Cultures fight wars with one another. They must do so because
> values can only be asserted or posited by overcoming others, not by
> reasoning with them. Cultures have different *perceptions*, which
> determine what the world is. They cannot come to terms. There is
> no communication about the highest things.[6]

There is truth in this, and a great deal of truth in the context of modern
western Europe. To follow David Blackbourn, progress had to fight piety, at
least in Catholic Europe, not necessarily because piety opposed progress –
those who have studied the ramifications of Trent in subsequent centuries
have shown this is not inherently so – but because progress was so nakedly
aggressive and elitist. It had to fight all the harder because piety was the
stronger, more popular cause, not in terms of arms and tangible power, but
because it could draw on deep wells of belief and the loyalties that belief
created. Piety was part of the fabric of life, in ways progress could not hope
to be. Nietzsche, almost alone, saw this clearly, if from a loftier vantage
point than that of the archival historian, but he traced the limits of ratio-
nalism and above all admitted its battle with the soul in uncompromising
terms.

This was an epic struggle. Those who insist on the assured, relentless
march of reason – Marxist or not – do not do justice to the nature of the
beast, and discount the greatest crisis of the West. This is not an obvious
assertion, in the context of an archival monograph, and caution should
dictate that it offers only ammunition to those with finer, more abstract
minds than my own. I wrote it with Nietzsche – or, more correctly, with my
thoughts drawn from Nietzsche – close to heart. Napoleon was, indeed, all

that Goethe believed him to be, a breaker of worlds, but the gods he fought were not quite dead yet, the natural bonds between men not quite dissolved. Above all, for me the Christianity of the late *ancien régime*, with its admixture of an atavistic popular culture which spanned the social spectrum and the high culture of the Baroque, was the last manifestation of a genuinely European 'folk religion'; it was the spiritual manifestation of a society that predated 'the last man'. The struggle against Catholic culture – against barbarism, ignorance and superstition in their discourse – became a battle mythic for both sides which involved sacrifice and on which the fate of their world hung. It did not admit relativism, at least not for long. Those on both sides were aware of the hardening of the lines, at least in the early stage of the conflict that took place in Napoleonic Italy. Europe in the wake of the Enlightenment, in the face of the Enlightenment project, was no place for relativism.

More personally, it has been remarked with surprise at times along the way, that an Ulster Protestant should acquire such an interest as this. When the work, of its own accord, invoked Nietzsche, I found it hard to turn away. It seemed to me something fundamental in a wider context, however limited in its own parameters. I do not feel it odd, however. This was not an attempt to expiate 'post-colonial guilt', to atone for the sins of the fathers. My politics are my own and are shaped by my community, if not uniformly of it. There, really, is the deeper answer. Confessional allegiance aside, I was instinctively drawn to a struggle between sides who abandoned relativism in the face of deeper realities: that to defend cultural values, to preserve a social cement, you had to be 'fierce', in local parlance. It is not attractive, it is not to be admired, but it is real. It endures – and can imbue life with meaning – when relativism fails the individual and impoverishes the soul. The first, perhaps the only real point, is that nothing is easy, nor should it be made to seem so. It is the duty of a scholar – of anyone who thinks – to remember that. I did not need to have the bonds of lay confraternities or the importance of communal, collective rites spelled out for me. In some ways, I envy that closeness, those bonds and – if Nietzsche is right – the myths which inspire and bind. Their consequences can be – usually are – diabolical, to risk an all too apt reference. Yet they matter, especially in a society bereft of them, through which one wanders rather than walks. Bonds shape even the most recherché life. It was the lack of them in a previous post that drove me back to the archives and the friendship of Paris and points Italian over so many years. It was the comradeship and warmth of my new home, in Aberdeen, which at last gave me the will to write.

The scion of a police family – forbidden from following Rangers in the name of *la chose publique* and the dignity of the dark green uniform – I can also see the other side: Ignorance, bigotry, intolerance, plain hooliganism – be it inspired by a local saint on top of an Apennine mountain or William III in my own street – is part of this, and I brought it to the book. No one had to tell me about the tensions of summer processional seasons, or the jangling nerves around a police barracks at Easter time. Throughout, I found much to engage my own experience as I went along. My paternal grandmother was a visceral *républicaine et reformée* who had no trouble turning Unionist when transplanted to Ireland. She named her son and grandson after her hero, Clemenceau, and told me, at the age of five, disaster loomed if the Catholics were left in their ignorance. My maternal grandmother was a direct descendent of Richard Talbot. Setting my sights on other cultures has not led me away from much that is ingrained in me.

The interest in the power of Catholic faith – for that is the word – is not detached. To fail to admit that, would be a lie. In the course of my adult life, I have stood in deep respect of the example of a Catholic life, lived truly, imbued as it is with an unsentimental compassion, just as I wondered in my youth at the courage and dignity of my police family. Cora Flyn in my student days; Jim McMillan, a friend and mentor, who might be surprised to find himself acknowledged in this way, throughout my working life; Philippe and Claire Béchu in the course of the research, especially; John and Elaine Wickstrom in the final phases of the writing. They have all set living examples to one unschooled in such things. Theirs is a faith I cannot share. My temperament – probably for worse than better – shall always be with the eagle of empire and its restless, ruthless quest for Something Else, rather than with the inner peace of the lamb of God. That does not preclude respect and admiration.

This work began with Liz, long ago and far away, but the circumstances in which it was completed brought home that part of me will always belong to her. It ended with Sue, my wife, without whom there would be nothing, so much has she given me. With all its faults and failings – and amidst the clash of cultures – this book is an offering of love to her.

St Patrick's Day, 2001

ACKNOWLEDGEMENTS

The author wishes to thank the British Academy for two Small Grants in aid of research, which helped finance trips to Paris and Florence. Thanks are also due to the editors of *The Historian*, for permission to reproduce here, material previously published in 'The War Against God: Napoleon, Pope Pius VII and the People of Italy, 1800–1814,' *The Historian*, Spring 2001, pp. 16–21; to the editors of *War in History*, for permission to republish material in Chapters 2 and 3, from 'Noble Romans and Regenerated Citizens: The Morality of Conscription in Napoleonic Italy, 1800–1814,' *War in History*, 8 (2001) pp. 249–270. Chapters 2 and 3 also use material from my article 'Cultural Imperialism in a European Context? Political Culture and Cultural Politics in Napoleonic Italy,' *Past & Present*, 170 (2001) pp. 152–180, and is reprinted with kind permission (World Copyright: The Past and Present Society, 175 Banbury Road, Oxford, England.) Luciana O'Flaherty first signed this book for UCL Press, thanks to the support of an anonymous reader, and at Routledge Vicky Peters has been an excellent and supportive editor throughout. Very special thanks are owed to the directors of the Scotland–GLCA Programme, who granted me a six-week Fellowship, free of all teaching obligations, in 2001. This enabled me to finish the book and to revisit my old colleagues at that paradigm of all that is excellent in a liberal arts college: Kalamazoo College. My former colleagues and many new friends made me more than welcome. Warm thanks are owed to the staffs of the Archivi di Stato of Turin, Cuneo, Genoa, Bologna, Parma and especially Florence, where many vital sources were uncatalogued and located thanks only to their expertise. The staff of the Archivio Comunale of Genoa were outstanding. The Archives Nationales de Paris yielded their riches thanks to my friends and colleagues Gérard Hérmisse, Philippe and Claire Béchu, Pierre Portet, Jacky Plaut, Eric Dufour and many more now retired. M. and Mme Charles Bonis lubricated the wheels of work in Paris for many years, while M. Fleury and Mme Auffray of the Institut de la Francophonie often provided *soigné* shelter. The research seminars of the Universities of York, Strathclyde, Ann Arbor, Aberdeen, Reading and St Andrews all heard earlier versions of this work, as did the Society for Eighteenth-Century

Studies in Bordeaux (1994) and the Western Society for French History (1991). My lasting thanks go to Allan Macinnes, who delivered me from evil and into the warm, vibrant department at Aberdeen he had done so much to shape. To Jean-Michel Chevet, Jim McMillan, Anthony Wright, Colin Lucas, Lucy Riall, Michael Biddiss, Robin Evans, Alan Dabbs, Sue Broers and – the first of all – Liz Butler, thanks just for listening! Finally, our 'Scots Grey' tabby cat, Onic, often sat with me as I wrote. He fell on Waterloo Day, 2001, and is much missed.

1

THE LAST BARBARIAN
INVASION?

There are four great constants in the conflict between the Napoleonic empire and the Catholic Church during the *epoca francese*: the two protagonists in the struggle were the political forces of the Napoleonic regime and the post-Tridentine Church; the geography, both physical and human, in which they struggled was composed of the centre and periphery of the states of the Italian *ancien régime*, which the Napoleonic empire overthrew and annexed, and over which the Church had exerted a powerful influence. The next chapter seeks to analyse the role of geography as applied to the conflict between Church and state; the present chapter attempts to outline the characters of the protagonists in that conflict.

Most of the Napoleonic reforms centred on the introduction of the French Concordat of 1802 into the *départements réunis*, and the creation and enforcement of a parallel Concordat for the Kingdom of Italy. The Kingdom of Naples does not enter into this study, largely because its religious affairs were handled differently by Joseph and Murat, and also because the Church in the Mezzogiorno was organized in a very different way from the modes prevailing in the north and centre.[1] At a more structural level, Mario Rosa has remarked that, in comparison with northern Italy, 'in the south, a more tragic and dark picture [emerges], so that we can properly speak of two Italies'. Spiritual belief in the Mezzogiorno is generally agreed to have been markedly more a-Christian – perhaps neo-pagan, a 'natural religion' – than the popularized forms of essentially orthodox piety found in the north and centre.[2] Therefore it was in the north and centre that the reforms of Trent had made their most sustained impact on Italian society from the mid-sixteenth century onwards. Here too, subsequently, French rule was most effective, and so reached down to the grassroots of the village and into the periphery with most force. However incomplete its application or brief its duration in the *départements réunis* and the Kingdom of Italy, the power of the Napoleonic state was such in these areas that its intentions were felt throughout its domains, which was never quite the case in the Mezzogiorno.[3] The north and centre were the core of French hegemony and, therefore, of the struggle.

1

When the French pushed over the Alps in the course of the revolutionary wars, they found waiting for them in Italy a Church whose presence and influence were more pervasive and significant in the lives of most of their new *administrés* than the secular states of the *ancien régime*. The conflict was between the greatest source of authority and influence in the old order – and the only such institution common to all the states of Italy – and the most powerful political entity the peninsula had known since the Roman empire itself.

The motives of French rule in Italy

When Napoleon led his ragged troops over the Alps for the first time in 1796, he told the peoples of the lands he was entering that he had come to liberate them from oppression, to bring liberty and the ideals of revolutionary fraternity. He told his troops that they were entering the richest plains in the world, that they would be well fed on their produce, that they would all soon be rich with the pickings of the material civilization of the great cities of northern Italy. From the very outset, the French occupation of Italy had two faces. What drew the French? Was it the torch of civilization and revolutionary fraternity, or the spoils of war? Did they wish to help or exploit those they came to rule south of the Alps?

In material terms, the French exploited their Italian territories from beginning to end. Conscripts were wrung from the mountain valleys and the cities and hamlets of the plains, to the point where regions such as Piedmont and Lombardy became better sources of recruits – however unwillingly they came forth – than many parts of France.[4] When Italians rebelled against this, the French replied with fire and sword, as in 1806 in the Piacentino – the mountain region between Liguria and the Po valley – or in 1809 in central and north-eastern Italy. 'Burn a village', was Napoleon's own answer to one of the earliest manifestations of this.[5] The extension of the Continental System to the Italian territories of the empire and the Kingdom of Italy was an ill-concealed policy of economic imperialism that made of Italy a mere supplier of raw materials to France.[6] The disillusionment of the Italian Jacobins with the authoritarian – as much as the exploitative – nature of Napoleonic rule soured into a combination of sullen withdrawal, reluctant collaboration from fear of popular reprisals and, finally, clandestine anti-French conspiracy. In many cases, their most ideologically motivated supporters at the outset of the occupation were among those most bitterly disenchanted by the end. Carlo Botta, the disaffected Piedmontese revolutionary, at several points in his *Storia d'Italia* and his longer history of the Western world described Napoleon's Italian campaigns as the last in a long line of barbarian invasions.[7]

Exploitation and political betrayal were the most obvious negative aspects of Napoleonic rule in Italy, although it has been argued often and at length that they contained within them the germs of modernity. The French brought an unprecedented degree of political unity to the peninsula; by 1809 it divided into the mainland Kingdom of Naples, the Kingdom of Italy in the north-east and centre-east, and the imperial departments – the *départements réunis* – in the north-west and centre-west. In the two latter polities, French institutions, French administrative practices and the introduction of French property laws are widely credited with the general advancement of the society and economy of the areas they penetrated most deeply.[8] The French certainly introduced higher standards of policing and law and order than had existed anywhere in the peninsula hitherto, and they did this most effectively in the Kingdom of Italy and the *départements réunis*.[9] It is not the intention of the present study to deny the positive and effective impact of French rule on Italy, which I have written about myself. Rather the present purpose is to go deeper than these essentially functional aspects of Napoleonic rule.

There was a highly subjective element to the imperial experience in Italy for both the rulers and the ruled. Italian resentment was not confined to the more explicit, material or strictly political forms of exploitation or repression. There is much in what follows to argue that these resentments actually intensified in those cases where the French most wanted to avoid exploiting their *administrés* and begin providing Italians with what they regarded as the benefits of French civilization and culture. The politics of religion in Napoleonic Italy turns, in essence, on the hostile reception Italians gave to these initiatives; they proved among the most detested changes they endured in the *epoca francese*. The intensity of the trauma endured, too, and the determined opposition the religious reforms provoked, gives a clear indication as to how different were the cultures of rulers and ruled. They are a reminder that concepts of 'the other' and of cultural imperialism, although fraught with complexities, have a place in a purely European context and are not the preserve of relations between Europe and the extra-European world.

When the Napoleonic regime made its peace with the Catholic Church with the French Concordat, it did so largely on its own terms and to suit the needs of France itself. These needs have been aptly defined as:

> not primarily a return to Tridentine Catholicism with its hierarchy, doctrines, catechism and confessional, but a religion concerned with parish life, centred on church services and the familiar rituals of baptism, marriage and burial.[10]

This was not the case in Italy, but it was the core of a Concordat that co-opted the Church into the Napoleonic state, rather than admitting it as a real partner in social control. Jansenist and Richerist[11] ideals had made a real impact on those elements of the French Church that Napoleon came most to trust. The real genius of the Napoleonic Church, however, was to absorb a great deal of Jansenism as it was practised in the parishes, while divesting it of those politicized elements that led it into defiance of authority. Whether or not Olwen Hufton's definition of the emergent *Tiers Partie Catholique* is correct in the context of the late *ancien régime*, it corresponds well to the ethos of the Church of the Concordat at the level of the episcopate and the Ministry of Religion. For Hufton, the *Tiers Partie* meant

> those who found a Jansenist approach to the conduct of life and worship totally desirable but who refused to embroil themselves in the theological pros and cons of *Unigenitus* and hence to erect the issue into a political conflict.[12]

This was perfect. The efforts of bishops, particularly in the Midi, to 'strengthen and reform Catholic practice very much along the puritanical lines of the Jansenists ... to place Catholicism beyond reproach'[13] were reprised after the upheavals of the revolutionary decade, but loyalty to the authority of the state was axiomatic. The style of official French Catholicism was set, however: practising Jansenism under the secular eye of Enlightened scepticism. Men of the Enlightenment were comfortable with an established Church of this kind, even if they were hardly enamoured of it. If religion there had to be, it should be an austere, rigorous, elitist religion, in keeping with the intellectual traditions of the French elite. The Counter Reformation had arrived later than elsewhere, according to Chartier, and became imbued with a severe native Augustinianism, even beyond Jansenist circles.[14] This was the kind of Church favoured and fostered by the *idéologues* who were so influential in the first years of the regime, typified by Antoine Roederer, a prominent Napoleonic imperial official in Italy and Germany, whose son became a prefect of one of the *départements réunis*. Privately a sceptic, he told his colleague Beugnot that 'the people have no other need of religion, than as a source of morality'. Roederer was one of many 'peaceable anti-clericals' in the regime, prepared to work with the French episcopate to restore social stability, and to appease them, better to gain their help for the secular authorities.[15] The French saw in this sort of Church an instrument of a very French form of civilization: rational, moderate, well ordered, but still independent minded. It was an extension of a cultural and political confidence that informed every aspect of Napoleonic imperialism. The Gallican Church was subordinate to the imperial cause and to the regime that guided it.

This was what the French then sought to impose on Italy and, when they did so, the Concordat found itself trying to take root in very different soil. It is not possible here to explore how correct Chartier, following Tocqueville, might be in his assertion that 'eighteenth-century France underwent a process of abandonment of Christian practices unequalled in Europe'.[16] However, there is much in the reactions of French officials to Italian piety to

support it, not least their seeming ignorance of many of the rites and practices of the Counter Reformation, such as the Forty Hours. Whether the
French masses were as estranged from the Church as Chartier and others
have suggested is not the central theme here. The Napoleonic occupation
fostered a meeting between members of the French elite and Italian society.
It would expose just how estranged that elite was from the Counter
Reformation as it had evolved in northern and central Italy. The encounter
also revealed how different had been the development of the Counter
Reformation in the French and the Italian Churches. By the time of the
Napoleonic conquest of Italy,

> the Revolution, through its declared hostility toward the old reli-
> gion, revealed to all eyes the reality of a transformation in belief
> that had already occurred.[17]

The application of the Concordat in Italy revealed it even more.

The Italian Church had suffered none of the privations of its French
counterpart. Its monastic lands had been pillaged by the Army of Italy, but
not until the reconquest of 1800 was there any question of their wholesale
confiscation; the regular orders were still flourishing, if not quite on the
scale of the seventeenth century, in contrast to their steady decline in
France. However tenuous clerical control over the laity might be, nothing on
the scale of the dislocation of parish life that affected France in the 1790s
occurred south of the Alps. Perhaps more significantly, there was very little
trace in Italian society of the dechristianization some have seen as all pervasive among the French laity and all admit was a powerful presence, however
regionally qualified.[18] The French were not the Godless horde of counter-
revolutionary propaganda – although they did, indeed, have a Godless
element among them – but they were an alien, heretical horde. Thus the
application of the Concordat would appear less the selective, largely appropriate restoration that it seemed to be in France, than an aggression. It
emerged for many Italians as, probably, the most barbaric aspect of the last
barbarian invasion.

The position of the Tridentine Church

If French intentions for their Italian *administrés* were Janus-like, the Italian
Church itself was hardly a monolith. In the context of the post-Napoleonic
Church in the Rhineland, Jonathan Sperber has outlined an institution 'at
war on two fronts', as it were, caught between the threats to its orthodoxy
posed by the 'externally originated secularization' of Enlightened officialdom – followed by the French – and the 'inherent laicization' embodied
in traditional popular piety.[19] The Italian Church of the late *ancien régime*
faced a not dissimilar threat. If that of 'externally originated secularization'

was less sustained than in France or much of Germany, it was still a raw wound after the traumatic confrontations between the Church and the reformers of the Bourbon and Habsburg states in the 1760s.[20] Yet, over the course of the century, the Church may still have been moving closer to this view of the need for reform, even if its position could hardly be described as one of 'liberal' or even reforming Catholicism, as Owen Chadwick puts it.[21] The struggle against popular religion was part of a truly *longue durée* and it absorbed the lion's share of ecclesiastical energies throughout the early modern period. This challenge, more than any other, revealed the Church as anything but uniform. How best to curb popular religion divided Jansenists from Jesuits, the epsicopate from the itinerant orders, the priests from the people, more clearly than most other issues. Attitudes to the style and tactics of missionary activity, particularly, betokened wider, deeper religious divisions among the clergy.[22]

At the heart of the history of religion in the politics of Napoleonic Italy lies the central sea-change in the attitude of the Church to its two major adversaries. The result of the conflict with the Napoleonic regime reversed the tentative, complex rapprochement between the Church and 'externally originated secularization'. Instead it made its peace with popular piety, to an extent unthinkable in the previous century. Thus 'inherent laicization' not only ceased to be perceived as a threat, but was no longer perceived as a process of laicization. It was transformed into a source of strength that had to be mobilized in crisis and deferred to, even imitated, in the darkest hours of Napoleon's persecution of the Curia. The Church emerged much changed from the struggle, less complex, perhaps, but still a strong influence in Italian society, battered but not dislodged by the Napoleonic onslaught. This is the story of a Napoleonic defeat to rival that of 1812 in Russia, or indeed Waterloo, of a magnitude only enhanced by its bloodless nature.

2

CENTRE AND PERIPHERY
The power and limits of a concept

The concept of states with clearly defined centres of political and economic power and cultural pre-eminence has proved remarkably apt for the study of the *ancien régime* in Italy.[1] In the wider context of modern and early modern Italian history, the acceptance of this concept by scholars has relocated the historical geography of the peninsula away from a tendency to search for the present north/south divide in earlier periods, and made central Assante's observation that 'every province had its "South"'.[2] The distinctiveness between the urban and lowland centres of every Italian region from the Alpine and, even more, the Apennine uplands formed the fundamental internal divisions of all the states of Hesperia in the north and centre, as well as in the Kingdom of Naples. This represents the most useful framework for Italian historical geography, at least before the mid-nineteenth century.

The topography of most of the states of the north and centre that concern this study, fit this pattern securely. Turin, Genoa, Milan, Parma, Modena and Florence – the capitals of the old states – together with their subordinate regional centres like Piacenza, Siena or Brescia, were all lowland or coastal cities, surrounded by mountain valleys which were clearly their peripheries. Chris Wickham, writing of the early middle ages in Tuscany and the Abruzzi, has concluded that 'no "Apennine society" may ever have existed … but a matrix of social tendencies characteristic of the Apennines … can be delineated'.[3] Although the detailed circumstances of the Apennine spine and the states along it had obviously altered greatly over the intervening millennium, the general point is still valid for eighteenth-century Italy. Apennine valleys differed markedly from each other, but they were all a clear periphery in relation to the urban centres. Topography corresponded well to political geography under the old regime: each state had a clear centre, an obvious capital, and none of them were located in the highlands of the Alpine or Apennine peripheries. By the eighteenth century, political, social and cultural authority of all kinds – secular and sacred – was based at the centre, and the centre was urban and lowland.

Centre and periphery remained distinct entities in *ancien régime* Italy, however. Italian states were heterogeneous because, although the centre possessed authority over the periphery, it could seldom translate it into territorial power or control on any permanent basis. Nor, in some cases, did it actually wish to do so. As Osvaldo Raggio has pointed out in a Ligurian context, it is misleading to predicate early modern Italian history on the study of the growth of the state and its organs, for not only did the state often fail to subjugate the periphery, there were many cases – Genoa among them – where it was not within the nature of the political culture of the centre to try. To concentrate on the advance of the centre in these circumstances produces 'only a partial and deformed image of the creation and transmission of legitimate public authority'.[4] Centre and periphery remained distinct and separate in terms of formal authority; the links between them were forged through economic interdependence, by ties of patronage and clientage, rather than through formal administrative structures. Indeed, a millennium later there was still truth in Wickham's observation that:

> The self-identity of the mountains and the political, social, economic and cultural influence of the cities must be recognized as coexisting, at every stage in history … in opposition to each other … . Not only can one not understand the mountains without recognizing the influence of the city, but one cannot understand the history of any … city without seeing it against the background of the mountains.[5]

It is just that these influences did not work through channels that are conventional in terms of the modern state. It is equally mistaken to regard the periphery as static, devoid of political life, although that life took forms that seldom corresponded to the institutionally based public life of the centre. The periphery was far from an immobile world, its outward stability the product of intense and incessant action among communities and clan networks, as Giovanni Tocci rightly stresses.[6] This internal dynamism was, however, just that – internal – and did not affect the life of the centre any more than the centre, by and large, sought to affect it.

The picture emerging from most recent research reveals states which functioned by arbitration coupled with occasional direct intervention on the periphery, but also centres and peripheries in constant, complex contact with each other. Put another way, the mountains were isolated only from the constituted authorities of the centre; the periphery was, indeed, a physical, topographical reality, but it was also a specifically political reality, and few secular authorities challenged this for long. It was a question of *de facto* independence, not isolation.

Nevertheless, the centre was the centre when the life of the Italian states is fixed in the currents of European history conventionally regarded as mainstream. Within their own confines, the centres of the Italian states subdivided into the urban centres and the rural lowlands around them. There was a marked town/country divide at the centre, but in the lowlands it was a case of direct, effective control of the plains by the city. The lowlands shared little in urban culture. Village life contrasted sharply with an urban populace linked by guilds, wealthy confraternities and the long talons of official patronage networks, but the plain had none of the political autonomy of the true highland periphery.

Political life at the centre revolved around the patronage of the courts, as well as that of individuals or families, and was usually beyond the reach of the micro-elites of the periphery. The centres of justice, ecclesiastical and secular, lay here, as did the institutions of the state. Elite culture – high culture – was essentially urban culture.[7] Whereas the mountains were full of small, poor bishoprics, in the states of the centre and the north the great sees were, in the purest sense, metropolitan. In the Piacentino and Liguria, the valleys were bereft of bishoprics altogether; their priests looked to Piacenza or Parma, to the north and east of the Apennines, or to the coastal cities on the southern and western side of the mountains. What forces of order the states of the *ancien régime* possessed were overwhelmingly concentrated in the cities. Corsican soldiers went out from Genoa to the valleys of the Ligurian periphery, and then only, as a rule, when requested by local factions or officials.[8] The Republic of San Giorgio also concentrated its *sbirri* in the capital, sprinkling only a handful of isolated individuals across the valleys, which made of them more a spy network than a police force. In the Duchies of Parma and Piacenza, and in Tuscany, a similar pattern prevailed. Even in the territories of the House of Savoy policing rested only with the army, based in the provincial capitals, from which it went out when ordered. In contrast to this, the cities of northern and central Italy abounded with urban police forces, official and semi-official. Above all, the cities were the repositories of the greatest arm of social control available to these weak states: the *annone*, the public grain stores provisioned by the municipalities of the great cities and the state, itself, an exercise made possible by the control exercised by the urban over the rural centre. The cities, too, were the major centres of the wealth, and thus the charity, of the Church. In times of crisis, the city was both a magnet that attracted the desperate of the periphery and a bastion to be defended against this influx. Whether through tight, effective controls on entry and residence,[9] or by stout resistance to siege, the centre – urban and rural – could still see the periphery as a source of dark, barbarous violence, directed at its wealth and prosperity. Alongside the very real ties of clientage and economic interest were also atavistic suspicions and dread. The economic crisis triggered by the first French invasion unleashed just such forces over much of northern Italy between 1796 and 1799.[10] A further reminder of the very real, potent animosity between town and country came during the peasant revolts of

1809 across central and north-eastern Italy, when most of the great cities rallied to – and around – the French for support in the face of huge, if unco-ordinated, assaults on the lowlands by peasants from the Alpine and Apennine valleys. The national guards of Bologna, Padua and Vicenza – cities hardly known for their love of the French – all stood firm against the rebels.[11] The same climate of suspicion prevailed in the cities of the Veneto and in Milan, at the height of revolutions of 1848–9 when the embattled urban rebels refused all cooperation with a like-minded peasantry in the struggle against the Austrians.[12] The volatile but complex relationship between centre and periphery was always tangible, and it survived Napoleonic rule as well as pre-dating it.

The framework of centre and periphery sets the states and societies of the Italian *ancien régime* in their essential context. It is the basic fact of life about northern and central Italy that must be acknowledged from the outset, if their historical experience prior to, during and after the Napoleonic occupation is to be understood. Its salient presence is also an admission that the concentration on religious issues cannot be taken as an attempt to analyse the impact of Napoleonic rule in Italy in its entirety. Giovanni Tocci's judgement that the study of local factionalism and clien-tage – of the *comunità* – is the key to the periphery, is in no way negated by a study which places religion at its centre.[13] Clientage is equally central to the urban history of the late *ancien régime*, as are the wider concepts of associa-tion and *sociabilità*, although the part played by the Catholic Reformation in shaping elite mores and channelling popular association has increasingly come to be regarded as very central to the evolution of urban life and culture in those centres which have been studied most recently.[14] It must be stressed that the religious issues raised by the imposition of the Concordats and other Napoleonic reforms are part of the history of the *comunità* on the periphery; they are a segment of a wider whole, although it is equally the case that the religious element is central to that whole. At the centre, too, the issues surrounding religion were but one part of the deeply pervasive impact of Napoleonic rule, and a study centred on them cannot embrace the economic and financial reforms which possibly offset the unpopular measures examined here.[15] The impact of Napoleonic rule on the *comunità* and on urban patterns of clientage and patronage will, it is hoped, form the basis of a future study. The task in hand is confined to a particular set of issues but, it is contested, the politics of religion as they unravelled at local level, on the centre and at the periphery, are as important to the history of Napoleonic Italy as they are neglected by historiography.

The framework of centre and periphery, as a pragmatic approach to the governance of northern and central Italy, was accepted, if never quite formulated in such modern discourse, by both the Tridentine Church and the Napoleonic regimes in Paris and Milan. It was their point of departure and the concept translated well, particularly where the material condition of the Church was concerned. The wealth – or lack of it – as well as the personnel and administration of the Italian Church were all fundamentally conditioned by the importance of centre and periphery to Italian life.

However, as will emerge, a singular – and significant – aspect of any attempt to analyse the impact of Napoleonic rule on Italian piety is where it breaks down. The pressures put upon Italian Catholicism by the Napoleonic reforms reveal many continuities between the piety of the periphery and that of the centre. Perhaps most significant of all, the experience of the *epoca francese* provoked a coming together of the hierarchy and the urban masses through the new found readiness of the former to adopt many aspects of 'peripheral' piety, and to promote them in an urban context in ways and to a degree unlikely under the *ancien régime*. The impact of the French reforms revealed Trent in a light very different from that of a rigid, centrally driven attempt to standardize Italian religious life, although in earlier periods it had certainly been that. Rather, when confronted by the enormity and unpalatability of the Napoleonic reforms, the heirs of Trent proved themselves very malleable and able to compromise with other elements of the complex, varied matrix of Italian Catholicism. Compared to the Gallican Church imported over the Alps, the heirs of Trent emerged as ready to be tamed by the laity as to try to tame it. This would emerge in the course of the imposition of the Napoleonic reforms, however, not at the outset of French rule.

That Italy was divided into a centre and a periphery was received wisdom: the French received it from the Church and found the experience of Trent compatible with their own, in this respect, despite the very different imperatives from which Trent and the French worked. It was where they both started from. This is important in itself. The Tridentine Church and the Napoleonic regimes did not conform in their aspirations or their methods with those of the *ancien régime*. The insights of Tocci, Raggio and other scholars of the secular old order cannot be applied to either of these powerful presences in Italian history, for neither contented itself with a non-institutional, indirect presence on the periphery, or with any form of oblique arbitration at the centre. That is, neither were content with influence rather than authority; neither accepted the desirability of a sporadic, as opposed to permanent, presence on the periphery; neither would accept anything but a monopoly of power in their respective spheres. This was how each, in turn, approached its self-appointed task in Italy.

The periphery: First impressions. From 'nuestras Indías' to 'a thousand Vendées'

The forces of the Catholic Reformation, and the Jesuits in particular, 'discovered' the lost Europe of the Italian periphery in the mid-sixteenth century. So awestruck were they by the levels not only of basic doctrinal ignorance, but also of general isolation, violence and social indiscipline, that they instinctively turned to missionary activity. The missionaries did not perceive a purely religious problem, in the strict sense; these regions were usually too isolated to be threatened by the Reformation. If the Jesuits interpreted the roots and the likely cure for the vendetta culture of the periphery to be spiritual in nature, they were also attempting to fill the void in social control left by the political culture of the *ancien régime*. They found the best way to tackle these regions, mainly in the islands and the Apennine valleys, was to deploy the tactics they had developed for the populations of the New World and the Far East. The Italian peripheries were soon dubbed 'nuestras Indías' – 'our Indies' – and the missionaries themselves were schooled to look at these regions 'through foreign eyes'. It was not difficult.[16] None would have challenged Gramsci's assertion that the Catholic faith was developed and systematized by an intellectual elite, and that it was meant to acculturate and tame those forms of 'popular religion'[17] that were orthodox in origin, but which the laity had adapted too readily to their secular culture. They were still tolerated and even encouraged by the Church, for their exuberance was to be curbed rather than extinguished. It was also meant to stamp out what has been termed 'natural religion', something quite distinct which embraced a matrix of non-Christian customs and practices 'heavily tinged with superstition and sometimes wholly foreign to religion'.[18] It was a distinction the Counter Reformation found easier to make than the French, and this doctrinal clarity was the key to their adaptable, sophisticated approach to the civilizing of the periphery. They knew where 'magic' ended and 'religion' began, however overlaid by folkloric practice popular religion might be. The Tridentine missionaries sought to redeem and purify existing customs, if they were essentially orthodox, as well as to introduce new ones of their own.[19] Behind the external exaltations of the Baroque, there was a subtlety utterly lacking in later, state-inspired projects to regenerate the peripheries.

Nevertheless, however 'accommodating' or 'gradualist' the tactics of the missionaries or the urban Church hierarchies, those involved never doubted that their mission went far beyond inculcating the doctrines of the faith in these regions. The Catholic reformers, the Jesuits in particular, well understood the difference between 'popular' as opposed to 'popularized' piety, as well as the wider distinction between 'popular' and 'natural' religion.[20] This was a concerted drive by the missionary orders and by the secular hierarchy through its seminary-trained parish clergy to change the culture and social mores of the peripheries, in ways and through a level of social control unthought of by the political authorities of the *ancien régime* states. It was a question of public order based on disciplined personal morality, but it was not imposed by the institutions of a secular state; it did not rest on force, at least in the first instance. When this is remembered, the success of Trent, however qualified over time, is remarkable. Much of that strength lay, indeed, in that very capacity to let itself be qualified. The Church learnt to discern carefully between what it itself defined as superstition and those extraordinary aspects of devotion that fell outside the fixed patterns of the liturgy and the festivals of the official calendar, such as pilgrimages and personal enthusiasms for particular cults or miracles. It accepted that its preferred Christocentric devotions were not as popular as those surrounding the Virgin or local saints, and that many aspects of archaic piety were expertly preserved and integrated into official celebrations. In return it saw Easter confession and communion become virtually universal even in the remotest parts of the periphery, while the Rosary, the Forty Hours and the litanies that went with them became absorbed into popular practice. The continued efforts of missionaries throughout the eighteenth century, as well as the persistence of truly popular piety, are the clearest evidence that no one believed the process was complete. Yet alongside the perseverance of the post-Tridentine Church was its ability to accept that its own initiatives had themselves been tamed by the communal structures of the periphery. Experience had taught the clergy the complexities of mountain society. The experience of the evangelical onslaught of Trent had revealed in those same communities a capacity for cultural and religious adaptation under the outward cloak of that 'sense of immemoriality that one can persuade oneself to feel when looking at a technologically "backward" society in the Mediterranean', as Chris Wickham has observed.[21] It is as spurious in the context of religiosity as it is in that of the rural economy.

In terms of the permanent relevance of the periphery as a concept for contemporaries, successive generations of clerics felt it was a problem that did not go away. There was no permanent cure for the masses of the periphery, only constant, increasingly regular and structured vigilance and exhortation. Seen another way, the periphery – and also many parts of the rural centre – also proved Gramsci right when he discerned in 'popular religion' not just conservative or reactionary 'fossilized relics' of traditional custom, but also

> a series of often creative innovations, arising spontaneously from actual, changing conditions which were opposed to, or merely different from, the morality of the ruling classes.[22]

These differences became more obvious in the course of the seventeenth and eighteenth centuries as the mores of Trent acquired a more pervasive grip on the urban centre.

Thus there was a great deal about the periphery that the French found unchanged when they came to rule it as the Napoleonic empire expanded. Equally there was a great deal in what had been changed by Trent that they failed to understand or to accept as change for the better. In essence, the French found societies they – and the Church, for that matter – considered still to be violent, backward and superstitious. Like Trent, they saw spiritual backwardness as part of the problem. However, they also came to regard much of the work and the preferred methods of the Tridentine Church as contributing factors to the problem of the periphery, rather than as palliatives or progression. The Church could be blamed directly for many aspects of the perceived savagery of the highlands, particularly for its complicity in the great revolts of 1799. This formed, after all, the first and seminal experience of the periphery for the future imperial rulers of Italy, and it was not something they could afford to put behind them. Whatever role the clergy did or did not have in the 'great Vendée' of 1799, these revolts proved to the French, beyond contradiction, that the Italian peripheries were dangerous. Whether inspired or condemned by their clergy, the highland communities had displayed a capacity for collective violence on a widespread if localized scale.[23] If Trent had sought to create a passive, non-violent society – and what the French found at the centre predisposed them to think so – then it had failed.

During the longer period of occupation after 1800, French impressions simply reflect a belief that, if its goal was to civilize the periphery, the work of Trent had sunk without trace. The barbarism of rural life was driven home to Paris again and again by those on the ground. They perceived a society largely unchanged since the Middle Ages, pricked by the Renaissance and the Counter Reformation only in a few urban centres like Siena. Beyond that lay an inferno. The prefect of Ombronne, the Tuscan department that was virtually synonymous with the old state of Siena, did not place the blame for the general 'current depraved state of morality' on the clergy of either the city or the countryside, nor did he believe that they were worse now than in the past.[24] The problem had much deeper roots:

> You would have to go back to the very distant past to find the cause
> of the depraved state of Tuscan morals, for Boccaccio in his tales,
> and the historians who have written after him, have given us most
> assuredly unflattering impressions.[25]

Other French officials were less discerning in their search for the source of the illness, but they were just as disparaging. In the autumn of 1812, Norvins, the Director-General of Police for the Roman departments undertook a tour on horseback of both departments which lasted three months. His verdicts were damning, not just of local politics but of the deeper cultural roots he believed they stemmed from. On finding orphanages full of illegitimate children in Civitavecchia, he exploded to his superiors in Paris:

> The corruption of morality is the same in all Italian towns, and
> especially in those of the ex-Roman states. Society is in a perpetual
> state of scandal, and only time can change that. It is easy enough to

establish these moral excesses by [counting] the number of children left at the hospital.[26]

More detailed, personalized instances of this kind of behaviour reached the French all the time from the periphery. Francesco Assereto, the son of a notary and municipal secretary of the commune of Uscio in the Apennines near Genoa, was obviously a man that Trent could not tame. Like his father, Francesco was judged a violent character by the local authorities. A police report described his conduct thus:

> he picks quarrels, he disturbs the peace of families by bringing dishonour and shame among them, by ruining young, inexperienced girls. This young man, devoid of morality, takes pleasure in insulting the mayor, the priest and the Gendarmerie, who all want him exiled.[27]

Although married, he had chased his wife from the house and installed two young girls in her place. It is true that the parish priest was among the loudest voices to demand his exile. The wider point was, however, that cases of this kind convinced the French of the continued existence of 'nuestras Indías' and that more was needed to civilize them than the Church had to offer.

If the towns provided the sex, the countryside offered the violence. In the hill town of Frossione, Norvins seemed to have found his vision of hell:

> The inhabitants of the towns and the countryside look like savages …. . There is no trace of civilization in these small towns perched on the slopes of the Apennines. The Popes called this district their Tartary … . This savage spirit prevails even in the wealthiest landed families … I intend to fight the brigandage of the mountains and the barbarity of the towns.[28]

If Trent had done no harm on the periphery – and given the prominent role of the clergy in the revolts of 1799 this was not easy to assume – it had certainly left no appreciable trace of what good it had sought to do. Nevertheless, Norvins' vow to regenerate and civilize the Roman periphery resembles earlier Jesuit reactions enough to be remarked upon. Unlike the political authorities of the *ancien régime* – and the Papal government behaved no differently from lay states in this respect – neither the Tridentine clergy nor the agents of French imperial rule were prepared to ignore the 'civilizing mission'. Their targets were the same.

The flood of denunciations and reports of violence on the periphery that reached the new French rulers from every corner did little to convince them that the work of the missionaries or the other efforts of Trent had brought 'peace to the souls' of the communities of the periphery. Neither confession and communion at Easter, nor the ritual reconciliation of estranged neighbours at the foot of the mission cross, were reflected in the dossiers of the French police. What shocked them were their unsolicited origins. Lagarde, the French Director-General of Police in Florence, told Paris clearly that:

> I have little liking for lightly taken measures and information coming from one sole source, for this channel is usually wrong, especially in Italy, which is a country of timorous, but also hateful passions. I never take severe measures without making enquiries on several different sides and ... I regard the municipal authorities as essentially partial, especially in the smaller places.[29]

The violent society that emerges from the many local denunciations that reached the French was even more shocking to the new regime than the levels of duplicity and mutual animosity which inspired them. The same apparent savagery that they had found directed against them in 1799 seemed to be turned inwards, in ready fashion, on peripheral society itself.

The legacy of a weak *ancien régime* was, at least to the Prefect of Genoa, 'a country where spirits are naturally heady, where shots are never long being fired'.[30] What the French hated was the legacy of discord they believed this weakness engendered. Left rudderless, a culture of vendetta and feuding was only to be expected. This was certainly Nardon's opinion of what he found in the Piacentino, the hinterland of the duchies and the theatre of the revolt of winter 1805–6. The experience of the revolt of the Apennine valleys of the Piacentino was formative for French perceptions of the region.[31] Just as important as the occurrence of the revolt and its immediate causes were the social climate and culture of anarchy that had given birth to it:

> this country must be governed ... there was a list of hideous crimes for every day during March which, although private in nature, pose no less a threat to the social order [than the recent revolt] ... . These morals, customs, passions, are the tragic effects of a very old pattern of impunity.[32]

The Apennine spine of Italy was treacherous country for any kind of authority; its populations were judged at best as laws unto themselves and at worst as prone to slip into an atavistic barbarism if not 'policed'.

The Tridentine Church did not entirely disagree with such verdicts, but the French did not see it as capable of playing anything but a subordinate role, at best, in their project of taming the periphery. They felt their own experience had generated enough evidence of the Church's inadequacy as an agent of social control, although it must be stressed that the French most often laid the blame for the degeneration of the periphery at the feet of the *ancien régime* states themselves. In imperial eyes the Church had failed to play its part on the periphery, but that might have been no bad thing for the prospects of the Napoleonic project. In this milieu, the Church was either isolated and powerless in the face of a society so at odds with its mores, or its lower clergy – regular and secular – were simply part of the culture of vendetta and amorality the French felt still prevailed on the periphery. It was the opinion of the French prefect of the department of the Apennines, east of Genoa, that the Genoese government had deliberately weakened the power of the bishops, for example, thus undermining their authority over the lower clergy. As a result, indiscipline was rife; in this sphere, at least, restoring and bolstering episcopal power was regarded as 'a thing that is quite necessary in this country'.[33] The revolt of 1799 convinced the French that this lack of discipline went far beyond lax personal conduct, however. It produced a lower clergy all too much at one with the violence of the society of which they had become too much a part. In the northern Tuscan town of Pontremoli, according to the French police, an Augustinian friar Celestino Ferrari led the revolt against them in 1799, 'dressed as a cavalryman on horseback, at the head of seven or eight armed peasants'. Ten years later, during the Wagram campaign, he threatened the administrator of the property seized from the monks under the Concordat that 'he would carve him into little pieces, should the government fall'.[34] Cases like this underlined the complicity of the lower clergy in the politics of counter-revolution. But, at a deeper level, they also seemed to the French to reveal the failure of Trent in these areas. After their own experiences in the Vendée and elsewhere, the French had come to expect little else but counter-revolutionary sympathies from the lower clergy. However, cases like Ferrari's were just as significant because they exposed how integrated were many clergy with the culture of the laity. Many such cases convinced the French – and the Italian episcopate – that the mountain clergy could be pre-Constance as much as pre-Trent. To support '1799' was one thing; to lead – literally – from the front was quite another.

Those who supported the counter-revolution, but held to a priestly conduct, faced the different charge of using their intellectual superiority to lead the ignorant and superstitious astray, of abusing their own gifts and their position for secular – as much as seditious – ends. Typical in this respect was the official view of the *parocco* of Castelnuovo, on the border between Parma and Liguria. Taneridi was an ex-monk, a good preacher, a serious man with considerable theological expertise which he used 'to win the support of the foolish and devout'. He came to the government's attention in 1811 because he denounced the Concordat's ruling that only parish priests be allowed to predicate and used this as a platform to attack the regime more widely.[35] Taneridi conforms to the Tridentine model in many ways: an intellectual placed in the midst of a savage people, capable of doing good but, in the political circumstances of the *epoca francese*, using his talents in the immediate cause of disorder and in the wider purpose of blocking the advance of Enlightenment through French rule in general and the Concordat in particular. At least this was how it seemed from an official point of view. Even in its 'proper guise', the Tridentine Church was not to be wholly trusted. For the clergy, the superstition and volatility of the mountain were there to be manipulated or joined; for the French, there did not seem to be much of a choice. It was not a propitious point of departure for the new regime.

For all that, there was at least spirit in the communities of the periphery. Violence betokened martial inclinations. Francesco Assereto and many like him were regarded as good military material. There was a strong sense among the French that, if Trent had failed to civilize these regions, at least it had not emasculated them. The ephemeral presence of the Church had saved the Umbrians from a worse state than isolation:

> being far from the centre, they were less under the yoke of the priests, and their industrious spirit found it easier to resist the influence of a government bent on destroying all national spirit in its territories.[36]

Industry and enterprise in a society so imbued by Tridentine Catholicism could assume singular forms, however. The French authorities took good note of one such form in the Ligurian Apennines. However superstitious and ignorant the people of the periphery might be, they were enterprising and, essentially, amoral in the eyes of the imperial authorities. In a handful of very poor mountain communes in Liguria, a particular practice emerges from the French archives. Groups of men went out annually from Boronasia, Mezzanego and Sopra la Croce, as far afield as France, Spain and Portugal, as nothing short of 'con artists', to beg for money under a traditional false pretext that their relatives had been captured by the Barbary pirates and were being held hostage. They played on an old Christian duty to help ransom such captives. They were known locally as the *batti birbbi*. What most intrigued the French, however, was that this practice was not the preserve of the very poor. The authorities believed that all the wealthiest landowners in the area had been *batti* in their youth, the mayor included, and that it had become something akin to a rite of passage in the area.[37] For the French, here was mountain 'piety' encapsulated. It had little to do with real faith; it drew on communal solidarity; it preyed on a still more superstitious centre. At least it possessed nerve and aggression, for where Trent really did seem to have fulfilled its mission – in the lowlands and the cities – the French found a more easily governable society but also a culture even more repellent to them than that of their 'thousand Vendées', as General

Wirion – a veteran of the western departments – described Piedmont in 1801.[38]

The centre: Saints or soldiers, Catholics or citizens?

The wild peripheries of the old states were a perennial presence – and problem – for whoever ruled Italy. The process of taming them was part of a long continuum. Under the old order, the urban centre had been regarded as the counterpoint to the peripheries; it was the fount of civilizing influences. The French turned this on its head, for the religious problem as it posed itself at the centre was fundamentally different from its place on the periphery. Whereas the mountains at least possessed the crude, untutored elements of regeneration, the rot in Italian society started at the centre and spread out from there. Italy was, in French eyes, rotten at the core. The continued strength of the concept of 'regeneration' at the heart of the French Revolution was nowhere more apparent than during the French rule of the urban centres of Italy.[39] Thanks, at least in part to the influence of the post-Tridentine clergy, the French prefect admitted that 'The city of Siena probably sees fewer crimes committed than anywhere else'.[40] Nevertheless, the price for this order was almost too high to pay. It warped and twisted the natural intelligence the French readily accorded the Italian elites. Roederer was far from seeing the Umbrian nobility as noble savages, but rather as cunning, worldly and highly intelligent: 'We find ourselves in a country where the upper class is very clever. They take the slightest hint'.[41] In similar vein, the prefect of the Apennines awarded grudging praise to the local notables of the Ligurian periphery:

> We have to cope with the kind of men who are used to calculating the danger as much as the reward, and who act only in proportion to the interest or the risk that must be run.[42]

None of it translated into civic virtue, as derived from the Revolution, however.

French contempt for the elite culture they perceived at the centre makes Napoleonic rule in Italy an almost unique period, although the first Austrian officials to govern Tuscany under the House of Lorraine were also shocked by the amorality they found among the Florentine elite.[43] In the context of its religious policies, the disdain the regime developed for that culture stemmed from the dominant influence of Tridentine Catholicism on the urban elites and masses. Here the French could watch and assess how the Catholic Reformation could transform a society in which it took root, and they did not like what they found. From this stemmed their determination to effect a cultural revolution in imperial Italy, which led to direct conflict with the Church. Essentially this turned on what the French saw as the emasculation of the Italian centre. There was too much enervating religion at the centre and they came to see it as the main cause of the malaise of the Italian elites. Weak government and narrow political horizons had created a vacuum into which the Tridentine Church had stolen, imparting values to the elites that drained men of the martial spirit so essential to their immediate war effort and that eroded morality and undermined the powers of reason throughout society. Indeed the French throughout Italy reached the startlingly uniform conclusion that they were faced with a corrupt, effeminate and irrational – if cunning – elite. In these circumstances the French were at a distinct disadvantage from Trent in their cultural assault on the highlands. Trent had built a secure base for itself at the centre – the French soon found out for themselves exactly how secure – whereas the new imperial order felt it had none. Conversely, the French felt they had more promising – if highly dangerous – material to hand on the periphery than did Trent. It is here that the profundity of the gulf between the Borromean and Bonapartist visions of the world emerges.

The proof of how decadent and degraded the French felt the centre to be, emerges starkly in the measures they took to try to regenerate its future leaders and, indeed, in the fact that they concentrated on the younger generation having despaired of what they found. They also felt a compunction to work fast, before the clergy – literally – corrupted the youth of the Italian elite. In the city of Parma, the French official charged in 1806 with its administration had very emphatic, precise views on the impact of clerical influence on Parmense youth:

> a morality which is inseparable from a pure and firm piety is rare here, and vices exist because of the absence of any check to moderate them ... . You would probably be surprised if I told you how familiar venomous, back-stabbing sarcasm is to the youth of all classes! You would probably be revolted to know that young creatures of eight or ten are sold into prostitution ... the state must attack this propensity for licence at its source ... . The number of priests must be reduced.[44]

Such judgements singled out the Church as a source of active harm in Italy.

There were plenty of aristocratic youths to go around the numerous priests of Parma, thanks to the presence in the town of one of the greatest and most exclusive boys' boarding schools in Italy, the college of Santa Caterina, which had attracted the sons of noble families from all over Italy since the seventeenth century. A Jesuit foundation, the school had passed to the Oratorians on their dissolution; the French inherited its boarders in 1805 when they annexed the Duchy. To reorient Parmese youth, in particular, and the scions of the Italian nobility, in general, the French soon reopened the college, but with a very different ethos and very clear goals. In the words of its French director:

> I can gather together 150 young men of the leading noble families of Italy, and I have got these little counts, marquesses and princes to enact *Le Dragon de Thionville* and *La Bataille d'Austerlitz* ... . You can grasp all the political and moral advantages. It is complained that I am giving too military an education to these children; that is to say, it is not exclusively monastical ... I am breaking their ties to home a little, and their attachment to their families' values. It gives a small taste of the right subjects that carry abroad the love of the laws and practices of my country.[45]

Parents withdrew their children by the score and, by 1807, the college collapsed.

As a statement of intent, however, there can be few more emphatic committed to paper. Here the army was to become *l'école de la nation*, just as in France, but the French firmly believed that there was much more schooling to be done, to the point where links with home and family had to be 'broken' – nothing less – and a wholly new culture instilled in the youth of the Italian nobility. That culture was entirely military in its ethos and avowedly opposed to the values fostered by a Catholic education, in the eyes of those who shaped imperial policy. The Administrative Prefect was very clear as to who was behind the collapse of the *lycée* and his line of reasoning sheds great light on the extent to which the French saw the pillars of Italian culture as diametrically opposed to their own. He told his superiors that:

> The superb institution that is the College of St Catherine is slipping from my control: the holidays, the ignorance, the intrigue, the local rivalries, all combine to oppose my project ... . The ambassadors, the ministers, the references, the importuning of every conceivable type, the tears of some mothers, who have been misled – these are the tactics they use.[46]

A week, later he added an old enemy to this list:

> Provoked by Jesuit lies, and by those of the teachers who have remained, in the spirit of a discredited system, those who cannot tolerate a few salutary changes in the college cannot abide an educated, hard-working Frenchman among them: the result is that, daily, parents withdraw their children ... . It seems impossible to struggle against the flood which is engulfing this fine establishment.[47]

These tirades provide a revealing list of those opposed to the French vision for a regenerated Italian youth, all the direct enemies of militarism: the strong tradition in weak *ancien régime* states of reliance on patronage – itself a breeding ground for selfish corruption – which places private concerns above public duties; the parochialism inherent in the life of weak polities; and – perhaps the greatest evidence for French imperialists of ineffectual government – the undue, indeed overweening influence of the clergy and of women on the destinies of their sons. In the last years of the empire, the French sought to bring the sons of the leading families of the Italian *départements réunis* and the Kingdom of Italy into the official fold through their enlistment in the *gardes d'honneur*, a socially elite branch of the National Guard. In an Italian context, the creation of the *gardes* assumed the magnitude of a campaign of moral regeneration that was itself the culmination of an arduous process of fostering a martial spirit in the hearts and minds of Italian males. For the French officials who imposed it, the creation of the *gardes* carried more than a hint of cultural imperialism and, more specifically, of anti-clericalism. In April 1813, Antoine Roederer, the French prefect of the department of Trasimeno, singled out a particular youth for the *gardes*. He was worth more than 100,000 francs in rents and carried 'le plus beau nom d'Italie', Connestabile Stoffa, but this was not Roederer's reason for 'targeting' him for active service:

> His father is dead and his mother treats him like a little girl. She is a respectable woman who imagines she could not do better than to have three priests bring up her boy. This young man is eighteen. Judge for yourself what a blow this will be for the poor mother! It creates a great good chance for this young man. There have been attempts to exempt him under thousands of pretexts.[48]

Roederer had a duty to regenerate Connestabile Stoffa, just as much as to the imperial regime, to ensure that no young *notable* was exempted 'when it was a question of someone rich and important'.[49] Roederer's words are replete with ethnic stereotypes, both in their direct intent towards the unfortunate, inoffensive young Umbrian aristocrat and in what they reveal about the ethos of imperial France and its fundamental incompatibility with Tridentine Catholicism, as least as it had touched the Italian elites. The reaction of Roman families such as the Patrizi was predictably hostile to this thinly disguised policy of the conscription of barely pubescent Italian nobles, giving rise to an upsurge of clericalism and overt piety.[50] It had also thrown several ancient Piedmontese families into the arms of the Jesuits by the end of the period. In his memoirs, Massimo D'Azeglio recorded movingly the impact of the forced departure of his older brothers to, respectively, the military academy of St Cyr and service in the Council of State, as well as the fact that the former, on his return, became a Jesuit with his father's blessing. Indeed Massimo's own education was entrusted to members of the clandestine order. But the aggressive character of these French policies not only shattered their own goal of *ralliement* among the Italian nobility, it altered sensibly the cultural world of many members of the only true 'warrior aristocracy' left in Italy, in Piedmont.[51] Michael Carroll has traced a psychological link from the 'father-ineffective family' through Marian devotion to the culture of machismo in southern Italy;[52] whereas the French thought they detected many men too closely bound to their mothers in northern and central Italy, they did not detect a great deal of machismo among them. However, on the periphery Marian devotion did seem to them to produce the aggression Carroll associates with the cult in the Latin Mediterranean – if for different reasons.

Although militarism was intrinsic to the culture of imperial France – and the cultural ethos of the revolutionary and imperial regimes was very masculine and warlike[53] – the French contempt for the Italian elites and the role the Tridentine Church played in their decadence went far beyond this lack of martial virtue. The French remained imbued with the Enlightened concept that the only true civilization was both *polie et policée*[54] and, as the Italians fell down on both these counts, they stood in need of the moral regeneration propounded by the Revolution. However, many of their reactions to the decadence they perceived in Italy also reveal the persistence of an older, more widely defined concept of corruption, expressed by Jean-Claude Waquet as

> the depravity of morals ... governed by and closely related to sin ... [C]orruption was the weakness of human nature, the depravity of mankind, the failure of virtue, the triumph of the passions, the outbreak of sin ... . Its meaning was then extended to cover the wider notion of corruption having almost metaphysical qualities.[55]

The French beheld an Italy full – too full – of churches and clergy, and the conclusion the new imperial rulers drew was not that Italians continued in their corruption in the face of the admonitions of their priests, as Waquet has posited for *ancien régime* Florence, but that the Tridentine Church itself was part of the corruption, that it had left them rudderless. The French distrusted the confessional not just as a ready weapon of the counter-revolution against the Revolution – although this was very strongly felt from the top to the bottom of the regime – but as a morally corrupting influence in itself. Thus the universality of Easter confession and communion, and the power of conscience exerted by confessors,[56] were not regarded by the French as a miracle of administrative policing and social control in the otherwise hapless world of the *ancien régime* state. They came to see it not just as a strictly political threat.

Whereas the early modern concept of corruption and depravity saw them as individual faults, however diffuse in human society, a view shared by the first Austrians in Florence, the French believed they stemmed from political and social circumstances. This is what made their relationship with the Italian elites unique. The weak, clientistic nature of the secular governments of the *ancien régime* were regarded as breeding grounds of decadence; the fiat of imperial conquest had created a new set of circumstances from which regeneration could begin. The Church, however, was seen as the breeder of corruption on the ground the *ancien régime* state had vacated. As the old states disappeared with the advance of the empire, the Church emerged ever more clearly as the root of all evil. The *ancien régime* state was a real but passive source of the problem; the Church was the active agent of the decadence of the Italian elites. Ignorance and amorality might be predictable on the periphery but the French saw at the centre, proof that the Church was actually a force for ill. It had, at best, left the urban elites rudderless; at worst, it had fostered their decadence and corruption. The empirical result facing the new rulers seemed to be a society permeated by false values and perverted moral codes. They found it everywhere, and they came to blame the Church not the lay elite for this state of affairs.

The most striking examples of the correlation the French made between piety and moral corruption are probably not those drawn from public life, or from the point where familial culture, public obligations and religion meet, as in the case of the *gardes d'honneur*. Rather, the best indications of how far 'the rot' went within the Italian elites, and of how closely bound up it was with religion, emerge in French attitudes to Italian upper-class women. The incongruity of the piety and loose morals among Roman society women is expressed in the official literature in the starkest terms. Degerando, a member of the provisional administration charged with organizing the ex-Papal states into French departments, told Paris in his 'Statistical Report on Rome and the Roman States':

> High society women are very corrupt, but without the slightest hint of coquettishness about them. This corruption is a very deeply rooted thing, it is accepted, and does not stop them being devout.[57]

There is, of course a logic to this perceived incongruity. Women were the most pious and 'priest-ridden' sector of Roman society, so it stands to reason they would also be among the most morally corrupt. This was not at all a disengaged, official reaction, dispassionately elucidated by one the regime's leading intellectuals. It was reflected in the personal correspondence of the Comte de Tournon – a young nobleman, himself from a conventionally Catholic background – who was appointed the Prefect of the department of Rome in 1810, specifically because Paris hoped he would prove acceptable to the Roman nobility. As it transpired, the female aristocracy proved unacceptable to Tournon, whom they saw as a very eligible bachelor indeed. He told his mother he would not bring a woman of less than twenty to Rome as his wife because:

> she would be too prone to adopt the mores of this country which, in all Europe, are the most set against happiness. I swear that, although I am not jealous by nature, I would only marry in Rome with considerable distaste. 'Putting it about' – for that is the term for it – is so general, so open among the higher nobility, that I would almost never want my wife to live alone, among these society women.[58]

Tournon and Degerando were both struck not only by the cheek-by-jowl existence of piety and promiscuity, but also by how joyless the whole business was. This shocked Tournon at least as much as the immoral goings on. This was all the more reason for breaking this culture down.

The French had a diverse cultural arsenal they unleashed on the Italian elites. The witty, polite conversation of the salon was to replace the unseemly manoeuvrings of Italian society; the more cerebral tradition of French theatre would oust the more vulgar enthusiasms of the opera. Saints and sinners were to become soldiers and citizens.[59] At the heart of the battle, however, came the role of the Church.

The French opinion of the Italian cities and lowlands came to resemble Edward Said's concept of 'orientalism' in so far as they regarded these parts of Italy not as primitive in any way. Indeed, it is clear that they often felt they were too sophisticated for their own good, although at a deeper level held in a form of ignorant innocence by the Church. As with Western views of the Ottoman Middle East in Said's thesis, so the administrators of imperial Italy viewed urban and elite culture as old centres of civilization in decline. They were stagnant, atrophied cultures and, as a result, they had become 'trivialized'.[60] Unlike Western views of the 'East', the French found clear culprits for this process of trivialization and decline, the Tridentine Church chief among them: as the cultural arbiter of *ancien régime* Italy, it was obviously responsible for moral and cultural decadence.

Tridentine Catholicsm, as it had evolved in French eyes by the time of their rule, produced effeminate mothers' boys and sluttish, coldly calculating women, bereft of personal happiness. The impact of Baroque religiosity on all spheres of Italian public life, as interpreted by the French, was as pernicious as it was pervasive.[61] It soon became clear that this was also a regime which was not prepared to leave such cultural mores alone. The Napoleonic empire was the standard bearer of a new moral order and its obvious target in the quest for regeneration was the Tridentine Church, because it held that Church culpable for the moral decadence it saw all about it.

It is already evident that the French decided to arrest this state of decline with a very heterogeneous mixture of militarism, social and intellectual refinement, and a return to the 'primitive Church'. There is nothing in contemporary discourse to suggest they sensed any irony or incongruity in this. Jansenism had long ceased to be a source of subversion of constituted authority, as had often been the case before 1789,[62] and had evolved into a pillar of the Gallican Church, as embodied in the Concordat. The Gallican articles were included in the Concordat, despite the Vatican's objections; Portalis, Napoleon's first Minister of Religion (Cultes), was an avowed Gallican. Nor was the state alone in its Gallicanism; many French bishops felt Napoleon had conceded too much to Rome. Although the Concordat actually spelled the end of Gallican independence for the French episcopate, this was not how it appeared to contemporaries, least of all Pius VII.[63] The Jansenist element of the Concordat would emerge less in the high politics surrounding the Concordat than in its terms and the zeal with which they were applied. The regular orders did not return under its terms, nor did the abolished saints' days or the right to process publicly on them. The ecclesiastical courts, the vast Church properties nationalized in 1790, all remained unaltered. These were terms to be extended, along with the empire, not softened or adapted to local conditions.

This was the spirit in which the Concordat came to Italy. The opposition the French faced, and their implacable repression of that opposition, destroyed one of the few constants Napoleon had hoped to pursue in Italy: peaceful cooperation with the Church. In 1796 he exhorted the Army of Italy – largely in vain – to remember they were in a Catholic country and to respect the clergy.[64] By the time he had finally torn up the Concordat and imprisoned Pius VII and most of his cardinals, Napoleon had already decided Italy was too priest-ridden for its own good.

3

THE RELIGION
OF THE RULERS

In the autumn of 1810, after a walk in the hills, the new Prefect of Rome, Tournon, wrote to his mother that 'I sat on the ruins of the temple of Jupiter Latinus, now a convent that will soon, itself, be a ruin'.[1] This was no flight of fancy, nor an idle threat, but a clear statement of policy, for the Papal states, as the last territories to be annexed in the Italian peninsula, would now feel the full force of the terms of the Concordat in a line that stretched back to Piedmont in 1801. The French enforced its terms as rigorously as they did those of the Civil Code or the laws on conscription, for it was just as important to them. Turning convents into ruins was exactly what Tournon had been sent to Rome to do, unless they were fit for offices, barracks or schools, for this is what had happened everywhere else. It would be no different now that the French had assumed responsibility for the very heart of the Roman Catholic world.

They did not have it all their own way, however. The imposition of the Concordat on the peoples of Italy met with resistance everywhere, at every level of society and on the periphery as much as at the centre, embracing the clergy and laity alike. Yet the regime never wavered in its attempts to impose its religious policies on Italy: to be an imperial subject was to be an adherent of the Gallican Church, as defined by the Concordat. Indeed the empire's meridional possessions were singled out for particular attention in the uncompromising words of a memorandum from the Ministry of Religion to Napoleon in November 1809:

> The limits of our empire … embrace almost all of Christendom … . Now it is notorious … that the Alps and the Pyrenees have always been barriers that the purity of the principles of the Gallican Church have not been able to cross. This diversity no longer exists … [and] your Kingdom of Italy must now be taken as the model for uniformity of discipline in the Church [which] is the surest guarantee of its perfection.[2]

His brief comment on the religious organization of the new Piedmontese departments throws the nature of 'Gallican imperialism' into stark relief: 'I feel it is important to place a French bishop in the former Piedmont to galli-canize the clergy of that country'.[3] The challenge to superstition was thrown down emphatically in a report to Napoleon in 1806, which took Montesquieu's justification for organized religion as its starting point: 'Dogma supports and sanctions morality. It preserves reason, in the face of the desolation of uncertainty'. Parish priests were to be trained in mathe-matics and science:

> These two sciences can provide the clergy with weapons against the kind of impiety that often tries to attack religion through facts of nature; they will put them on guard against the sort of superstition that often abuses natural occurrences to corrupt Religion.[4]

Clearly, Gallicanism meant more than simply a change in the sources of executive ecclesiastical authority.

The determination to impose this 'purity', 'reason' and 'uniformity' on Italians forged a striking degree of *amalgame* among the French, for the struggle against Italian piety drew the same sense of purpose – and the same virulent anti-clericalism – from nominally pious patricians like Tournon and D'Auzers, as it did from scions of the moderate Revolution, personified by the Alsatian Protestant Antoine Roederer, chiming – at least in this context – with the latent *Hébertisme* of ex-Terrorists like Nardon. Their contempt for every conceivable facet of the religious culture of their *administrés* led the French to see themselves as part of a *longue durée* which pitted the more rational, civilizing forces, originating at the political and cultural centres of the Italian states, against the latent barbarism of the hinterlands. The sub-prefect of Sarazzana, an arrondissement embracing some of the most remote valleys in Liguria, pointed directly to the lack of real clerical influ-ence on the people of the region.[5] They appeared to all those in authority – French or indigenous, lay or ecclesiastical – as lands that had forgotten Trent, even if the heirs of Trent had not forgotten them. Here the struggle was perceived – often only with partial accuracy – as a confrontation between unreconstructed religious archaism and the forces of modernity, in which the Napoleonic state and Tridentine Catholicism became allies in a common civilizing mission. Nor, the new regime soon found, was the need to carry on the work of Trent confined to the peripheries. The urban confrater-nities had shown themselves active and resilient in the face of the reforms attempted by the Synod of Pistoia, in Tuscany, in the 1780s, especially in Prato, the very diocese of the Synod's leading light, Ricci.[6] Equally, a circular issued in 1811 by the Minister of Public Education of the Kingdom of Italy on the persistence of folklore, superstitions and unorthodox reli-

gious festivals revealed what might best be described as 'a-Tridentine' practices to be widespread – and thoroughly denounced and opposed by the
local clergy – throughout the *pianura padana*, as well as the foothills of the
Dolomites. That is, the centre was far from free from archaism more readily
associated with the periphery, even in a region that might reasonably be
thought of as the 'Borromean heartland'.[7] The experience of Enlightened
reformers before them, and their own investigations, showed the French
that the imposition of the Concordat might not follow the pattern of
passive centre, recalcitrant periphery. It did, however, strengthen their
conviction of a common purpose with Trent that, in practice, singularly
failed to work.

Their contempt for – and assault on – the religious culture of the hinterlands is wholly predictable. Perhaps less so was their withering contempt for
the spiritual decadence they perceived at the centre, among all classes of
lowland and urban society. It was the corollary of French disdain for the
perceived lack of Italian martial spirit. With the introduction of the
Concordat to the *départements réunis* and the Kingdom of Italy, that
contempt found its true institutional target: the Church itself.

D'Auzers, as the Director of Police for the departments of Piedmont,
Liguria and the former Duchies of Parma and Piacenza, was the official
with the longest and widest perspective on Italian piety: his remit was wide,
as were the territories for which he was responsible, and his tenure was the
longest of all his colleagues. He could claim to know his *administrés*. In
1810, after almost seven years in Italy, his distaste for Tridentine piety is
manifest in his description of the great *festa dei lumi* held for the
Assumption at Chiavari on the Ligurian coast. The whole town was illumi-
nated for several days and nights, and this always included the houses of rich
and poor alike, as well as the churches and public buildings. This was a post-
Tridentine ritual *par excellence*, and D'Auzers pointed less to the archaic
disorder attendant on its celebration, than that Tridentine ideals had
triumphed too thoroughly among the urban people of the coast:

> What will become of the public servant? He can't avoid being
> caught up in the crowd. If there is trouble, how can he control his
> *administrés*? The religious festivals are almost as important to the
> people as the law – and when the altar is not used to stir up
> fanaticism, they might guarantee him control, but not when the
> festivals are prolonged ... when they lead to disorder. The people
> thus see only God and his ministers and, believing, obey them;
> they then become deaf to the public servant, who speaks for the
> law.[8]

D'Auzers also added that this particular year – the first of the Pope's
captivity at Savona, just along the coast – the *festa dei lumi* had lasted a

whole week, longer by several days than was usual. He did not remain unsupported in his desire to curb the *festa*, for the Minister of Religion replied that in future it would be confined to Sunday and the illuminations restricted to the churches, in accordance with the terms of the Concordat.[9] D'Auzers emerges as a Voltairian, shadowing the entry on 'Superstition' for the *Philosophical Dictionary*:

> The superstitious man is to the rogue what the slave is to the tyrant. Further, the superstitious man is governed by the fanatic and becomes fanatic.[10]

His criticisms reveal more than the predictable exasperation of a Voltairian of his generation, however. Here D'Auzers is not aghast at the barbarousness of the 'nuestras Indías' of the periphery, at rude people untouched by the currents of civilization. Rather he fears the power of a well-disciplined, Tridentine clergy over an urban population, for it is just such a clergy – in his eyes – that is turning the *festa dei lumi* into a disorderly event at its own behest. What should have been a peaceful, relatively brief exercise in public piety was corrupted by its very guardians and creators into something more atavistic for short-term political goals. Turned on its head, this analysis points not only to the power wielded by the secular clergy in this sizeable Ligurian port – the type of place where Trent made itself felt – but also to a tendency among the clergy to coalesce with more atavistic forces latent in the laity, to project mass forms of passive – if often rowdy – resistance to many aspects of French rule. D'Auzers, as a policeman, was quick to discern this trend. In Genoa at the same time, after a 'spate' of miracles, the Prefect there also lamented with undisguised contempt the uses to which priestly power were put in the city:

> It is pathetic, in this century of Enlightenment, that of Napoleon the Great, [that] there are still those sordid enough, impudent enough, to agitate public credulity, as they dared to do here, last night.[11]

The fragile, if not quite artificial, nature of any 'alliance' between Trent and the French is here exposed.

Others found deeper, cultural reasons to disparage the religious culture around them. In the same letter to his mother in which he foreshadowed the 'arrival' of the Concordat in the Papal states, Tournon contrasted the robust, imperial past of his *chef lieu* with the servility of what he found:

> The temple of Jupiter that once dominated the eternal city is a far cry from the humble cells of the Passionists! The [Roman] triumphs brought exotic spoils of conquest to this place; the mendicant friars

bring to it only the alms given them by wretches poorer than them-selves![12]

As the scion of a royalist family who had fled the Jacobin sack of Lyon as a child in 1794, Tournon's contempt for Baroque charity is all the more striking, with its clear resonance of Gibbon. Tournon's conventionally pious background make many of his disparaging remarks about Roman piety all the more revealing. He was pious enough to pay for several masses to be said for the soul of his father on his death in 1810, even if he had to rely on juring priests to do so.[13] Yet his loathing of indigenous religion is omnipresent. Tournon thus embodies the extent to which the Catholic Reformation had diverged in its French and Italian contexts. The gulf between rulers and ruled was not all the fault of the Revolution.

While Tournon, the aristocrat, despised the ignobility of Roman piety, Degerando, the secular-minded, intellectual voice of the regime, turned his scorn on the superficiality of religious culture among the Roman elite. Yet whereas Tournon drew almost instinctively on his classical education and a code of honour-through-glory, Degerando based his distaste on contempo-rary French notions of a more cerebral approach to the sacred than he found among the highest secular magistrates of the city:

> Religion, such as it is conceived of by Enlightened men, and felt by virtuous men – such as it exists generally in France – [is] the fruit of a reasoned and reasonable conviction, its principle is the improve-ment of morality. [This is] scarcely even perceived among the Romans ... . Worship is only an expression. Relics, indulgences, the Forty Hours, the Rosary are what interest them; reading the Scriptures would appear profane, and a Roman would suspect heresy in these august, simple truths ... the author of all things would pass only for an atheist. The Gospel exists no more in Rome, save in the paintings which decorate the basilicas ... . How many thousands of men who come to kiss the feet of the statue of Jupiter – transformed into that of the prince of the Apostles – even suspect that a Gospel might exist![14]

Degerando's specific targets are as revealing as his more general observa-tions. He derides the minutiae of Tridentine devotion, rather than a failure by Trent to impose itself on the laity, for the Forty Hours and the Rosary were the most renowned and readily accepted of Tridentine innovations. To single them out as barriers to the attainment of piety struck at the heart of orthodoxy, and Degerando knew it. Yet he could not see that such practices were actually part of a concerted 'anti-folklore strategy' to create alterna-tives to archaic popular traditions.[15]

In Parma, Nardon, an ex-Terrorist, revealed – almost unwittingly – how vast and unbridgeable was the gap between the French and Baroque piety in an urban setting. In 1806, recently installed in the city, he remarked with puzzlement on the very existence of the ceremony of the Forty Hours, when 'day and night, processions of the confraternities and the [religious] corporations go about the churches'. More predictably he added 'moreover, these nocturnal ceremonies are often the occasion for scandal and trouble'. Clearly some forms of fun were all right and others not, for 'on the other hand, all the theatres are closed' for two days, something the two French regiments stationed in the city found 'very singular'. Nardon was particularly proud that he found a compromise by which 'each followed his own tastes and principles'.[16] This compromise foreshadowed the terms of the Concordat regarding religious ceremonies, and pointed to his desire for a virtual state of apartheid between the French and the locals in such matters. This is the official decree issued by Nardon:

> We are French, we are led by French laws and customs:

> I will permit the religious ceremonies of the Forty Hours [to take place] because there is freedom of worship in France; I forbid and prohibit they be prolonged after eight in the evening, because to allow them to continue later would lead to scandal, for Religion itself, and for the public peace. I order the theatres be opened, as normal, as each will see fit; this is the essence of true civil and religious liberty.[17]

Nardon's decree is replete with significance at multiple levels. He simply regarded the Forty Hours as an unknown, alien practice which, if disreputable and exotic, should be tolerated in keeping with the principles of his own political culture, but alien and exotic it certainly was. Nor was it to impinge on what the French themselves regarded as normal. Predictable condescension pervades his opinions. Yet – and this marks out the difference with any previous experience of the French 'interior' – there is also a complete sense of the Other. The Forty Hours was an explicitly Tridentine form of ritual devotion developed first by the Capuchins in Borromean Milan in the 1530s; it centred on the Eucharist, that most anti-populist of objects of devotion, which the Capuchins made the core of their 'Easter strategy' which tried to ensure that the public, collective Easter celebrations had an orthodox 'high point'. The Jesuits developed it further, making it overlap with the last three days of *Carnevale*, which were usually the worst for public order and sincere devotion, '[thus] establishing an alternative to other forms of popular devotion, in strict accordance with their more general anti-folklore strategy'.[18] Perhaps the manner in which the Forty Hours had come to be celebrated in Parma showed signs of that 'loss of effectiveness' that allowed the masses to absorb Trent and evolve their own devotional forms, blended partially with those of the Counter Reformation and partially with 'the remains of paganism, various superstitions and numerous elements which were properly Christian', as also characterized the French masses in the late eighteenth century. [19] All this was lost on Nardon, less because he sensed these cultural trends, than through total ignorance of the origins and purpose of the Forty Hours. Whatever, he had his superiors right behind him. The Minister of the Interior told him 'You have done well to forbid the prolongation of this ceremony beyond eight in the evening' and echoed Nardon's views on public decency and order, adding:

> I also approve of the fact that you have forbidden the closure of the theatres ... . The principles of religious toleration, which are the bases of the Concordat, do not intend to deprive citizens of amusements which pose no threat to decency or public order, for religious motives.[20]

Tolerance had its limits, nonetheless. As at Chiavari under D'Auzers, the *festa* was to be restricted in scope and time. Freedom of religion was freedom as defined by the French Concordat, not by local practices.

Nor were the French satisfied by the more sober expressions of Italian piety cultivated by the Counter Reformation. This, too, was very different from castigating the neo-paganism of the 'nuestras Indías' of the hinterlands, or even the excesses of the urban masses. To lament the savage ignorance of the mountain was one thing; to attack the urban elites who had thoroughly absorbed the religious culture of Trent was quite another, revealing French contempt for the decadence they perceived at the heart of elite Italian civilization. Norvins, the secularized ex-noble, despised the Romans for their attempts at *gravitas*, speaking of 'this people, who prefer the procession to the dance, and the sermon to the theatre'.[21] Indeed, he condemned Tournon and Miollis, the Governor of Rome, for suspending the theatre during Lent and got his way.[22] That is not to say that there were some elements of that culture above Enlightened criticism or that deserved to survive.

For better, as well as for worse, the French were determined to impose religious toleration on the heartland of the Inquisition, and the heritage of the Revolution could be rekindled by what they found in Italy. Napoleon's commitment to Jewish equality is well attested, as is the strength of Tuscan anti-Semitism.[23] The Concordat specifically banned the traditional passage in the Easter sermon condemning the Jews for the death of Christ and, during their first, tense Easter as the rulers of Tuscany, the French deployed troops in all the churches of Pisa during Mass to enforce the ban.[24] Only two weeks earlier, the Archbishop of Pisa had tried to evade the change, saying it was 'too last minute' and that the Pope would not allow it.[25] Brute force made him back down. The Pope's response was to publish a small, popular prayer book, emphasizing the Easter message in its traditional form, and distributed it throughout Tuscany. Several copies were found in Siena and the Prefect was very critical of Chigi-Zondadari and his Vicar-General, who had 'turned a blind eye'. Even if it was not a crime legally, 'The evil is in the intention' said the Prefect:

> Once upon a time, fanatics and the common people believed that on a given Sunday, heaven would take its vengeance on the enemies of the Catholic faith; the Jews were already considered 'marked' victims of this vengeance. It is, then, for me to warn those who would use this as a pretext to attack the Jews … . But, on the one hand, the public can see that the supposed revenge of heaven has not happened, and that, on the other, the power of the state is ready to strike against anything opposed to it. Open your eyes to your own true interests every day, and remain under the law.[26]

Siena had seen a pogrom in 1799 and the Prefect well knew the force of public opinion he faced. Only weeks before, he had uncovered a plot in Siena to 'raise the lower classes' of the city against the Jews, 'as in the year seven' (1799). The occasion had been the sale of properties from the closed regular houses and the agitators played on the fact that Jews were prominent purchasers, but also on the loss of alms and charity for the poor and the sick as a result of the closures. He believed several nobles were agitating the artisan families they patronized: Senese anti-Semitism could cross class barriers. Troops were posted at the houses of Jewish families, and more were asked for because the Prefect admitted that his 100 troops were not enough to contain real trouble. The whole panoply of the counter-revolutionary coalition seemed to be bearing down on the French, but the Prefect was defiant:

> Your Excellency knows how the spirit of the lower classes can be influenced by some monkish malcontent or some indiscreet noble. If the strengthening of the visible physical force dissipates any idea of insubordination or riot, the moral force it supports gains a double strength, and emerges enhanced by going out to confront the opinions of the fanatics, and the agitated.[27]

The Gendarmerie arrived – this emergency providing the spur to its installation in Siena – along with more troops, and the Prefect was encouraged to arrest 'several leading people' and send them to Florence for questioning.[28] The same menace that was used to enforce conscription protected minorities from the darker side of Baroque piety, but such incidents only hardened the contempt felt by the French for Italian Catholicism. When similar sales in Rome had by 1812 provoked a series of disorders and complaints, Tournon – acting more in his originally conceived role of conciliator – halted them, but only under protest from Janet, the ex-republican head of the *Domain*, who said it was giving in to 'fanaticism'.[29] For his part, Pius VII lambasted Napoleon in his Instruction of 22 May 1808 for 'his indifference to all religions, with the exception of Judaism, the implacable enemy of Jesus Christ'.[30]

The paradigm of cultural imperialism, as usually applied to extra-European circumstances, has a clear relevance in the assessment offered to Nardon on his arrival in Parma by a member of Moreau's administration about the 'religion' of the Piacentino:

> I think that we have made a huge mistake about religious attitudes in this area. I have looked at them closely, and I am convinced they do not stem from sincere piety, nor from superstitious fanaticism; only the habits acquired under the last Duke[31] still retain the appearance of superstition, and mean nothing better than this, to those who seem more attached to religious practices [than others]. In a word, the morality that is inseparable from a holy and firm piety is rather rare, and the vices [which exist here] are the direct result of this absence of a moderating check on them.[32]

The shift from patronizing tolerance to civilizing mission was now under way. The same memorandum initiated the revival the College of Santa Caterina. If anything, Nardon's future experience of Parma hardened him to such even-handed tolerance, but at this early juncture his attitude – and that of his superiors – more resembles the bemused, innately superior tolerance detected by Said among a later generation of imperial administrators.[33] It would not last. The system of cultural apartheid was not left to stand for long.

Like D'Auzers, Degerando and Tournon are revealed as Voltairians to the core when their observations are set beside Voltaire's entry 'Bishop' in the *Philosophical Dictionary*, where he recounts an encounter between a young Swiss Protestant and a wealthy prelate in the Papal states, who is, however, walking on foot:

> 'You are doubtless on your way to comfort a sick man, Monseigneur?' 'Sir, I am on my way to my master's.' 'Your master? That is Jesus Christ, doubtless?' 'Sir, it is Cardinal Azolin; I am his almoner.' 'What! You are in the pay of a cardinal? But do you not know that there were no cardinals in the time of Jesus Christ and St John?' 'Is it possible?' cried the Italian prelate. 'Nothing is more true; you have read it in the Gospel.' 'I have never read it,' answered the Bishop; 'all I know is Our Lady's office.' 'I tell you there were neither cardinals nor bishops, and when there were bishops, the priests were their equals almost, according to Jerome's assertions in

several places.' 'Holy Virgin,' said the Italian; 'I knew nothing about it: and the popes?' 'There were not any popes any more than cardinals.' The good bishop crossed himself, he thought he was with an evil spirit, and jumped out of the carriage.[34]

Lagarde, in Florence, concurred: 'Tuscans are superstitious, rather than religious. The crime of the priests here, is to absolve anything, which makes for "big" Fridays and Saturdays!'[35] In Nardon, and even more so in his subordinates, there is a sense of something more militant at work, however. Parma brought out something of the ex-Terrorist in him; his uncompromising revolutionary outlook saw him sent to Spain in 1812 to confront the demons that he first met in Italy writ large. Moreover, French officials at the very highest levels were implementing policy with cultural stereotypes firmly in mind, and a blindness to the complexities and richness of indigenous Italian religious life. Their strongly expressed personal prejudices, often predicated on private tastes, are transformed into matters of historical consequence because the terms of the Concordat – and the opposition and discontent they provoked in Italy – gave these men the chance to act on their views. Each of the opinions expressed above found its place in Napoleonic religious policy and spurred on its implementation, in a near perfect meeting of private and public cultural dispositions. Put bluntly, contempt for Italian religious life in all its myriad forms less dictated imperial policy, than reflected it.

Paradoxically, their highly selective approach to the Italian past also allowed men of such opinions to see themselves as the heirs of the Borromean paradigm. It was not entirely absurd. Degerando, as the official intellectual of the regime, discerned the wider points of contact with Trent, even while disparaging its details:

> The last and longest Council of Trent … renewed in part the old, severe rules of discipline, and intimidated even the morals of this same Court [of Rome], or, at the least, served warning on it of the need for a more austere morality in the face of the Protestant Reformation. In effect, from that time onwards, the throne of St Peter has seen more virtue and less scandal.[36]

Nevertheless, he believed that in the intervening centuries '[t]heology had replaced Christianity', that Roman theologians did not go back to the sources and that 'ecclesiastical history is on the Index'. In his reaction to this, he assimilated to the original reforming zeal he saw in Trent:

> the moment has come to return religious ideas to their ancient and true spirit, to reveal Religion, itself, by stripping away the veils that have disfigured it, by giving a still uncertain century both a moral

and reasonable direction, to set religion in the place of the priests, morals in the place of devotions ... . If carried out prudently, this Revolution might work without damaging Catholicism; the true tradition of the Church, directed by able men, would be enough to bring it about.[37]

Nor were these the visions of a powerless intellectual. The Minister of the 3[e] *arrondissement* of Police saw the suppression of the monastic houses of Tuscany as a vital step in just this direction:

in the present circumstances, it is appropriate to prove [our intentions] to the peoples of Italy by carrying out great changes in this part of the Empire, through reforming the abuses that weak and vicious clerical government has allowed to be introduced; in the abolition of the religious orders, the government is seen to attach great importance to the eradication of libertinism, thus reimposing those severe morals which will benefit religion and return it to its ancient purity, replacing the degraded mores which emerge from such bad institutions [as the regular houses].[38]

Whereas Degerando's views were formed by Enlightenment writings on the nascent discipline of anthropology, those of *le grand flic* appear more rooted in the subversive literature of the 'forbidden books'[39] and Diderot's *The Nun*. The words of both men, themselves so different, reveal a penchant for confidence based on selectivity, authoritarian uniformity in the face of complexity, and a mixture of zeal and self-assurance that equate with cultural imperialism.

Yet Degerando was all the more inaccurate in his vision of the future, in believing that it also had native roots. His views represent less a real attempt to bridge a cultural divide, than a projection of his hopes onto an unreceptive past; his construct soon decomposed in the face of Italian realities. The French missed three essential points about the post-Tridentine Church in Italy that were exposed at every step of their own attempts at reform. The first was how very pluralist Trent had been as regards the institutions of the Church. Although there had been initial plans to amalgamate all the regulars into a single order, and all the confraternities into a unique corps, that of the Holy Sacrament[40] – and the Concordat mirrored the former provision exactly – their selective approach to history ignored the essential point, that the Tridentine Church acknowledged, adapted to and then tapped the impulses of revival and renewal within the regular orders; that it fostered Jesuit missions and subsequently supported the emergent Redemptorists and Passionists in the same work; that it made use of regulars as predicators to bolster an under-staffed secular arm. Indeed, by the seventeenth century, post-Tridentine bishops proved adept at using particular orders in special ways: the Jesuits and the new orders as missionaries to the periphery, the Dominicans within the cities, and the Capuchins in the surrounding countryside, the 'rural centre'.[41] This flexible structure allowed them to adapt to 'the social, political and economic contexts of individual states and specific geographical areas within them',[42] something utterly at odds with the Concordat and lost on the French. Just as the National Assembly chose to ignore the findings of the *Commission des Reguliers* of the 1760s,[43] so its successor regime set aside the process of compromise, adaptation and evolution that was a defining element of the work of Trent. Borromeo and his adherents certainly envisioned the partnership between the secular arm and the other components of the Church as an unequal partnership, but they hardly saw the future in terms of the annihilation of the regulars enacted under Napoleon. The French neither saw – nor wished to see – that the reforms set in motion by Trent were allowed to evolve: Degerando saw only what Trent had been initially, not what it had become; he stressed only what he saw as its degradation. In practical terms, this meant the French had no grasp of the many ways in which the Church contributed to the process of social control that was so essential to their own projects.

Of course, the French did not outlaw confession, the Forty Hours or the Rosary, but they did stamp out the 'policing structures' which had been carefully put in place to enforce them since the sixteenth century, even when not specifically banned by the Concordat. Most significantly, they outlawed the effective method of parochial control of attendance at Easter confession, the issue of *biglietti* – tickets – to parishioners in Holy Week, to be handed in at confession which, in turn, admitted the holder to Easter communion. In contrast to the ramshackle, ephemeral world of secular policing, this system worked with ruthless efficiency and accuracy, even in remote areas. The names of those who had neglected their duty were posted on church doors, with some effect.[44] Ironically, it rested on a vision of society shared by the Napoleonic state and Trent, that of sedentary communities, for the Italian episcopate shared the distrust of the Napoleonic police for the transient populations of the hinterlands. The *biglietti* were seen as one way to exert at least a modicum of control over them.[45] This appalled the French, its distinct resemblance to the *livret du travail* and the internal passports favoured by Police-Générale not withstanding. This was not a case of the state trying to harness the power of the Church and failing. Rather it was the triumph of cultural sensibility over utility. The French Bishop of Casale in Piedmont believed this practice produced 'truly deplorable consequences, [stemming] from outdated, inquisitorial injunctions … . [It is] a dangerous and useless practice'. He knew, however, that many of his curés were deeply attached to it[46] and his circular to them passed it off as an oversight on their part, even referring to the use of *biglietti* as 'a practice which had a good effect, in a period when the piety of the faithful had been discernibly weakened'.[47] His private comments to the Minister reveal stronger feelings based, interestingly, on a dislike for the explicit invasion of personal conscience and privacy they effected. Their continued use came to light in the diocese of Vercelli in 1809, when a rural canon denounced it to Paris.[48] The Bishop defended himself, arguing that he had revived it because people were 'back-sliding', that it was still authorized by the Lateran Council. His main argument, however, was that it was by demand of the heads of household – *les pères de familles* – and so it was a matter of 'domestic discipline' more than of ecclesiastical practice. The Bishop pointed to a change in religious observance under way in this part of Italy, the longest under French rule:

> it is clear that the young will not communicate without a reason, and it is a fact, that where communion, at least at Easter, disappears, morality and the Faith disappear from view … . In fifty-six years, there was only one excommunication in Piedmont. Now, a good third of the faithful of our churches do not communicate, especially since the Revolution: One says nothing to them. One does not ask for their ticket … . It was only ever applied to the lower classes, to the country folk: Everyone would have said, had they not been issued, that the government had a secret policy to destroy Religion entirely, step by step. It was my hope … to make the government respected.[49]

The Bishop's case is stunning, all the more so because he was very pro-French. The vast implications for the secularization of this part of Italy are striking in themselves, but equally striking is the fact that the regime was not moved by it. It stuck to its original policy. Secularization was less of a threat to it, in its own eyes, than the attack on the principles of freedom of religious conscience that was embodied by the use of the *biglietti*.[50] When news reached Paris that the practice still continued in Tuscany, three years after the region's annexation, the Minister of Religion ordered the Director-General of Police in Florence to get the *maires* to intervene to prevent their issue and ordered the Tuscan bishops to do the same, concluding to Napoleon:

> there can be no more question of the tickets, which are counter to the spirit and the interest of religion. Counter to the spirit of religion, which should not resort to coercion or still less this sort of public denunciation that facilitates great scandals. Counter to the interests of religion, since a great many of those who appear to fulfil their Easter duties, do so only to mislead their pastors.[51]

French officials at the highest level expressed their contempt for this practice in the clearest possible terms. The Minister spoke of the empty spiritual content of the exercise, echoing Degerando's views on much Tridentine practice, showing contempt for the quasi-official, publicly sanctioned use of denunciation which was made all the more distasteful by its introduction into the sacred sphere. His sensibilities approximate in no small measure to the revulsion felt by many French police officials at the readiness of their Italian *administrés* to deploy denunciation against each other. It was another aspect of the clash between the culture fostered by the Inquisition and that of *citoyennité* under the Napoleonic police-state, for the *biglietti* had become incongruous in any practical sense and reflect, rather, the lingering revolutionary and liberal aspirations at the root of the regime.

When the long history of hostility between the Revolution and the confessional is recalled, the subjective objections to these practices emerge as all the more central to the antagonism felt by the French towards this Tridentine practice. It was his failure to reach a refractory confessor at the Easter of 1791 that convinced Louis XVI to flee Paris, and the uneasy relationship developed from there. This baggage was carried over the Alps and the French were always convinced that the dark, secretive space so meticulously prescribed by Carlo Borromeo[52] was now a powerful influence against them. Yet, even surrounded by this sense of menace at what was preached in the confessional, it was its wider context, as a form of social coercion, and the methods used to 'whip in' the laity, that drew direct French fire. It was not just their own position they felt to be threatened, but the dignity of their *administrés*. Clearly the Napoleonic state and the Tridentine Church had developed very different concepts of the line between the public and the private sphere.

The missions were the other major weapon of social control in the Tridentine arsenal deliberately suppressed under the French, something not originally stipulated by the Concordat. The decree abolishing all non-overseas missions in the empire and the Kingdoms of Naples and Italy was issued on 26 September 1809,[53] thereby enshrining in statute the hostility to the missions felt among Italian reformers since the mid-eighteenth century: Du Tillot issued a 'blanket ban' on them in Parma during his quarrel with Rome in the 1760s,[54] as did the Leopoldine legislation in Tuscany.[55] Joseph II banned Jesuit missions in the urban areas of Lombardy in 1767, although he did not interfere with their work in rural areas,[56] perhaps something of a backhanded compliment to the importance of the missions as a source of contact between the centre and the periphery. All this confirmed a growing distaste for the demonstrative, traditional work of the missionaries among reforming governments and sections of the urban educated classes, as well as more longstanding Jansenist criticisms.[57] However, the frequent assertion that the missions were increasingly discredited in the late eighteenth century ignores too many signs of their strength and popular appeal in Italy. This does not equate to their decline in France after the 1770s, when the Superior of the Mulotins – a new order founded in the late seventeenth century to evangelize the remote west – declared that 'a false delicacy prevailed so that we would be censured if we tried to put on these pageants of religion'.[58] In Italy, by contrast, the missions survived and prospered in the face of direct attacks by reforming governments – a circumstance which did not apply to France – and even the suppression of the Jesuits. The Redemptorists and Passionists had gained sufficiently in numbers and effectiveness to compensate for the absence of the Jesuits, and also learned to moderate the demonstrative Jesuit approach to predication and collective participation in the religion of the missions, largely through the writings and example of the Redemptorist Alfonso de Liguori, who dominated missionary work from the 1740s until his death in 1787. Liguori rejected Jesuit tendencies to stir up emotions to extremes and their penchant for collective processions of the laity, nor did he dwell luridly on sexual transgressions. Liguori's work showed that the Italian missions could – and did – adapt successfully to the changing circumstances of the eighteenth century without losing the support of the masses.[59] This was obviously lost on the Napoleonic regime, but Liguori's stress on 'the conversion of sinners' by 'convincing the intelligence and winning over the will'[60] was hardly out of keeping with Degerando's approach to religion.

Even mainstream, non-Jansenist elements in the Church often criticized the missions for their failure to make a lasting impact on the laity. Indeed, the Jesuit model of the mission that dominated the sixteenth and seventeenth centuries was evolved as a direct response to the obvious failure of the Franciscans and Dominicans to achieve only the most superficial results through the mass baptisms in the New World.[61] Later Liguori's critique stemmed from his questioning of the results achieved by the Lazzarists in the Maremma in the 1740s, where he felt too much stress was placed on 'fervour'.[62] Using new methods and working closely with the bishop, by 1795 it was generally felt that improvements had been made in the spiritual and, therefore, behavioural life of even this extremely remote area.[63]

The missions were easily revived in those states where they were banned in the 1760s and 1770s, perhaps the clearest tribute to their role in the workings of the *ancien régime* state, as well as their special place in the life of the masses. In Parma and Piacenza the respective bishops, Turchi and Cerati, soon deployed the re-formed Jesuits to teach open-air catechism classes in the cities and on missions to the hinterland during the mid-1790s; Jansenist criticisms were vocal and Turchi in particular was careful of them. Ultimately, however, they were impotent.[64] In the Tuscan Maremma, by the 1780s and on into the 1790s, the missionaries had resumed their important role of reporting to the Bishop on the state of the clergy, as well as of the laity.[65] Alone among the revolutionary regimes of the *triennio*, the Ligurian Republic appreciated the possibilities offered by missions as a means of reaching the communities of the periphery. In 1799 they planned a series of 'national missions' to the countryside, staffed by pro-patriot clergy, although this came to nothing because of the war.[66] After 1800 the restored Republic allowed traditional missions to continue, thus furnishing the French with first-hand evidence of this aspect of 'Baroque piety' in action.

The role of the missionaries, working with the Inquisition, was central to all efforts by the centre to exert social control on the periphery. However, perhaps the real loss to the Napoleonic regime came less in the realm of policing, in the light of its own formidable ability to gather information, than through the loss of the help of a potentially kindred spirit, even among the ritually castigated Jesuits. From the outset of their work, the Jesuits in particular were sensitive to cultural differences; they were as shocked by the savagery and ignorance they felt existed on the periphery as any French official, and even coined the phrase 'nuestras Indías' to draw the direct parallel with the untamed New World; above all, they learned 'to look at your own country as if through foreign eyes',[67] thus initiating an anthropological approach to social control on which the Enlightenment drew shamelessly. That is, their cause was harmed less by the lack of the information gathered by the missionaries, than by the skill and spirit with which such information was gathered. Their sensibilities led the French into the same quagmire as the mid-century reformers, Peter-Leopold and Du Tillot especially, but which figures as diverse as the Ligurian *giacobini*, Turchi the post-Tillot Bishop of Parma and Ferdinand III of Tuscany had all tried to reconstruct: this work was now aborted. In their predisposition to recoil from these methods of social control, the French inadvertently set themselves against the tide of the 'civilizing mission' in its most successful manifestations in Italy up to that time. Unlike their indigenous predecessors, the French possessed real powers of coercion and so avoided paying a direct price for their ignorance.

As ever, it was a mixture of distaste at the external workings of the missionaries they saw at first hand, their own traumatic experience of the Vendée and an inability to distinguish among the many currents at work in the late eighteenth-century Italian Church that led them to discard this most powerful weapon in the struggle of the centre to control the periphery. There was a difference of opinion about the nature of the missions at the apex of the Napoleonic state that turned on conflicting interpretations of their role in the Vendée, before and during the Revolution. Revolutionaries of all shades felt the missions of Grignion de Montfort were the real origins of the Vendean revolt, a fear made all the more intense because his missions were thoroughly orthodox in character and so was Vendean piety. The Royal and Catholic Army fought under the Christocentric Sacred Heart, rather than the more atavistic Madonnas that rallied the Italian masses in 1799. Although 'more to do with Revolutionary phantasms … than factual reality'[68] this prejudice was alive and well within the Napoleonic police. Two years after the abolition of special missions in 1809, Savary, Fouché's successor, lashed out against them as an active source of subversion in France in a circular to 'All Prefects and Police Commissioners':

I have told His Majesty many times about the bad consequences of the missions ... . These men, outsiders in the areas where they exercise the important ministry of preaching the word, are almost always distinguished by their fanatical, gross sermons ... . I expressly advise you to see to it that all missions are banned in your jurisdictions, and to arrest any priest not in a parish who tries to preach.[69]

Earlier, in 1806, the Minister of Religion had stressed the importance of the missions for reconciling parishioners to their own clergy; exactly because they were outsiders: 'The missionaries have re-established civil and religious peace in many dioceses. They have done incalculable good.' The report asked for a minimum of 500 missionaries to serve the whole empire.[70] Needless to say Napoleon trampled on the request, but in 1806 he did not yet share all the prejudices of his police. In criticizing the proposals made by the Ministry of Religion, he noted that the only part of the empire where missions might be useful was, indeed, the Vendée, and that only twenty priests, all trained in Paris, would be needed.[71] By 1809 even this view had changed, another instance of the regime moving not to the 'right' over time, but back to its Revolutionary roots, as the views of Savary's police prevailed over those of even the most Gallican elements in the Church, even over the protests of Fesch, who told his nephew directly that the news of their abolition had 'terrified all the bishops and all French Catholics'.[72] He got nowhere, but his worries were supported even by the new French Bishop of Piacenza, who informed Paris of 'the very bad effect' the decree had made at the moment the missions traditionally began and which he thought a very useful institution:

Sunday morning begins with prayers and then Mass, catechism in the afternoon, vespers, a meeting, and then the benediction ... . [T]he result is a useful education.

The Bishop hoped for their reinstatement, otherwise 'we all run the risk of provoking disquiet'.[73] His colleague in Parma, Caselli, a Piedmontese ex-regular noted for his loyalty to the regime,[74] agreed: 'these missions are sometimes necessary to recall Christians from their errors'. Whereas his French colleague painted a picture of missionary work for Paris, the native prelate pointed to the practical disruption the ban would cause. The parish clergy could not leave their posts during Advent and Lent, when their presence was most needed to 'police the faithful', but this was also when good, constant preaching was most needed; the parishes were short-staffed as it was. Nor were there enough truly good preachers to go around.[75] The different emphases stressed by the Frenchman and the Italian reveal the shock felt by the former at the lack of religious education among his new flock, akin to that felt by the original missionaries of the Counter Reformation, while the argument of the latter stemmed from a solid knowledge of the shortcomings of his clergy and an ingrained sense of the intrinsic place of the missions in the work of the secular arm.

In the course of 1808, between the report of 1806 and the abolition of 1809, much empirical evidence from Liguria poured in on the nature of missionary activity. Liguria offers a unique opportunity to examine the attitude of the French to missionary activity in Italy, because it was quickly brought under control in the Piedmontese departments when they were annexed in 1802 and in the same year, when they occupied the Duchies of Parma and Piacenza, Moreau de Saint-Méry swiftly republished Du Tillot's anti-clerical legislation, which included a ban on missions.[76] Tuscany and the Papal states were annexed after 1809. It is not possible to establish a direct link between its acquisition by the offices of Police-Générale and the suppression of the missions in 1809, but it does reveal that the opinions of French officials in Liguria were divided on why they opposed missions, even if they would all support Police-Générale against Religion. Predictably, there were sharp differences of interpretation within the French administration about the missions organized throughout Liguria in the summer of 1808. The French Police Commissioner admitted they were done legally, on the orders of Spina, who was rapidly becoming infamous for his ability to organize multifarious forms of passive resistance to the Concordat, while staying just the right side of the law. Spina deployed secular clergy from Genoa, there being no more regulars in his province, drawn from his newly organized 'Congregation of Urban Missionaries', centred on the Cathedral Chapter of San Lorenzo, to which he assigned the considerable sum of 500 francs for their work.[77] The Prefect of the Apennines, Rolland, noted dryly that the missions had been 'held down low' under the *ancien régime*, when government permission had been needed for them, but under the Concordat Spina actually had a much freer hand, to the point where civil officials had no control over the missions.[78] Although both officials condemned the missions, they stressed different reasons. The Police Commissioner remarked that, whereas missions in previous years, before the quarrel between Napoleon and Pius VII became overt,

> preached against sloth, drunkenness and about morality, now they preach only about Religion, about the obligation to support it, and about dying rather than let it be changed.

The sermons were about martyrs' deaths and the heresy of the terms of the Concordat.[79] The implicit political message was obvious to the Commissioner and it was paramount for him. If the main thrust of the missions was, indeed, to warn of the dangers of imported heresy and the threat to the Papacy, then Spina had knowingly returned them to their original purpose and away from the more 'structural' work they quickly assumed when it became clear by the late sixteenth century that the Protestant threat would not cross the Alps.[80] Although the Commissioner noted – and was repelled by – the 'terrible discipline' of the self-flagellation of one of the missionaries at Rivarolo, he really feared that the missions were being put to political ends. This was all the more pressing because of their popularity with all classes: in the Val di Polcervera, 'people of a certain standing went to the mission, barefoot' and handed out more alms than usual, the churches were 'well attended', the confessionals were never empty, there were more processions than ever – and they were big. At Sestri, they preached to a crowd of over 4,000 in a wood outside the town and were followed by a rapturous throng for nearly two miles, when they moved on after the usual five days' work.[81] It was the turning away from the work of 'social control' to counter-revolutionary agitation that drove the Commissioner to demand 'several severe examples of punishment to arrest their progress'. He was very alert to the 'regression' in the external presentation of the missions from the more restrained models of the eighteenth century back to the 'enthusiasm' of the Jesuits, but there was a deeper history behind what he interpreted as mere 'playing politics'. The Church had a very long tradition of confronting secular challenges it felt to be heretical or even diabolical. Also evident in the missionary preaching in Liguria were elements of the earlier Franciscan tradition of prophetic preaching, which stressed divine signs of change and fate.[82] This was more than a calculated political challenge to French rule; it had echoes of a return to an orthodox atavism within the ranks of the clerical intellectual elite. Ironically, a grudging respect for missions as they once were is evident, if hardly dominant, in the thoughts of the Police Commissioner.

The Prefect was much less suspicious, but even more damning, in his assessments. Rolland had been the Prefect of the Piedmontese department of the Tanaro before crossing the Apennines – and noted that missions in Piedmont were much less demonstrative than in Liguria. For all his experience, he was both a Protestant and a Frenchman, and his insistence on banning the missions was cultural, not political. Rolland insisted they were not politically dangerous; indeed, under the *ancien régime*, the government used them to persuade people to hand over their arms. They were sickening, for all that:

> These missions are exceedingly ludicrous things for Protestants, accustomed to the immobility and monotony of their preachers … .
> To the French, an Italian priest in the pulpit seems like a demon, and so a missionary who has to appear even more forceful than the regular preacher … has to reach his audience through actions that can only appear mad, extravagantly absurd … [self-]flagellation has always been a part of it, for without it, the oratory would have no

effect. Gendarmes who speak the local dialect said there was nothing seditious preached during the mission at Sestri, as have other reliable sources.[83]

Yet he concluded that 'For my part, I think the missions are very bad practices, just as the confraternities are very bad institutions'. His analysis took no account, indeed showed no awareness of, the style of mission developed by Liguori from the 1740s onwards.

Fouché handed down a severe sentence, ordering that the Archpriest of Comogli who had led the mission at Sestri be sent to Fenestrelles under Haute Police. When D'Auzers passed on the order, the reason given was not that of politicizing, counter-revolutionary agitation. Rather,

> This priest, amidst several scandalous scenes and challenges to the public peace, after having preached in a damaging way, allowed himself to be almost skinned [alive] in his pulpit, and to bleed like a flagellant. This excess of fanaticism took place before more than 4,000 listeners.[84]

The first attempt to arrest the Archpriest failed, causing a minor riot in Comogli. The gendarme charged with it said he would have preferred to arrest his quarry on the road to Genoa, but felt time was short, as he had to stop him taking part in another mission.[85]

When Fouché then tackled the Ministry of Religion about this, he blended the two strands of official disdain. The missionaries at Sestri preached

> in a style that could only appear ridiculous to reasonable men, were it not also a dangerous influence on an ignorant and naturally superstitious fanatical people.

However, they had also been playing on 'the events that have occurred at Rome', which was a loss because, parroting the words of his subordinate

> the preachers no longer stress morality. They take as their only standard the dangers to religion, the need to defend it, and the absolute loyalty owed the Pope and the Church. The clear intention here, easily discerned, is to whip up their spirits, and drive them to excess.[86]

There was more than state security at stake in this incident; indeed, the Prefect of the Apennines went so far as to say he did not see state security as an issue: Fenestrelles was felt to be the best corrective to 'old-time religion', regardless. In the years ahead, prison would increasingly become the destination for clergy opposed to the regime. There are many worrying aspects in the behaviour of both Church and state in these incidents. French lack of awareness of the different traditions of Italian missionary activity is already clear, but parallel to it was the persistence of 'archaic' tendencies, chiefly self-flagellation and 'hell-fire' preaching of the kind Liguori and his collabo-rators had largely abandoned from the 1740s onwards. Even leaving any potential for true counter-revolutionary agitation aside, this represented a worrying trend within the Church: These missionaries were not Jesuits or Capuchins, orders steeped in the tradition of this genre of proselytizing; rather they were high-ranking secular clergy, handpicked by the Cardinal Archbishop of Genoa for the task. This would seem to indicate a deliberate shift away from the main currents of the eighteenth century towards a return to more atavistic – populist, as well as popular – forms of devotion. This trend is discernible in many other aspects of Spina's actions and, arguably, it is the clearest evidence of the Church's efforts to reforge an alliance with the masses in the face of the Revolutionary threat. Indeed, the other striking feature of the missions of 1808, from the point of view of the Church espe-cially, is how popular they were, both at the centre and on the periphery. Large, fervent crowds supported the missions not only in the 'Indies' of the Val di Polcervera but also in the maritime cities of Liguria. The populist forms of devotion expressed in the missions spanned regional divisions; they had roots everywhere and the Church was now playing to them rather than trying to curb them, as had been done in the preceding decades. Even according to the French, this was the case. Spina's tactics were a far cry from the insistent demands of the Bishop of Grossetto in 1776–7, when he banned flagellation, that all missions be 'wholly devoid of din'.[87] French prejudice was not wholly unfounded, it would seem, in matters of sensibility and, even by the standards of his own Church, Spina was playing a dangerous game. Liguori – to say nothing of Jansenist and reforming critics – would have disapproved. These events depict the closing of a vicious circle: in the face of a Church becoming defiant and difficult to work with, even within its own rules, the regime resorted first to arbitrary arrest and then to suppression, rather than trying to adapt the work of the missions to a purpose avowed useful by all. For his part, Spina turned towards true populism, setting the Church on a collision course with the French regime. This was not a conflict about politics in the strictest sense – the missions spoke about defending the Church, not reviving the Republic of St George – it was, in truth, far worse than that. Church and state were pulling away from the little common ground they possessed, willingly. Spina and French officialdom together undermined what should have been their greatest common cause: the struggle over a truly *longue durée* to achieve 'the pacifi-cation of souls', a cause that should have been approximate to that of creating a *société polie et policée* – and French officials of very anti-clerical stamp were aware of this. The concrete, quasi-secular scope of the missions

– 'to facilitate reconciliation between enemies and restore peace in communities troubled in any way', in the words of one historian[88] – was rejected by the French for reasons that were a mixture of politics and taste, being too hedged in with cultural compromises to be adapted to the service of the new regime.

There is something of a 'sliding scale' that is often, and naturally, applied by historians to the forms of resistance which were driven by religion, whether wholly inspired by it or not: the violence of the *Viva Maria* risings under the *ancien régime*, or the *Santa Fede* and the other revolts of 1799, take precedence. These are followed by the peaceful but very public confrontations between Church and state at High Days.[89] Bringing up the rear is a seldom manifested but more widespread sense of alienation from the reforms of the Concordat, all the more important, perhaps, for being so. Protest and resistance in religious matters were overwhelmingly peaceful in character, but that should not detract from their intensity, particularly when it is recalled how deeply some aspects of the Concordat struck into the fabric of family life. The French ignored – as they had in France a decade earlier – the fact that their reforms clashed with those of Trent exactly in those aspects of the work of the Church dearest to the laity. Civil marriage and divorce came as shocks to all classes all over the peninsula. They first caused consternation in Turin, where the Piedmontese magistrates so lauded by the Dal Pozzo and Degerando for their high degree of assimilation admitted only eight divorce cases – and granted only three – between 1802 and 1814.[90] In Naples the provisions for divorce were never actually published, so great was Joseph's fear of elite reaction to their very existence. Indeed, under Napoleonic rule there were only nineteen divorces granted in the two satellite kingdoms and the *départements réunis* combined.[91] It should be remembered, too, that divorce was an upper-class issue. There are signs that civil marriage was intensely disliked among all classes. Only a handful of civil marriages, without benefit of clergy, were ever contracted in Piedmont during the *triennio*, for example.[92] At one end of the social scale – and of degrees of resentment – the respected Piedmontese jurisconsult J.B. Ferrero, published a university textbook in 1808, *Jurisprudence du mariage sur le rapport moral: Traité tendant à concilier les lois du Code Napoléon, de l'organisation des cultes et de l'enseignement public*, the title of which is self-explanatory; at the other, among the demands set out in the petitions of the rebels of Val di Trebbia in the Piacentino in 1806, was that marriages take place 'only according to the rights of the Holy Church'. Indeed they also demanded 'the re-establishment of the monks, and the full restitution of their properties'.[93] There are even signs that by the late eighteenth century the better organization of diocesan administration meant that canon law made a significant impact on the laity, at least in urban centres, that

The application of the laws of the Church influenced individual conduct, and in the course of this process, a new equilibrium took shape in the Catholic conscience.[94]

In Siena, by the last quarter of the eighteenth century, the Church seemed to have developed its own way of defending married women, an increasing number of whom came forward to the Ecclesiastical Tribunals to request – and often be granted – separations from their husbands, a process which might be interpreted as a renewal of faith in the Church courts.[95] They were certainly more sympathetic to women than the Napoleonic legislation. In this case, at least, the Church and the laity seemed to be finding a *modus vivendum* to which the Concordat could contribute nothing of worth. In Piedmont the Church was under much tighter government control than in Tuscany, with a clear duty to support the state in stifling scandals that 'troubled the public peace'.[96] Here, predictably, the *ancien régime*'s attitude to separation within marriage was much closer to that of the French and few were granted,[97] but as has been seen this also meant that opposition to the institution of divorce was equally strong.

These were what might be termed 'structural' assaults by the Concordat on the intimate traditions of Italian family life, in that they bit into the fabric of existence rather than manifesting themselves publicly at 'high points', as was the case with the changes wrought by the Concordat in the Church calendar or by the closure of chapels, churches or regular houses: the latter aspects of the Concordat were very visible affairs and provoked well-documented, highly visible responses that will be discussed below. However, within these more demonstrative protests were often embedded resentments bred by more 'structural' issues, such as marriage, and the petition of the rebels of the Piacentino is a case in point, its mention of marriage set alongside a long list of more 'profane demands'. Direct attacks on the Concordat's provisions for divorce were among the themes emphasized by the Ligurian missionaries in 1808, and were regarded as a very powerful weapon by the French police.[98] Widespread Italian dislike of civil marriage becomes intriguing when the provisions of the Concordat are juxtaposed to the priorities of Trent: whereas the Tridentine reforms sought above all to ensure that the couple entered into marriage of their own accord, free from external pressures,[99] the Code gave considerable powers to the parents, to a degree where either could prevent a marriage. Emphatic conclusions are impossible to draw from the nature of the available evidence, but the Code was clearly not at odds with Italian habits of marriage strategy *per se*. The widespread penchant for the use of dowries to control husbands in many parts of the peninsula in the early modern period[100] was also attacked by the Code, and resented, but on another level their use might point to a more fundamental shared interest between Italians and the framers of the Code: a desire to thwart the Tridentine ideal of freely contracted union. In practice, it did not work this way for the French: the symbolic, binding significance of dowries and Church marriages as *de facto* legal contracts certainly continued to outweigh the provisions of the Code. Such attitudes become equally interesting when set beside the far clearer materialistic opposition to the institution of divorce: simply that it could ruin carefully constructed marriage strategies. The Code threatened nothing of the kind; Trent might, yet Italians of all classes throughout the peninsula stood by Trent in these matters. In the pressing concerns of family life, the provisions of the Code left the new regime stranded between one of the few Tridentine strictures viewed ambiguously by the laity and that same laity's distrust of the presence of the state in such matters. The French sensed this and were extremely sensitive to any sign that civil marriage was being defied. This was more than a matter of keeping the *État Civil* up to date, as shown by the case of the Archpriest of Rapallo in 1810. He was denounced for carrying out marriages before the civil ceremony had been performed. His political views were not sound and one of the weddings in question was that of a leading local civil servant.[101] The reaction of the civil authorities was revealing in its intemperance; both the Procureur of the Criminal Court and the Prefect wanted him brought to trial. The former stressed the influence wielded by the clergy in the coastal port and that this conduct proved 'that ignorance, fanaticism and prejudice are still set above the Price and the laws of the Papacy'.[102] The latter believed the public trial of a priest over such a matter would have a good effect in the area, stressing the need for the government to assert itself over the formalities of civil marriage once and for all.[103] On Sunday, 29 May 1808, shortly after the annexation of Tuscany to the empire, the parish priest of Pitigliano near Arezzo preached against civil marriage from the altar at the reading of the Gospel. He urged the people to keep faith with the Church's sacraments and that it was only the sacrament that made marriage a contract. The police captain who heard the sermon noted 'there were some approving murmurs among the ignorant, which could have dangerous consequences'.[104] In contrast to its reception in France, the Code satisfied no one here. These were the deeper currents of dislocation and resentment which recalcitrant clergy would draw upon in their more open, dramatic confrontations with the new regime. Perhaps the depth of the chasm between rulers and ruled in the realm of marriage is found in a report by Tournon in Rome in 1810. He 'discovered' the Congregation of the Holy Annunciation, composed of 200 Roman laymen and founded in 1460. It had no formal pious obligations, but existed either to provide dowries for poor girls or to place them in convents. Tournon was amazed at its success and its extensive resources, as they came wholly from private donations. The Congregation was abolished by the patriots in 1798, but revived thereafter, and in 1810 it was worth 30,000 francs.[105] The Code outlawed dowries, and the Concordat convents.

Nothing shocked or surprised the French in the barbarous, backward or counter-revolutionary culture they found on the periphery. All this was well known to them from their experience of their own periphery in the Vendée and the Auvergne. Indeed, this experience was a constant point of reference, in their religious as well as secular confrontations with the Italian hinterlands. Yet two things did shock them and convince them that they were dealing with something markedly – if hardly entirely – different from the problems of the 'interior'. The first was how extensive the Italian periphery was in comparison to that of France. Whereas it was felt in 1806 that only the west and the Massif needed missionaries – and only a handful, at that[106] – those French officials in Italy who did not oppose missions on principal saw a huge need for them, in the right form. The French did not perceive a large 'block' of Italy, comparable to that north and east of the future 'Maggiolo Line' that was already taking shape in the minds of Napoleonic officialdom, a generation *avant la lettre*. Although Mirabeau *père* bemoaned the failure of the French masses to attain 'that softening of behaviour, that urbanity, that civility … that is virtue' in the 1750s,[107] those of the next generation felt that it had made far more progress than in Italy. Moreover, there was a discernible 'civilized core' to both the country and the elite that was lacking beyond the Alps. The second major difference with France was that the culture of the French centre in no way equated with that of the Italian centre. This has already been explored in a secular context, and the French examination of Baroque piety in its urban, elite and lowland contexts only confirmed their belief that these differences were rooted, essentially, in religious differences. Degerando, Tournon, D'Auzers and Nardon were criticizing the devotional culture of some of the largest cities in Europe; D'Auzers and Rolland castigated not only the piety of the highland valleys in Liguria, but that of the substantial cities of the Riviera as well. They were not blind to the nuances involved: the periphery was dominated by archaism, neo-pagan devotional rituals, even a complete lack of interest in the 'true religion' of the rational heart. Here, in ironic – if wholly predictable – similitude to the early Jesuits, the French sometimes had hopes of a return to 'the primitive Church', as they conceived it, much as they hoped to harness highland ferocity to their military machine. In contrast, they pointed to the enervating, degenerating consequences of the success of the Tridentine Church. Thus they conceived a two-pronged assault on the Italian Church, in every corner of their possessions, touching every arm of the Church and every element of Italian society. The introduction of the Concordat was meant to cut to the roots of a whole culture.

4

THE RELIGION
OF THE RULED

There was little in Italian piety that was wholly alien to the French, as opposed to what they misunderstood. Nor were there many battles which had not been fought before between the Italian laity and, successively, Trent, the Jansenists and the Enlightened reformers of the mid-eighteenth century. Indeed, French officials had fewer problems in recognizing the more archaic aspects of Italian religiosity – those of 'nuestras Indías' – than in disentangling them from Baroque orthodoxy. It was often Tridentine rituals like the Forty Hours that seemed new to them, not those rooted in archaism. The new regime emerged from a world full of popular superstition, a multiplicity of Madonnas and, at least in the Midi, the lay confraternities, which embodied that 'meridional sociability' Agulhon calls 'a valid global intuition'.[1] Although the associative life of male confraternities had declined over much of France by the end of the *ancien régime*, particularly in the north,[2] most other forms of popular devotion, and the cults of local Madonnas and saints, were widespread well into the nineteenth century, alongside the quasi-Christian folk beliefs that sustained them.[3]

This is exactly what the French had chosen to turn their backs on, however. The roots of the break may, indeed, lie deep in the *ancien régime* in both a social control operating through the Church, at the apogee of absolutism,[4] and in a more recent Enlightened revulsion for popular superstition and organized religion, although these trends were subject to significant regional variations between north and south.[5] In Napoleonic Italy the Concordat enshrined this dislike in statute, and when it entered the *départements réunis* and the Kingdom of Italy it had already left no room for that compromise Agulhon defined as an 'anti-ideology that Catholics will judge Voltairian, and republicans as reactionary'.[6] The ensuing conflict found its most public, overt confrontations with the laity in exactly those aspects of popular devotion the French had already learned to hate at home: the cult of the Virgin and the miracles surrounding it; the associative, public life of the lay confraternities; and the local saints' days, which the Concordat first abolished and then sought to overlay with its own festivals. The final confrontation, which brought the laity and the clergy together, arose when the regime sought to infiltrate the Mass itself with new prayers. These were the most obvious 'flashpoints' between the state and its *administrés*, not just in terms of religious practices but in the challenge of the conception of political life embodied by the Napoleonic state and the more intricate, atomized political culture – the *campanilismo* – of the Italian *ancien régime*. Confraternities, local festivals and shrines, and even the Mass itself were all central to this political world, and so at the forefront of a wider clash of cultural values. There is a strong body of evidence to suggest that the newly ruled knew what they were defending and that the experience of so doing served to intensify those very bonds of corporatism the new regime had determined to break. The defence of traditional, popular piety drew otherwise divided communities together, as much in the larger provincial centres as in the countryside and the highlands, thus having a similar effect to the collective resistance to the imposition of conscription.[7] Religious inspired resistance proved all the more awkward to repress because it usually took pacific forms. Nevertheless, the new rulers knew what they were set on destroying and made the conscious choice to do so.

The Napoleonic regime expressed its dislike for public forms of popular devotion directly through legislation. Napoleon took up the cause of the Habsburgs, through a policy 'conscious of the need to consecrate the solemn times, but also to reduce the number of holidays which distract people from their work'.[8] The Concordat reduced these High Days – drastically in the case of most parts of Italy – and confined almost all of those that remained to Sundays. In 1806, Menou and the Archbishop of Turin – both reliable, loyal Bonapartists – were upbraided for allowing the *Fête-Dieu* to be held on a Thursday: only Easter, Christmas, the Ascension, the Assumption, Corpus Christi and All Saints days could be celebrated on a day other than Sunday. The character of Sunday itself was also altered, however. While it was considered too much for shops to open, a report by the Ministry of Religion in 1807 stressed that

> a worker who thinks he needs [to do] a job, can work … . Religion
> must not contradict people's views. In religious affairs, as in the
> natural and civic orders of things, necessity overrides all the rules,
> and suspends them.[9]

The French in Italy pursued this enthusiastically. In 1812, the Sub-Prefect of Novi fumed that

> It is impossible to stop people going to church on the days of festi-
> vals abolished by the Concordat, but it is easy enough for the police
> to prevent the preaching of useless sermons.[10]

Some did not see a problem with the former, however. This was the difference between the new regime and the old. The Gendarmerie could interpose itself with particular brutality to enforce the law. In 1808, while looking for refractory conscripts in a village near Piacenza, gendarmes found a banned *festa* in progress. According to the – French – Bishop of Piacenza, 'A gendarme entered the church, sword in hand, hat on head, and insulted the priest, using very obscene expressions'.[11] Aggressive acts of this stamp reveal the lasting heritage of the Jacobinism of the Army of Italy, but they do not represent a phenomenon that waned with time.

There was more to this than Josephine utilitarianism. The cheerful brutality of the Gendarmerie on such occasions reveals how politicized these confrontations were. This was a battle for public space, and for the monopoly of civic ritual so important to both cultures. As the regime attempted to impose the celebration of its own High Day, the feast of St Napoleon, after 1806, and to enforce the new prayers for the Emperor in the Liturgy, such scenes became more common. French hatred of popular religion had a future in Italy, as well as a recent history; it had ready 'enforcers' at local level to support the policy-makers on high. The people of Empoli in Tuscany were wrong in the letter – but not necessarily in the spirit – of the Concordat, in their fear that the French were about to abolish Christmas on the eve of annexation in 1808.[12]

Madonnas and miracles

The new regime could not ban miracles, nor did it try to outlaw devotion to the Virgin, in whom Italian popular piety soon found a familiar refuge and focus of resistance. This, at least, was something the French were prepared for. In both cultures, shrines and statues to the Virgin were widespread, especially in the countryside, and the French and Italian masses sought the same help from their madonnas – often more profane in motive than sacred – in the same ways. The use of the plural throughout is deliberate, for the concept of separate, individual madonnas, almost as per statue or shrine, was a widespread, common heresy in both France and Italy.[13] Familiarity bred contempt well before the annexation of large parts of Italy brought official distaste of such things into contact with Italian culture.

Nevertheless, there was a particular context to the relationship linking rulers, ruled and the Virgin Mary in Napoleonic Italy. Although Marian cults took almost identical forms in France and in northern and central Italy, there was probably a difference in volume. A detailed study of the cult in Italy reveals that, over the early modern period up to the late nineteenth century, there were more miracles, shrines and appearances of the Madonna in Italy than in other parts of the Catholic world. Within Italy, the highest concentrations were in the north and the centre.[14] The Ligurian Riviera was a particularly strong centre of the cult, with three major shrines: the

Madonna della Guardia near Genoa; the Madonna della Misericordia at Savona; and the Madonna di Montallegro at Rapallo.[15] Smaller shrines were also well supported. Cicagna, high in the Apennines, became a place of pilgrimage in the 1530s when a neglected statue of the Virgin began granting miraculous favours, following the introduction and widespread popularity of the Rosary of the Madonna into these valleys by the Jesuits. Cicagna presents an example of how deeply and swiftly the cult penetrated into this part of 'nuestras Indías'; the shrine still flourished in 1789, when a book was published about the *festa* of 1786 when the Virgin was crowned, a rare occurrence over most of northern Italy in this period.[16] In 1807 and 1808 the Vicar-General of Genoa reported ever increasing amounts of alms and other offerings – 'the pious liberality of the faithful' – at the small hill chapel of Our Lady of Vittoria. All the funds went to the upkeep of the chapel; none reached the parish. The Vicar-General complained that the local authorities were so attached to 'this fanatical devotion to the Virgin' that they did nothing to enforce the government's ban on nocturnal processions, which formed the devotions at the chapel.[17] Thus, when the French annexed Liguria, they entered one of the most intensely Marian parts of the Catholic world. Vittoria and Cicagna, outposts of the Jesuit civilizing mission in the 1530s, remained defiant strongholds of atavism, in the eyes of many, by the eighteenth century. The French occupation would bring the wheel full circle, however. When the Vicar-General's superior, Cardinal Spina, threw in his lot with 'this fanatical devotion', it grew stronger still, as it was deliberately rehabilitated – if hardly in need of actual revival – at the centre. The Vicar-General's identity of interest with the French over Marian devotion belonged to a passing era.

The omnipresence of the Madonna as a rallying cry during the traumatic revolts of 1799 all over Italy conditioned all French relations with the Virgin.[18] The place of religious motives in these risings, and those of the late eighteenth century against the Leopoldine reforms in Tuscany, is debatable among historians,[19] but clearer to contemporaries. Under the French, when a Madonna cried, moved, fell over or worked a miracle, French officials and the local *giacobini* reached for their guns. Over a six-month period in 1796, no less than 114 incidents of madonnas moving their eyes were reported in the Papal states, twenty-four of which were adjudged miraculous by the authorities. A report of 1797 argued they were warnings from heaven against earlier Jansenist outrages, rather than connected to the first French invasion.[20] The experience of the Concordat would prove there was little real difference between Jansenism and French rule. When a woman regained her sight in front of a statue of the Madonna in a church in Piacenza that was due to be closed and turned into a stable, it attracted tremendous popular interest, but the French were worried about more than a rowdy procession or overwrought crowds. The church was closed, the image locked away before the churchwarden removed it to safety. The whole thing risked 'fomenting fanaticism, [and] inspiring anti-French thoughts' in the lower classes, manipulated by the priests.[21] In Genoa in 1810, when a crippled boy walked again after looking at a statue of the Madonna, the police rushed to the scene, cleared the cathedral and then locked up both it and the boy. It all had to be 'severely repressed'.[22]

The French were not the first to dislike the cult of the Virgin, nor have they been the last. Michael Carroll has spoken wryly of 'liberal theologians for whom traditional Marian devotion is a bit embarrassing'.[23] For the Jansenists of eighteenth-century Rome, the purification of worship and the struggle against superstition were particularly directed at Marian devotion.[24] The Pistoian reformers and Muratori were averse to it.[25] Nor was Mary always warmly embraced by the mainstream of the hierarchy: her full acceptance by the Curia did not occur until 1854. Although Liguori propagated the doctrine of the Immaculate Conception, thus reinforcing the links between popular religion and missionary activity, it had yet to become official doctrine.[26] Devotion to the Virgin was still cultivated in the Jesuit Noble Colleges,[27] but the days when the Borromean reformers actively promoted the coronation of statues of Our Lady were long gone by the mid-eighteenth century.[28] The lessened emphasis on devotion to the Virgin was part of a wider trend in orthodox thinking that, while far less decided than that of the Jansenists or Muratori, 'did not wish to evoke aggressive religiosity in the faithful'.[29]

However, official disdain for the Virgin was matched in almost inverse proportion by continued popular devotion to her. The power of the cult on the Ligurian coast or on the periphery was not unique. In rural parishes of the diocese of Prato, on the eve of the reforms of Pistoia, half of all the rural confraternities were devoted to the Virgin, and these were all of recent origin as the older confraternities tended to be devoted to the Holy Sacrament.[30] The veiled Madonna in Pisa itself, another in the Church of the Nunziata in Florence – surrounded by legends of its power – and a third in Impruneta were strong foci of the cult in urban Tuscany, all of which the Pistoian reformers had attacked at their peril.[31] The popular rising against Scippione Ricci in his own see of Prato began in the spring of 1787, triggered by rumours that he was about to remove the Girdle of Our Lady which she had shed on her ascension to heaven.[32] In the hinterland of the diocese of Venice, there were fifty-four chapels to local saints and sixteen to the Madonna which were 'for the most part, the poorest, the smallest, the most neglected, abandoned, but they were never destroyed, even in the face of episcopal orders'.[33] It was the same in the Tuscan Maremma.[34] This evidence does much to support the general claim of Michael Carroll, based on Christian's work on sixteenth-century Spain, that most Marian shrines were rural and were maintained as part of the attempts of rural communities to assert their autonomy from the centre. To ensure their survival and avoid their abolition by a suspicious centre, the communities of the periphery had to keep producing 'evidence of divine intervention' that was clear and incontrovertible.[35] Thus Marian devotion remained intense from necessity, and came to symbolize the recalcitrance of the periphery.

Atavism and recalcitrance were only to be expected on the periphery. But the Virgin dominated the centre with similar intensity. Here the close links of the Marian cult and older forms of popular piety should be recalled. The earliest 'reform movement' in the Church, the Spiritual Franciscans, never attacked the cult, while the Flagellants, spreading out from Perugia, actively encouraged it and specifically argued that God was influenced by her intercession.[36] Although the lay brotherhoods were usually devoted to their own patron saints, the bonds between them and Mary were real enough, forming an informal coalition between those two aspects of popular piety that made authority, clerical and secular alike, most uncomfortable. A petition from the former members of the confraternity of the Sabbatini of Bologna in 1811 is a good example of the longevity and intensity of Marian devotion in this prosperous urban centre:

> From time immemorial and without interruption, it has been the custom of the Sabbatini to go, one Saturday in the year, to visit the Sanctuary of the Blessed Virgin of San Lucca, leaving the city three hours before the Mass of St Peter [Matins]. In whatever circumstances, and under whatever regime – and with its support – this religious duty has never been interrupted. Now, however, it has been suspended by order of the prefect.[37]

The regime had banned it because it was a nocturnal procession but, in suppressing the confraternities as well, it destroyed those who sustained this High Day. They did not give up, however. As for Marian devotion among the Romans:

> Their great popular devotion was directed to Mary, the Mother of God, who was worshiped in a frenzy of tenderness. In the popular faith, she was the chief power in heaven; she had made the world. She replaced the God Hermes of ancient times. No work was done, no enterprise or business launched without sheltering under the image of Mary. She was the repository of the city's collective memory and the rallying point of the Roman masses.[38]

In Piedmont, a very different society from that of Rome or Bologna, the Madonna of Vico remained, under royal patronage, the greatest shrine in the region. It was duly sacked by the Army of Italy in 1797 and its crown of pearls – a present from the royal family – was carried off to Paris, along with all the other treasures of the Grotto,[39] a warning of what was to come.

The revolts of 1799 are the most spectacular, politicized expressions of the importance of Mary in the hearts of the Italian masses. They bear comparison with the almost contemporaneous revolts in Mexico. In 1769 a localized, millenarian revolt fought in the name of Our Lady of Guadalupe; it resembled the 'Viva Maria' risings in Tuscany.[40] The next came in 1810 with the collapse of Spanish rule.[41] The Virgin increasingly emerged as the counterpoint to Enlightened reform and – more overtly – to Enlightened absolutism, wherever her cult was strong. Mexico, like many parts of Italy in the same period, felt the impact of the Bourbon reforms and reacted in similar fashion. In Mexico, as in much of Italy, the 1760s saw religious policies attempted that one historian has termed the replacement of a Baroque Church with a Church of the Enlightenment.[42] The imperial dimension of the Mexican and Italian experiences in 1810 is also worth considering. In both cases, subject peoples turned to the Virgin as a focal point for resistance. Late colonial Mexico may present more fruitful comparative ground with the religious climate of the new imperial power in Italy than late *ancien régime* France, where the Cult of the Virgin sustained far more direct and consistent criticism, and seems to have been in comparative decline.[43] Marxist claims for widespread dechristianization in France must be treated with great circumspection, but the trend was far more apparent there than in Italy.[44] In France, although traditional devotion to Mary continued unaltered, it had become increasingly, if not quite exclusively, a phenomenon of the periphery and of the lower classes. While in the Vendean *bocage*, a priest of the Counter Reformation '[in order] to win over popular practices, reach[ed] a compromise with his parish', the five traditional Marian shrines of the plain of the Sarthe – the bastion of republicanism in the west – had disappeared by the eighteenth century.[45] As J.-C. Martin has observed of the Vendée, the difference between the *bocage* and the plain was not of belief as such, but in ritual practices and, in the case of the plain, 'in a greater submission by the faithful to the clergy'.[46] Although the Catholic revival of the nineteenth century revealed the extent to which 'genteel Catholics inhabited the same miraculous world as the shepherdess',[47] there were still fewer genteel Catholics by the 1790s than south of the Alps. Moreover, it was often the product of a revival, not of a survival among them. France was too fragmented, spiritually, to rise for the Virgin.[48]

This was not so in Italy. The Italian masses, when thrown back on their own devices, rose for the Madonna in 1799, as they had for the Virgin of the Carmine in Naples in 1647 in the face of an earlier, Spanish imperialism.[49] Cicagna became a redoubt of anti-French resistance in the Ligurian Apennines under its priests, Pezzuolo and Connio, just as in the seventeenth century the shrine of the Madonna had been a repair for smugglers and other outlaws when Corsican soldiers were sent from Genoa to burn it down. Lannes took similar actions in 1798 when the only part of the church to survive his ravages was the chapel of the Virgin.[50] Yet Mary represented a particular form of revolt. There is no contradiction in the universality of

Marian revolts in 1799, which is not at all to assert any uniformity among them. The French threatened every shrine and image and, therefore, every shrine was to be defended. It is an irony coincidental on an objective level – but not wholly by chance – that the Madonna was not taken as the symbol of the largest, most coherent counter-revolutionary movements of the time: Ruffo's *Santa Fede*, the Royal and Catholic Army of the Vendée and Hofer's Tyroleans all fought under more orthodox, Christocentric banners.[51] Mary's was the counter-revolution of the guerilla; the Sacred Heart, that of the Crusade. The latter marched on Nantes and Naples, the former fought – splintered, incoherent, but tenacious – only for hearth, home and harvest. The Mexican experience juxtaposes Marian and Christocentric forms of resistance most powerfully in the contrast between the atomized, Marian-inspired Hildago revolt of the early nineteenth century and the highly coordinated resistance of the *Cristada* a century later.[52]

This iconography has a wider meaning than any politicized struggle, however. In the age of Enlightenment and revolution, the Madonna – more splintered than the Cross – remained close to the people. The judgement of the leading historian of the place of religion in the Hidalgo revolt holds just as good for Napoleonic Italy: 'An ardent veneration of the Virgin Mary served to justify both preserving the political and social *status quo* and mounting pressures against it'.[53] The imperial grip on Italy was far stronger than that of any Mexican regime of the time, Spanish or indigenous, but, when set in the wider context of 'Enlightened imperialism', the various expressions of the Marian cult in Napoleonic Italy offer an intriguing window on passive resistance and on the growing together of popular and elite culture in the face of foreign occupation. The Madonna had led the atomized counter-revolutions of the *triennio*, and she went on to assume a special place in the history of the French occupation, thereafter. It has been noted that 'Mary's decision to appear at particular places at particular times is one of the things that most clearly establishes her as a distinct supernatural personage'[54] and that 'the Virgin has favoured ... rocky uplands – areas of sheep and goats ... not the fertile European plains',[55] behaviour that makes her a fitting patron of *guerrillas*.

Outwardly the forms of Marian devotion were little changed during the *epoca francese*, because there was little the French could do to change them. There were still apparitions, miracles, pilgrimages and the great festival of the Assumption – just. The festival of the Madonna of Divine Love went on as usual in May 1812, when over 2,000 Romans flocked to her small hill chapel, nine miles from the town. The police said it would have been more, but for troop movements blocking the roads. Crutches were cast on the altar; an old woman – a domestic in a noble house – went into 'the most horrible convulsions'; no one was outraged when a distraught young woman soiled the altar cloth in her ecstasy, indeed three hundred of them cried 'Grace!' for her. Another woman placed a silver snuff box on the altar, promising it to the Virgin if she were cured; when nothing happened, she took it back in a huff. The whole panoply of popular Marian devotion was on display. Norvins was no stranger to this culture, even if he despised it:

> It was a morning passed in the extravagance of the silliest supersti-
> tion … . It is all about bread and priestly conniving, and the
> customs dearest to this people.

He took pride in the fact that it was better policed than under the Popes. French observers also noticed an older, indigenous struggle take place, at the height of the devotions, although it was not noted as such. It was not really the gendarmes who curbed the frenzy of the crowd, but the curé and the local police commissioner who led them in litanies,

> and then this throng, avid for miracles and furious at its own power-
> lessness to obtain them, suddenly calmed itself, and went back to
> Rome, peaceably and piously, singing the litanies.[56]

What Norvins had, in fact, witnessed were good missionary tactics, as practised by Jesuits and Redemptorists. Norvins knew he had local knowledge to
be grateful for, but he did not know its history. He had witnessed a classic
case of a priest and a local official caught in the middle, less between
Church and state than between popular, pre-Tridentine devotion and more
orthodox practice. Most importantly, Trent had taught them how to cope.[57]
As Peter Burke pointed out in the context of the Masaniello revolt of 1647
in Naples, the most effective way to fight social drama was with social
drama: the Neapolitan clergy used Christocentric devotion to calm the
popular rage focused on the Virgin. 'Order had to be restored in the supernatural as well as the natural world'.[58] This was beyond Norvins. Put
another way, left to its own devices French policy would have been unable to
curb 'excessive' Marian devotion, save by strong-arm tactics. Subtle struggles, of an older kind, meant nothing to Norvins.

Traditionally, the power of the Madonna manifested itself in several
ways. There was the power and veneration vested in the images, both statues
and paintings, and there were apparitions of Mary herself – or selves. The
differences between them are significant in themselves, in the wider context
of Italian piety.[59] However, the way all these things were perceived by all
those involved was henceforth conditioned by the memory of 1799. It was
also different when it happened on the periphery, not near a large, control-
lable city. The Madonna appeared, perched in a tree, to a group of
countrywomen led by their priest, all shouting 'Over here! Over here!' Under
the *ancien régime*, it would have been a matter for the diocese to investigate
and, probably, to forget unless great interest continued to be shown in the
tree. But it took place in a village in the volatile Piacentino in 1810. The

Prefect, Nardon, said it was all a priestly ruse to get money out of simple peasants, but he told Paris he wanted those behind it punished. The *maire* then ordered the gendarmes to cut down the tree:

> In this way, we have removed the means by which someone can abuse the credulity and faith of the highlanders. Since the oak no longer exists, the supposed miracles have gone away, and the fanatics and the superstitious keep their mouths shut.[60]

The point was that things were never going to be the same under the French, and it was the state's business to ensure as much.

Even at the centre, the French were wary of Marian devotion. The police commissioner of the Tuscan port of Livorno remarked in 1811 that the arrest and exile of the Pope would probably cause little trouble in the city,

> but they would rise in revolt, if any one touched the Madonna di Montenero, in whom they have great confidence. She saved them during a terrible earthquake, sixty-seven years ago, and they have always been grateful.

It was all part of a superstitious 'faith', concerned only with external devotion and devoid of dogma. However, this artificial approach to religion cut across class lines, for 'people of a certain rank only appear in church on Sundays and High Days'.[61]

This traditional mixture of intense devotion and lack of *gravitas* among the urban elites was undergoing a subtle but profound change under the impact of French rule. Old bastions of Enlightenment were crumbling. Florence saw a spate of Marian miracles in 1811, 'in this city of the superstitious' in the words of the Director-General of Police.[62] Lilies burst into flower before several of her statues on the street corners of the city, and crowds gathered rather than getting on with their work. Ten months later there were four more 'flowerings', and a Capuchin sister – whose house had recently been suppressed under the Concordat – regained her sight at Mass before a statue of the Virgin. The Director-General remarked, with routine condescension, that interest in these things was not confined to the lower classes, but that Florentines were not moved to raging fanaticism.[63] But there was nothing routine about this. It marked a very important cultural change and, in the context of the French occupation, perhaps a political point was made as well. The Madonna was finding upper-class support – if not necessarily respectability – in the face of the Concordat. In this casual remark, the whole trend of elite religiosity of the eighteenth century is seen being reversed, as is the fact that the French missed its full significance. This mattered in a Florentine context, because the city had been the cradle of the Jansenist polemicist Giuseppe Pujati, whose attack on the fervour and laxity of the use of Papal indulgences connected with the *Via Curcis* in 1782 won him elite support well beyond the circle of the political reformers.[64] Now the resurgence of upper-class Marian devotion indicated that the cultural process of the previous century was in conscious reverse.

A correlation has been discerned in Italian Marianism between a neglected holy image and its sudden propensity to dispense miraculous favours, even to the point that the former causes the latter.[65] French policy ensured the occurrence of many such instances. In the autumn of 1810 in the small mountain commune of Compiano, where Tuscany, the Piacentino and Liguria all meet, an isolated chapel was reopened, illegally as it tran- spired. In the course of the restoration a painting on an outside wall was uncovered from its layers of dust: the Madonna of Faggio. Then, D'Auzers reported, 'the rumours started':

> It was said it had somehow detached itself from the wall. Soon, they were adding that the bells were ringing by themselves. Angels were seen flying high in the air, celebrating, their voices joining in with trumpets from on high. A woman dressed in heavenly blue was spotted walking majestically on the clouds at night, surrounded by burning candles, when the image of the Virgin was uncovered … .
> When a wall collapsed, trapping three stonemasons, no one was hurt, even though they had been trapped under three feet of earth. It was all due to the Virgin. These happenings – continually changed and added to – attracted much attention.[66]

The imagery invoked and the patterns of behaviour described certainly reveal a very orthodox, almost standard vision of the Virgin and of Marian behaviour, notable evidence of conformity with the imagery of the hierarchy in the heart of the Apennines. More so, it might be added, than Bernadette's visions at Lourdes about which the Church remained uncomfortable – and quickly sought to readjust.[67] When the crowds came to admire the painting from Pontremoli (in Tuscany) and Bardi and Borgo di Taro (in the Piacentino), they expressed their devotion in the exaggerated manner the French detested:

> The most credulous walked up the mountain barefoot, and approached the painting in this state, where they all believed their sins would be forgiven. There was a priest from Ozacca, at the head of ten or twelve women.[68]

D'Auzers' contempt was palpable, but he attributed other motives to the timing of this local *cause célèbre*. The first miracle took place on the same day that twenty-seven Trappists from Cervara were being escorted to house arrest in Compiano for refusal to take the oath and receive their pensions, following the closure of their house: 'Several superstitious – or ill-intentioned – people asserted that the Virgin had shown herself to avenge the oppressed innocents'. D'Auzers took no chances and demolished the chapel,

> which is far from any dwelling, deep in a wood and was often more
> a refuge of vagabonds and refractory conscripts than a temple of
> the faithful.

Of course, it would be to such men that Mary would come, as the icon of the people. If D'Auzers was correct about the coupling of the apparitions and miracles with the arrival of the refractory clergy, the events in Compiano reveal profound levels of politicization in the heart of the periphery, even if the issues involved were rooted in tradition and interpreted in purely religious forms. French policy struck deep into these isolated communities as a result of the terms of the Concordat and the harassment of refractory clergy. The result was first to relate atavistic piety to contemporary politics, and then to leave a permanent reminder of French 'Otherness' and hostility in the area, not only through the arrival of the Trappists but also in the physical ruins of the chapel. In this case D'Auzers fought the whole panoply of Catholicism head on, leaving only ruins and – it is safe to presume – deep resentment in his wake through his effort to contain a set of events he assumed to be dangerous, revealed by his actions, and culturally repugnant, by his words. This was the periphery, at least. It was dangerous territory, but at least it was isolated. It would not remain thus, however. Other events would soon bring home to the French that Marianism, and the forces of resistance it represented, were finding other homes beyond the periphery, and new adherents at the highest levels.

Something happened in Genoa, under the occupation, that signalled a major change in Italian piety, and much more. In the autumn of 1805, before his departure from Liguria was postponed by the rising in the Piacentino, Lebrun, the French commissioner for the annexation of the region, made Cardinal Spina a parting gift of the statue of Our Lady of Charity, which had been impounded after the suppression of the monastery of Santo Spiritù. Spina thanked him warmly, and put it quietly away somewhere.[69] It was a mistake by Lebrun. A 'Virgin in reserve' was a dangerous cultural weapon in a country so devoted to Mary as Liguria, and even more so in the adroit hands of Spina. When his old friend Pius VII was deposed, arrested and gaoled in 1809, Spina did not try to raise Genoa in revolt. Rather, that July, he fetched Our Lady of Charity out of the episcopal cupboard, set her up in a new chapel in the Cathedral of San Lorenzo and held a vast, unauthorized festival to celebrate her transfer from a quiet side chapel to her new altar. It is tempting to equate this action to the tradition of unveiling a Madonna, normally kept shrouded precisely to heighten popular perceptions of her power, as happened in other parts of Italy and so hated by Jansenist reformers, although there are no references to such intentions in Genoa.[70] The episcopal celebrations lasted four days and embraced the whole city, not just the parish of the San Lorenzo.[71] When the processions, street banquets and open-air masses continued, unchecked and unrebuked, into September, the Police Commissioner exploded:

> A week does not pass when similar ceremonies do not get repeated several times – first in one church, and then in another. More often, still, these general solemnities are celebrated not in one neighbourhood, but over the length of the whole city ... . This is how the whole point of the Concordat is dodged, completely. It is time these unofficial holidays were restricted to Sundays, they are making people lose time at work and adding to their misery.[72]

It was an old attack, an eighteenth-century response to something newer than its expression might indicate. The French policeman missed the point, and it was not really that Spina's personal motive might have been to embarrass the regime over the arrest of the Pope. Whether this was his intention or not – and, circumstantially, it is likely – the true significance of the new-found passion for Our Lady of Charity is that Spina instigated and led it. The devotion of the laity was assured, but that a Cardinal Archbishop should play to it in so unrestrained a manner marks a fundamental change in official attitudes to the Virgin and, above all, to the popular piety she incarnated. The pressures of the Concordat, the traumas of the Revolution, the arrest of the Pope and the misery of a port devastated by the blockade, all came together in these festivities.

It is impossible to say from the evidence whether Spina had undergone a spiritual experience that led him back to popular piety, or if he was now playing what Allan Bloom has called

> a cultural relativist [who] must care for culture more than truth, and fight for culture more than truth while knowing it is not the truth.[73]

The latter seems the more likely. Whatever, Spina had become a populist, at least within the city. What had been thought necessary to hold in check a generation before was now sponsored and blessed. This was not an old High Day revived, but a new invention, built in defiance and fear of the Concordat. Spina's actions in Genoa represent a clear break with the recent past, but they were not the dawn of a new religious culture. Spina was planning for the future, but he was not ahead of his time. The new festival was not a forerunner of the tightly regulated, 'tamed' collective piety of the nineteenth-century revival. If the French police reports are to be believed, it drew on the traditional unruliness of popular piety and based itself on its traditional ritual space: the neighbourhoods of the city. Thus Spina was not a pioneer of the nineteenth-century revival in terms of social discipline. This was an alliance between equals, not an assertion of a new, clerical-inspired piety for the masses.

Nevertheless, he pushed the Church's relations with popular piety in a new direction; that this was so, mattered enormously in the conditions prevailing in Napoleonic Italy. His street parties were as great a volte-face as was Napoleon's coronation for Jacobins, probably more so. They were joyous, rather than vicious; wine, not blood, ran in the narrow streets of the old town; there was singing and laughter, not gunfire. Yet Spina produced a spectacle of cultural resistance to the new order as profound as any guerilla raid across the Balearic Sea. Above all, he had to change his own approach to devotion to achieve it. The ceremonies were repeated on the anniversary of the transfer of the statue in 1810.[74] That year saw a series of 'miracles' before the Virgin. Spina did not go as far as supporting them, but he cynically played for time. However, several of his senior clergy did take it upon themselves to promote the cult surrounding the image. One night in August, an old woman came to offer a whole jug of oil for the lamps of her chapel, in exchange for a few drops of the original oil. On the same night, a canon of the cathedral gave the Madonna a gold ring set with a precious stone. The police thought there were probably many more such gifts unknown to them.[75] The real point, lost on them, was the drawing together of popular and 'establishment' piety. After disdaining her throughout the age of Enlightenment, senior clerics in a major archdiocese were actively promoting this most populist of cults. The Church was on a new path in Liguria, even if it was not consonant with that taken by the later Catholic revival. D'Auzers sensed it when he demanded of Savary in 1811 that as many priests as possible be got out of Genoa and more reliable people appointed. He went as far as insisting that a second Vicar-General be appointed, and that the post went to a priest who was a police spy, to keep a close eye on Spina.[76]

Nor was Spina alone, even if, as the incumbent of a great see, he could put on the best show. Under the nose of a French Metropolitan sent to reform them, the Florentine clergy drew the wrath of the French police:

> There are festivities every day for the Madonna, there are octaves and the exposition of the Holy Sacrament in the Lady chapels until ten or eleven at night. In a word, the priests are inventing everything they can think of, to draw in the people, making them lose precious time off work.[77]

In Pisa, Spina's tactics were replicated, although applied to the relics of the patron saint of the city, transferred from one altar to another. The Minister of Religion reprimanded the Archbishop, reminding him that 'superstition is the greatest enemy of religion'. His account to Napoleon shows the strength of a different outlook:

> The whole population of the town and the neighbouring country-
> side moved itself to take part in these ceremonies. They lasted three
> days, and involved pilgrimages and offerings.[78]

Perhaps the greatest event of all took place at Savona on 8 September 1810, however. Pius VII, incarcerated there, said a Mass in honour of the well-loved Madonna of Savona on that, her feast day, which had been banned by the French. A crowd of 400 found its way, unsolicited, to his window to hear it. There was no trouble.[79] The very apex of the hierarchy had now embraced Marianism, in clear contrast to the reticence of the recent past. It seemed that French domination now threatened every Madonna with neglect, from those in the remote field chapels, closed by official order, to the occupants of the greatest shrines. Her – or their – power now grew accord-ingly, as Pius acknowledged.

As the Marian tide rose against him, Napoleon made his own spiteful riposte. In 1811 the government sold off the pearl crown of the Madonna of Vico, looted in 1799, to the Mont de Piété of Paris, for the huge sum of over 37,000 francs, enough to pay the pensions of 1,000 ex-nuns. In 1816 the restored government was still trying to recover it.[80] This was only a skir-mish.

The lay confraternities

The confraternities were the living embodiment of lay recalcitrance to Trent, the great 'irreducible' element in popular devotion, detested by the Church hierarchy, the secular authorities and reformers of all and every persuasion, Tridentine, Jansenist or Enlightened. For Nicholas Terpstra,

> Brotherhoods were the most public face of the Church, yet were
> almost entirely lay ... [I]t was their very ubiquity that made conflict
> and contradiction inevitable.[81]

The conflict between the empire of reason and the forces of 'obscurantism' was clearly drawn here, as was the more specifically political conflict between corporatism and the 'citizen state' of the Revolution. The confrater-nities were the driving force of *carnevale*, of public festivals that took over whole cities when they did not revolve around isolated, suspect rural chapels, dedicated to saints of dubious provenance, owned by the brotherhoods. To Trent, this epitomized impiety and archaism; to the secular authorities, simple disorder; to the Enlightenment, savagery and ignorance. Muratori attacked them root and branch in his *Antiquitates Italicae Medi Aevi, sive*

Dissertationes de moribus, ritibus, religione regimine of 1742, devoting the entire seventy-fifth dissertation to demolishing them. His disciple, Lorenzo Mehus, a Florentine cleric, echoed this in his *Of the Origins, Progress, Abuses and Reform of the Lay Confraternities*, written at the height of Peter-Leopold's wholesale abolition of the Tuscan brotherhoods in 1785. It sold only 200 copies, but mirrored government policy, blaming their decadence 'squarely on … the mendicant orders'. The government's own report of 1783 concluded of the lay confraternities of Tuscany that 'as far as piety and devotion are concerned, there is not even a hint of them, but everything revolves around mundane pomp and display'.[82]

Predictably enough, the Napoleonic regime stood foresquare in this continuum, to its own loathing of the brotherhoods adding the political defiance of corporatism into the bargain. But it succeeded neither in breaking this strong tradition, nor turning its assault on it into a source of *ralliement* with those elements in the Italian elite normally hostile to the effusive, often obstreperous character of public piety. Seldom did the Napoleonic regime come so close to living up to its claim to be the heir of Trent, but it was also in these reforms that Trent had most misjudged the faithful. The judgement of Maurice Agulhon on the confraternities of Provence on the eve of the Revolution is just as apposite south of the Alps:

> The phenomenae I have sought to isolate … are traditionally [seen] as those which defy rational, prosaic explanation. The irrational is the only opponent I have faced.[83]

Yet Agulhon's work also pointed to a decline in the religious element of the confraternities, and the accelerating, if gradual, process of the transfer of the meridional instincts of associative, public sociability from religious to distinctly lay bodies. He also noted a growing distaste of 'the France of Paris, of the north' for *la sociabilité meridonale*. John McManners concluded that the relative success of orthodoxy in eighteenth-century France was most felt when the hierarchy did finally harness and tame the confraternities. It turned them into instruments of parish administration, imposing a more serious intent on their devotions, a Pyrrhic victory:

> they had been attempting to turn the existing nominally religious clubs into devotional confraternities. Had they realized it, the choice before them was between the existing large membership with sociability or piety and few adherents. The period of the Enlightenment was the beginning of the process whereby the Church became a minority association.[84]

For McManners, the taming of the confraternities is a major turning point in a seminal process in the social, cultural and even political history of modern France. John Bossy, too, sees the success of Trent in this sphere as sowing the seeds of long-term failure: 'I should be inclined to blame the sociological weaknesses of Tridentine Catholicism'.[85] Chartier is even more emphatic:

> The ecclesiastical venture that aimed at inducing all Christians to share the clerical definition of Christianity was freighted with unbearable tension. Between the faithful and their Counter Reformation priests ... mutual incomprehension was unavoidable.[86]

The dilemma of this choice, made by the Gallican Church in the early modern period, is still felt. The *Dictionnaire de spiritualité ascétique et mystique*, a guardian of orthodoxy, admits that even though the confraternities had 'degenerated' into vehicles for petty, secular rivalries and 'the external expressions of piety had acquired too considerable a place', it cannot be doubted 'that at this stage of human development, the confraternity represented the solution most adapted to what we call today *Action Catholique*'.[87]

Nothing of the kind happened in eighteenth-century Italy, despite the best efforts of Borromeo, Muratori, the *togati* and Peter-Leopold. If the confraternities are, indeed, the key to transforming and taming popular religiosity, then the fact that France and the Italian states took such different paths is of major importance. Peter-Leopold found over 251 such bodies to suppress in Florence alone in 1783; his investigations revealed their wealth and popularity there, and his assault on them was soon undone in the face of popular fury.[88] The political battle was one thing for the regime – it had been fought and won before, within France[89] – the power of popular piety itself was quite another, and the French were less prepared for it. The battle was politicized – and it involved the defence of a political culture – but its mainspring was piety. In this context, the Concordat put two alienated cultures on a collision course.

The Concordat permitted but one confraternity, that of the Holy Sacrament, virtually synonymous with the parish committees, the *fabriques*, which administered funds and cared for church property. They were allowed their own chapels and banners but, as with all processions not connected with the handful of 'approved' High Days, they could only hold them inside the church. The hope was to give the curé complete control over all forms of religious ritual in the parish, not just the administration of the sacraments. This may not have mattered overly much in France, if even in Provence 'the festival – a heady time and a paroxysmic expression – was no longer the same'.[90] In Napoleonic Italy, it was like trying to put a tiger on a lead.

Italian confraternities existed layer upon layer, their variety of form and origins standing as a living testament to the inability of Trent or the secular powers to reduce them to orthodox forms, even if they were, at times, able to infiltrate them. The bastion of Tridentine orthodoxy was Easter observance, and most of the festivities of Holy Week have their origins in the seventeenth and eighteenth centuries.[91] The remarkable feat of the confraternities was to retain their stranglehold on the public festivities, even of Holy Week. Borromeo foreshadowed Bonaparte, in his efforts to create new confraternities under tight episcopal control – 'archconfraternities' in his parlance – meant to become the sole such bodies in every diocese and 'fronted' by the lay elite. Obviously, they were dedicated to the Holy Sacrament, rather than to the Virgin or local saints.[92] Although these bodies proliferated, they neither displaced nor overawed the older confraternities.[93] In Civitavecchia, in the Papal states, there were still three confraternities of practising flagellants in the city on the eve of French rule. They had their chapels in the Dominican house and dominated the Good Friday procession in the traditional style.[94] In 1805, in the early stages of the application of the Concordat, the police discovered a manual for flagellant ceremonies circulating throughout the Kingdom of Italy, 'which is producing some unrest, and spreads their venom against the lawmakers'.[95] An official enquiry of 1811 by the Minister of Public Instruction in Milan revealed the extent to which the rural confraternities set up by Borromeo had evolved along more traditional lines, dominating Easter Week with processions and rituals more in keeping with pre-Tridentine, flagellant brotherhoods. The prefect of Lario described the Good Friday procession in one village:

> telling the sad story of the Calvary, by getting a man to play the Nazarene, with gushing blood for his costume … . The little Virgins and the penitents followed him. None of the instruments of the Passion were missing, and there was a full contingent of barefoot Jews.

His colleague in the Adda said the brothers beat themselves 'to extirpate the excesses of *carnevale* and show their girlfriends how tough they were'.[96] This enquiry has already been cited as evidence of the weakness of the Tridentine reforming process in its own heartland. It also reveals that, left to themselves, communities would subvert Tridentine institutions and devotions in well-established, traditional ways: they had already formed their own concept of the confraternity, and of Easter devotions, to the extent that Trent was not just quickly subverted, but subverted in a specific way.

Only in Tuscany was their power broken by the time of the Napoleonic occupation. The ferocious resistance to the Leopoldine reforms had led to their reinstatement as legitimate institutions, but the confraternities did not get their properties back and so were reduced to almost nothing.[97] However, an exception had been made for the powerful *contrade* of Siena, whose highpoint was – and remains – the racing of the 'sacred grey' horses at *Palio*.

> The Tuscan princes had learned from long experience how attached
> the people of Siena were to their *contrade* … [T]hey not only
> preserved it, but put it under their protection.[98]

If anything, the *casacce* of Genoa had an even greater standing than the
contrade in the eighteenth century. Unlike the great *Palio*, their glories have
not survived into living memory. The French took advice in Siena they
seldom heeded elsewhere and the restored regime in Tuscany proved more
accommodating than the Piedmontese, who were as alien in Genoa as the
French. In their own time, however, the *casacce* were as legendary as the
contrade and their *Palio* are today.

The twenty-one *casacce* fraternities of Genoa[99] had their origins in the
flagellant movements of the late Middle Ages, and by the seventeenth
century they were independent of the churches, with their own chaplains
and oratories. They continued to escape episcopal or state control, because
of powerful noble patronage and their mass memberships, and their processions dominated Holy Thursday. They represented cross-class solidarity
within their narrow neighbourhoods, their processions attracting the
wealthy, whose sons would pay large sums to carry crosses and floats.
Perhaps their real power is best seen by their survival of so many demands
to suppress them in the second half of the eighteenth century from within
the Enlightened elite of the Genoa. The secular powers were too timid to do
so, and in 1748 the Archbishop openly admitted they were beyond his
control. In short, as the century progressed, they became more like themselves – secular, sociable, rowdy, tightly knit – not less so. Popular devotion –
popular in its pristine sense, for all classes were involved – was still vibrant
here on the eve of the Revolution.[100] In 1791 they attracted the disdain of a
Prussian traveller, von Archenholz:

> The Genoese have retained many devotional ceremonies … . There
> are more confraternities here, than in any other city in Italy … .
> Their costume is a long robe, and they are masked. Many of them
> hide weapons under these habits, hoping to strike an enemy, if he
> passes in the course of the procession. These foul deeds are not rare,
> and usually go unpunished: the brothers will protect the wrong
> doer, and refuse to name him. Most are working men; many devout
> merchants would not lower themselves to be involved in such things.
> But the nobles are proud to belong, and carry crosses in the proces-
> sion.[101]

The processions were interrupted during the fighting in 1797, but resumed in
1806 in their old pomp, attracting large crowds from far afield as was
normal.[102] No more emphatic proof of their durability need be cited, than
the capacity of the *casacce* to survive the ravages of the Revolution and rise

again, not immediately, but after a long interval – just in time for the French to ban them.

The strength of confraternities was measured in less ostentatious forms of devotion than those beloved of the *casacce*. Roman confraternities extended their social influence 'upwards', attracting many nobles to their ranks, even if their zeal for charity waned, thereby loosening their grip on the masses. Yet even in 'self-absorbed' Rome, charity was not unknown.[103] Elsewhere, as the suppressions of the French period revealed, confraternities devoted to burying the poor, caring for the sick and running the prisons were a useful part of the Italian urban fabric. However 'decadent' they had become by Tridentine standards, attempts to abolish them in the eighteenth century should have warned the French what they were in for. The thirty confraternities of Prato in the 1780s were not wealthy enough to survive on their patrimonies alone, and their magnificent oratories and processions were supported by the continuous contributions of their members. Many of the confraternities were avowedly popular as well, and over 50 per cent of the population belonged to them – 3,865 people. This was hardly a phenomenon in decline, although there was a marked trend towards secularization in that regular devotions and administration became the preserve of the few. The great festivals remained powerful expressions of confraternal solidarity, however. Rather than despising their archaism the new, rising urban bourgeoisie was determined to dominate the confraternities. When, in 1786, Ricci proposed remodelling them on Borromean and Muratorian lines, he attacked a live animal, not a corpse. Employed, respectable brothers were a significant presence in the rioting of 1787, which reversed the reforms, and calls for their restoration were among the rioters' demands.[104] The Senate of Genoa was probably wise to leave the *casacce* alone. This kind of reform had to await the arrival of the Gendarmerie.

The disorder and divisions sown by the associative life of the confraternities reached far beyond the rowdiness of their processions. They divided cities and the jealousies between brotherhoods were often almost rivalled by the in-fighting for power and precedence within them.[105] In the countryside, they could easily become yet another vehicle for the feud. This was the case just as much among the newer confraternities, founded in the wake of Trent, as among those with medieval origins.[106] Those directly concerned with policing the periphery were, predictably, troubled by a lack of clerical control over the religious life of a 'degenerate' laity. Loysel, the Prefect of the Po – a man with a republican past, unlike D'Auzers, and not noted for his religiosity – looked forward to the complete abolition of the lay confraternities in the *départements réunis*, largely for reasons of public order, as well as a sense of ingrained disgust at meridional piety:

> Their existence ... apart from adding nothing to the standing of religion, is damaging to public order. There are always rows

between the heads of these institutions and the *curés*. They organize clandestine meetings the police can watch only imperfectly, which serve other ends than the practice of pious virtues ... . There is a prevailing spirit among their members, of independence from clerical authority.[107]

He noted, too, that the House of Savoy had long cherished the hope of destroying the confraternities, and that the French stood in firmly in this tradition.

However, the most important clerical influence on the confraternities, particularly on the periphery, was provided by the regular orders. They, more than the parish clergy, guided the festivities and were often the chaplains of the oratories.[108] Thus, when the Concordat abolished the regulars, the slender grip held by the Church over the confraternities was weakened still further. The eighteenth century had been a long, losing battle by the Church to tame the confraternities. The parish clergy tried, in vain, to enforce the bishops' instructions to ban nocturnal processions, flagellants and people in costumes, whether in the Borromean heartland of Novara or in the true periphery of the Tuscan Maremma.[109] As late as 1811, the mayor of Budrio near Bologna in the Kingdom of Italy warned the prefect that the brothers of the Holy Sacrament had long ago wrested the right to appoint and sponsor the 'extraordinary predication' in the town from the *parocco*. They even had moved it from Easter to May, which was more convenient for the people of the surrounding countryside. It was, he added, best to let them carry on, for 'it is within the scope of the penitents' influence to maintain public order, quiet and peace'.[110] This had survived almost ten years of the Concordat. Even their own creation, the Confraternity of the Holy Sacrament, had slipped from episcopal control in many places and, a generation before, the Jesuits had set themselves the daunting task of trying to claw it back.[111]

The Concordat was exactly in line with this tradition. This was not really a question of fear of counter-revolution, at least to begin with. Judgements such as those by the *maire* of the Piedmontese town of Cuneo in 1810 on the three confraternities of the town were rare:

> These associations were a vehicle of the Sardinian government ... .
> In the present circumstances, a public official cannot be blindly confident of them, since these gatherings take place under a kind of mystery which could degenerate in a moment of crisis, and serve as a rallying point for a fanatical faction.[112]

This was a question of an old struggle, not a new phase in counter-revolutionary resistance, at least until the indigenous clergy began to change sides themselves. Even the *maire* of Cuneo admitted, however, that the confraternities still had their role to play: 'even now, their pious zeal for helping the poor and the suffering is to be acknowledged'. However, socially exclusive confraternities found it easier to evade the Concordat and did become havens for counter-revolutionary sentiments, if not of revolt. The venerable confraternity of *La Toricella* was the preserve of the noble families of Piacenza. It refused to recognize the authority of the French bishop, and the prefect suppressed it. This only resulted in a very insulting and well-publicized sonnet about the bishop doing the rounds of the town.[113]

The *casacce* continued to embody John Bossy's vision of the confraternities as a 'social miracle', binding all classes together.[114] Beside them, the brotherhoods of Cuneo and Piacenza are examples of that 'authoritarian parenthood' with which Borromeo and the *ancien régime* sought to infuse them.[115] The lay confraternities had survived into the nineteenth century in all their guises, and all of them provided the French with ready vehicles for that 'entryism' the Medici had practised so astutely in the construction of the Tuscan state.[116] The whole experience of the Italian *ancien régime* demonstrated the readiness of the lay confraternities as instruments of *ralliement*. Instead, the French chose to annihilate them.

The confraternities had been anything but 'corroded by the Enlightenment', nor had their traditional base among the bourgeoisie – urban or rural – been weakened,[117] save perhaps in Tuscany where Peter-Leopold's reforms dented their patrimonies. The archives of the Napoleonic period reveal the continued wealth of the confraternities in urban centres, as witnessed by the inventories of their suppressed oratories. In the country-side, the abolished festivals of patron saints were often stopped only by the Gendarmerie and the demolition of their field chapels. Powerful testimony to the importance of the confraternities to their commuities on the periphery can emerge less in their wealth, than their poverty. The oratories and masses of confraternities of the Apennine valleys above Reggio-Emiliano absorbed all their revenues, leading to the conclusion that they were supported not as sources of privilege or prestige, but from devotion to particular chapels and sites.[118] Their vibrancy straddled centre and periphery, although it took different forms. In urban centres they remained bastions of corporatism, centred on trades or neighbourhoods, while in the countryside their key role in public festivals made them the lynch-pins of communal solidarity. The evidence amassed in the course of enforcing the Concordat sustains the view that they were still strong and that, largely because of them, 'the omnipresence of religion in social life meant that no ceremony or public occasion could be wholly profane'.[119] This would cost the French dear, when they tried to usurp their place. First, they simply had to stamp them out, and the omens were not good. There were tiny rumblings in 1805 when the first steps were taken to close the oratories in Genoa: keys were withheld from timid local policemen,[120] the first small shot in a long war. Genoa was the unofficial capital of associative lay devotion in Italy and, by 1809, it had a degree of clerical patronage unimaginable under the old order. In July 1809 – following the passage of Pius VII into exile in Savona – the clergy made clear, common cause with archaism. Four suppressed feasts of patron saints were held in the town, with the assistance of the seculars – the regular clergy who normally fulfilled these roles being themselves abolished.[121] This simple fact, in town and country, must always be remembered. No clerical presence was possible in confraternal devotions, save that of a secular priest, after the regular orders were dissolved. In an earlier era, this would have been hard to imagine. No longer. In 1811, a curé in the city openly defied the police and celebrated the banned feast of Nostra Signore della Carema with full pomp, but he had refused to ring the bells for the victory of Wagram in 1809.[122] The priest was obviously politically motivated in a true counter-revolutionary sense. However, his way of building popular support was by supporting the laity in what he knew they held dear. To sustain this kind of feast day was to give pride of place to the confraternities. The other way to protect the confraternities, especially the *casacce*, was first to stress the vital public service they played in burying the dead, and then to elude the new legislation of burial, which struck deeply at local tradition. By 1808 it was clear to the French that when Lebrun 'rallied' the urban bourgeoisie and handed them control of the municipality in 1806, he had made a crucial error. The *casacce* were immediately revived and thus the new legislation on burials, which prohibited inhumations in church or within urban areas, was stalled repeatedly. It was 'all of a piece'.[123] Elite support for these forms of popular devotion was still prevalent in the great port, and continued to be so into the nineteenth century. The French finally banned the *casacce* in 1811, but they re-emerged after 1814 and were just as unpopular with the House of Savoy. Charles-Albert IV finally banned them, for good, in 1835.[124] The battle over burials continued under the restored monarchy as well.[125]

In 1805 the Sub-Prefect of Novi, a moderately sized town on the border between Piedmont and Liguria, warned his superiors that the local confraternities were trying to elude the decree closing their oratories:

> The matter seems of little importance to me, but the locals are very passionate about their own oratories. They set great store about dressing in their red or white robes, so I dare do nothing, without your orders.[126]

It was another first shot in that same long war, and the fear of this exposed local official is palpable. When the order came to abolish the confraternities in 1809, the last hope of the brothers was that some might be saved, because of the good works they undertook. It simply intensified the old rivalries and the Sub-Prefect discerned a mixture of political lobbying and uncomprehending rebelliousness. First came the politics. The Sub-Prefect reported a meeting with the heads of the confraternities on 9 December 1809:

> The rivalry between the oratories of the penitents will work wonders for the public good of this commune. The fear engendered by their coming suppression has led them to come up with projects I will do all in my power to foster. They would never have proposed such things, in the days of their brilliant, assured existence.[127]

The brothers of the Trinità swore to bury all the dead in the public hospital; their traditional rivals of the Misericordia promised to pay for a new public fountain. It took the threat of destruction to shake them from the decadence of the 'para-religious' state into which they had fallen, and to revive the older tradition of a civic pride that was itself predominantly secular. Paris was unmoved; the Concordat decreed their suppression. This was predictable and, from the perspective of the regime, essential: even at their most public-spirited, perhaps especially so, the confraternities incarnated a spirit of corporatism and *campanilismo* far more dangerous to the new order than meditated counter-revolution.

In any case, when the Sub-Prefect gathered them together three weeks later, their attitude had changed:

> I met with them three or four times, but it was useless ... . You can see from their replies, what kind of attitude is driving all the oratories ... . One of them had the temerity to say, to my face, that from that moment on, he was in protest against any further discussions. I told him that any such protest meant the death of his oratory.[128]

In his own anger, the Sub-Prefect told the brothers that theirs were worthless institutions and that the oratories of Novi amounted to no more than 'processions and the ringing of church bells – to which the Concordat has put a welcome end'. This was a red flag to a bull. In the heat of the moment, the Enlightenment had fired its usual salvo at communal corporatism and popular devotion. The reply came in style, and force. Large processions and much ringing of bells followed, not once but many times. In June 1810, the *maire* of the hamlet of Pasturana reported that not only had the brothers of his commune's banned oratory assembled to process to their small hill chapel for Corpus Christi, but that they had been joined by almost forty members of the confraternity of the Trinità from Novi. Their leader, Sauli, had with him their banner 'which he had obviously pilfered'. The procession took place 'with full pomp and solemnity'[129] and it was not clear whether any clergy had even been involved,[130] an interesting comment on how independent, but also how determined to carry on, were the brothers of Novi. The hill chapel was closed and the gendarmes impounded the keys; D'Auzers called it 'scandalous insubordination' and wanted Sauli punished. He was brought to Genoa, admonished by the Prefect and warned he could be arrested under Haute Police, as this case had got as far as Paris.[131] The

Sub-Prefect thought this would be the end of it, for the Trinità and Sauli – a wealthy merchant – were very influential.[132] He was wrong. A year later, he stood by helplessly as the populace celebrated the banned feast of their patron saint for two days – working days – with full pomp, led by the confraternities. Faced with such mass resistance, even the Gendarmerie – so fearless in campaigns against the bandits of the region – was powerless. All the Sub-Prefect could to was write an indignant letter to the Archpriest, 'who answered me calmly'.[133] In 1812, he reported that '[i]t is impossible to stop people going to church, on the days of festivals abolished under the Concordat'.[134]

This is an indication not just of continued lay resistance to the Concordat, but that, in the matter of the activities of the confraternities, the local clergy – once their rivals – were effectively changing sides. This was the provincial equivalent of Spina's behaviour in Genoa. At the height of the confrontations in Novi, the Prefect told Paris that he had asked the bishops to support him in curbing these processions.[135] It was a reasonable request by eighteenth-century standards, but things were moving on. In 1812 the Vicar-General of Casale – the immediate subordinate of a French prelate – showed signs of supporting this sea-change in his parish clergy. He calmly reported in 1812 that the parish of the hamlet of Castelnuovo Scivia allowed the officially recognized confraternity of the Holy Sacrament to process the streets in its traditional white robes on Corpus Christi. He added that the official confraternities also do this in Alessandria, Turin and in the Kingdom of Italy. Knowing it was virtually the norm, he did nothing, the terms of the Concordat not withstanding. Finally, he observed to the Prefect of Genoa of the Corpus Christi celebrations in Tortona, a sizeable town:

> following a very old practice, the Holy Sacrament was paraded through the streets, from one parish to the next, without this ever being regarded as a holiday. Only well-off people who do not have to do daily work take part.[136]

He would stop it next year, if the government wished. In 1813 the *maire* of San Quirico, a village between Novi and Alessandria, reported that the curé had allowed a robed, nocturnal procession in honour of Our Lady of the Rosary to continue, because those who took part were not a confraternity.[137] The recalcitrance of the Ligurian border-country is particularly poignant. Its tradition of banditry had been thoroughly rooted out by the French; it had been occupied longer than most other parts of the *départements réunis*, but popular piety proved a more difficult enemy to defeat than the great band of Mayno of the Spinetta.[138]

Popular devotion in the Italian *départements réunis* had lost none of its force, in either town or country. The vibrancy and outright rowdiness of the confraternities did not preclude powerful backing from the lay elites, who at least in some part must be counted as still sharing in popular culture. Now, having survived clerical disdain for so long, they were receiving its support, a pattern utterly different from the process at work in France itself.[139] As priests and people drew closer together, it was soon clear this support would have to be mutual. The clergy had its own public battles to wage against the Concordat and it found the laity on its side. In 1811, just months before their final abolition, the Prefect of the Apennines called the confraternities 'the last refuge of fanaticism, in opposition [to us] alongside the curés'.[140] He knew not all of which he spoke. A clear sign of how far the clergy had moved from its post-Tridentine position towards that of its flock came in Umbria, the medieval cradle of the penitential confraternities. There, in 1811, the clergy of Terni linked the high drama of the liturgy with a direct appeal to the most traditional piety beloved of the laity. After a very 'fraught' Holy Week, all the nobles, priests and ex-regulars turned out with a large congregation for midnight Mass on the piazza on Good Friday. All the laymen wore the black robes of the recently banned flagellant confraternity of the town. When the cross was raised for the Benediction, the candles were put out instead of saying the *Domine salvum fac Imperatorem*. Norvins noted that no priests said the prayers during Holy Week. There were no regulars or non-jurors involved in this.[141]

Liturgical resistance

The extent to which priests led their people or were led by them vexed the whole Catholic world in the early modern period, and the confrontation with the Revolution merely intensified it. In Napoleonic Italy at least this much is clear: certain of the liturgical innovations introduced by the new imperial regime gave the clergy a very public platform to attack or support the regime, in so far as they wished or dared to do so. It was, above all, a public platform, for the Mass was the most widespread public drama in Europe. The public nature of the Mass meant that acts of liturgical resistance – or collaboration – could not escape the attention of the laity, and this is what it has in common with the lay-inspired piety of the devotions attached to the confraternities. Whatever went on to do with the Mass was the business of laity and clergy alike. It could divide or unite them, but few clerics could have long sustained liturgical resistance, or liturgical reform, without the support, tacit or active, of their congregations.

If anything, the Concordat sought to intensify the omniscience of the Mass in the devotional life of the laity. This insistence on the centrality of the parish church, and thus the assembly of its entire population for Sunday Mass, was the response of a post-Enlightenment, secular, bureaucratic state to the same culture of vendetta that Charles V confronted when he sought to revive the *Pax* in his own empire.[142] The French tried to cut away all other sacred spaces where the Mass was said, concentrating it in the very public, state-financed confines of the parish church. The Mass symbolized peace and social unity in a divided society, whereas the oratories of noble families and the lay confraternities, and the churches of the regular orders, represented the foe of corporatism and privilege, while the hill and field chapels were the unpoliced havens of superstition and ignorance. When they tried to insert the new, imperial state into the same parish Mass, the power of which they so wanted to enhance, the French often united clergy and laity against them, not the reverse. By attempting to infiltrate the Mass and the Church calendar, the regime took a tremendous risk. It recognized the usefulness of the Church as a tool of social control from the outset; this had been the whole driving force behind the Concordat. However, what happened in Napoleonic Italy shows that the regime did not have the faintest idea how to harness it to these ends. It held too much devotional practice in too a great a contempt to attempt to manipulate the clergy on its surest ground, or to count on pressure from the laity to coerce their priests on its behalf.

The regime attempted three innovations in the devotional life of the Church, directly aimed at its own glorification: two were in the text of the Mass itself, the other in the Church calendar. Prayers were to be said for the Emperor at Sunday Mass, replacing those for the deposed *ancien régime* rulers. The High Days and local saints' days abolished by the Concordat were to be replaced by the singing of *Te Deum* at Sunday Mass for military victories and events in the life of the imperial family. Finally, the Imperial Decree of 18 February 1806 created St Napoleon's Day on the Emperor's birthday, 15 August, which fate had decreed was also the Feast of the Assumption. All of these initiatives proved disastrous. Liturgical resistance, when linked directly to the Sunday Mass, could insult the regime at the very moment when social unity should have been closest to becoming a reality, and it could be re-enacted regularly, almost routinely. The refusal to sing a *Te Deum* offered the chance to belittle the regime at those very moments it sought to make itself look glorious and – an important point, in the militarized Europe of Napoleon – invincible. The whole concept of St Napoleon's Day brought the new, statist, militarized – as very distinct from militant – Catholicism into direct conflict with its very antithesis – Marian devotion – in the most poignant manner conceivable. It was all made even worse in the practised hands of a post-Tridentine clergy, proficient in the well-defined ritual of the Mass. Borromeo saw the secular Church as the officers of a well-organized army – a diocese had its generals, colonels and captains[143] – a very ironic metaphor in the context of the confrontation of his successors with Napoleon. French incursions into the liturgy of the Mass gave these officers the opportunity to fight on their favourite ground, with the confidence of their parishioners, 'the ranks'. When the regime chose to fight on the Assumption, it stumbled onto the favourite ground of those same ranks.

In May 1808, following the annexation of Tuscany to the empire, the Tuscan clergy were ordered to say public prayers for the Emperor, as was the practice throughout the empire, and to precede them with *Domine salvum fac Imperatorem Nostrum Napoleonem*, thus ensuring the object of the prayers was known to the congregation. However, the Florentine clergy omitted the name, leaving the impression that they might have been praying for Francis I of Austria. Indeed, in a letter to the police, the Archpriest of the Metropolitan of Florence admitted that 'the usual practice' was being followed.[144] Initially brought to heel, the Tuscan clergy did not conform for long. Police-Générale raged to Religion, in July 1809, that the bishops had told their curés they could dispense with chanting the *Domine salvum fac Imperatorem*. Even when it was being sung, there had been adroit adjustments to the liturgy by the clergy themselves:

> The chant was being said only after the farewell blessing, whereas from time immemorial [that is, before French rule] it was done at the same time as the Benediction. As a result of this change, this prayer ends the service, and it is said when the congregation is noisily leaving church, when the servers are snuffing out the candles. In a word, aversion to the government is to be seen everywhere, and recognized by these characteristic signs.[145]

It was believed this 'adjustment' had originated in Genoa and entered Tuscany through Livorno, where it was common practice. Whether by coincidence or imitation, this was also common in the Roman departments, causing Norvins to say that the prayers were said only 'in the shabbiest fashion'.[146]

In Pisa, on Holy Saturday 1808, a priest said the prayers in the name of Emperor Francis, corrected himself audibly, and changed it to Napoleon. When arrested for this, twenty-one wealthy petitioners came to his support.[147] On Good Friday 1808, a Florentine priest said the prayers, but had the bells ringing and the organ playing as he did so. In the same service, he also took a public stand against the omission of the anti-Semitic prayers.[148] In the summer of 1808, at the moment when fighting first broke out in Spain, and at the start of the quarrel with Pius VII, the Bishop of Sarazana in Liguria ordered a prayer to be said throughout the diocese immediately before the *Domine salvum fac Imperatorem*: 'an Oration for all kinds of tribulation'. Traditionally it was said when war cut off sea communications with Genoa, and had last been said when the British were raiding the coast. The Gendarmerie said it had stirred up the area.[149]

In the Roman departments, things were often less subtle, but the timing was in keeping with the power of the Mass as a public drama. In 1813 a priest in Civitavecchia chose Good Friday as the first time he omitted the *Domine salvum fac Imperatorem*. A year earlier, in a remote parish in Umbria, a priest conducting the service left the altar at the point of the *Domine salvum fac Imperatorem*, stood silently to one side for a moment, and then returned to carry on the service. Roederer made no attempt to hide the impact he made by this action: 'Most of the congregation took it as the sign to start leaving church at that moment'. He was put under police watch.[150] A canon of Velletri, also in the Roman departments, was particularly clever when he answered a charge of not saying the *Domine salvum fac Imperatorem* on the grounds that he did sing a *Te Deum* for the pregnancy of the Empress and did not want to bore his congregation with needless repetition. It also transpired that all the churches of the town had omitted the prayers for the Emperor on Holy Saturday.[151] Anti-revolution was tipping quite easily into counter-revolution.

Te Deums were, perhaps, the most deeply embarrassing moments faced by the regime. The most infamous was unquestionably the empty stalls in St Peter's and the other great basilicas of Rome, which greeted Tournon and Norvins when they tried to celebrate the birth of the King of Rome 'in his own city' in 1811.[152] Tournon remarked in his memoirs that the clergy of Rome saw quite clearly how important all this was to the government, and let it play into their hands. This was a moment when a great deal was risked on their adhesion to external ritual. Instead, Tournon recalled, the clergy reminded the faithful that they did not recognize the divorce from Josephine, and came very close to calling the King of Rome a bastard. Tournon also felt, with hindsight, that things had not been helped because Miollis, from an older, genuinely dechristianized generation of Bonapartists, had himself failed to grasp the importance of clerical participation.[153] The French reply was swift and ruthless. Napoleon had already had those Cardinals who refused to attend the wedding stripped of their standing and exiled to various parts of France. The canons became among the first secular clergy to be arrested and sent into exile, but even the musicians and the choirmaster of St Peter's – all of whom had refused to participate – were first sacked and then imprisoned. Miollis admitted that their 'obstinacy' had created quite a stir in Rome.[154] The French had had fair warning, however. The first attempt to hold *Te Deums* in the Roman departments was in 1809, for the anniversary of the imperial coronation. It was held in Civitavecchia, but had to be sung by laymen as none of the clergy would do it. This was as successful as it got, because the Vicar-General the diocese of Viterbo ordered the clergy to boycott the ceremonies – and they obeyed. The Pro-Vicar of Montefiascone told the French police that it was not a ceremony of the Church in any case.[155] In 1810 the great basilicas of Rome had ignored requests to pray for the Empress when she was pregnant. This caused Tournon to request the arrest of the 'ringleaders', a step he considered to stop short of the violence he said he wished to avoid.[156]

It was but the tip of an iceberg, however. Open defiance spread to the provinces and was not confined to a few great occasions. Several clergy of Frascati were exiled to Corsica in June 1811 for refusing to sing the *Te Deum* for the birth of the King of Rome, but they were only scapegoats, for Miollis admitted that all the clergy of the city had stood together.[157] It took place in Montefiascone, but the President of the Civil Tribunal noted that only four priests even came and,

> The Mass finished, the celebrant chanted the *Te Deum*, but scarcely had he started, when the small number of people attending suddenly all walked out … . A priest had been stationed on the door, to persuade people not to come.[158]

Nor did they desist. The police were still arresting clergy for this kind of defiance throughout the Roman departments and Tuscany in 1813.[159] Nor was there only one way to defy government orders. In 1812 in Umbria Roederer reported that although his clergy had sung *Te Deums* for the birthday of the King of Rome, he found – after a thorough study of mass missals – that they had actually said prayers irrelevant to the occasion.[160] These were the greatest moments of defiance, but it was readily admitted that, on the periphery, passive refusal to sing *Te Deums* or say prayers for the Emperor was widespread. Nardon, in Parma, ominously reported that at the height of the Wagram campaign in 1809 the *Domine salvum fac Imperatorem* stopped being said throughout the Piacentino. The churches were full when there was news of French victories, but no *Te Deums* were sung.[161] There seem to have been relatively few problems with getting the clergy to sing *Te Deums* in most cathedrals and urban centres until the invasion of the Papal states. The question was, how. Inevitably, no one proved better at subverting it than Spina. When a *Te Deum* was called for in Liguria, for the first time ever, to celebrate the victories of the Wagram campaign of 1809, Spina decked out his cathedral and even the *Domine salvum fac Imperatorem* was performed. However, Spina did all this according to the old pre-Concordat calendar, which meant the official offices were performed on suppressed High Days. Moreover, although his pastoral letter ordered the clergy to follow suit throughout the Archdiocese, it did not indicate that the *Domine salvum fac Imperatorem* was to be sung every Sunday and High Day. The Police Commissioner concluded:

> I am not at all surprised that His Eminence should have concocted this little Jesuitical ruse to elude, as far as possible, the orders from Religion.[162]

Clearly, an artist was at work.

This pattern repeated itself, exactly, in 1859–60, as did official responses to this sort of clerical defiance. The Bishop of Pisa found himself 'deported' to Turin in 1860, and put under house arrest. It was a measure Cavour, the godson of Pauline Bonaparte, described as 'possibly not very legal, but usefully compatible to political wisdom'. Nonetheless, the unitary state soon learned that the prudent way was simply not to mention the clergy in the context of public ceremonies. The post-1860 festival of unification 'offered [its opponents] little room for provocation or confrontation', remaining secular and wholly official in form.[163] Napoleon did not learn this lesson.

The new festival of St Napoleon was an accident waiting to happen, at least in an Italian context. It represents one of the worst in a whole series of miscalculations made by the government in its quest for a legitimate place in the Church calendar. Created in 1806, the debates surrounding the new festival are very revealing of the preoccupations of the regime. From the outset, the intention was to 'pair' it with one of the remaining great High Days of the calendar, but not necessarily with Napoleon's birthday on the Assumption. Because outdoor festivities were regarded as essential, the choice was restricted to Easter, Corpus Christi and the Assumption. Easter was, indeed, toyed with by Portalis, on the grounds that it 'was trouble', but even Napoleon – and even in 1806, at the height of his success – thought this was taking too big a risk. Napoleon himself rejected Corpus Christi, because it was too close to the old *fête du Roi*, promoted by Louis XIV, and he did not want this festival to be associated with the old order, but rather to mark a new beginning for the empire: marriages involving veterans and serving soldiers would, it was hoped, come to be celebrated on this festival. Portalis, the Minister of Religion, had originally wanted to link the new *fête* with that of St Louis, but then convinced Napoleon that it could be easily combined with the Assumption.[164] The Piedmontese department of the Sesia was one of the most secure, pro-French of the Italian departments, and its Prefect reported that the new festival had been celebrated throughout the department.[165] Three years later, the Bishop said the same, but he hinted strongly that this had only been done in the mountain parishes, because, since 1806, he had made a point of touring them in August.[166] In 1811 Spina spoke of the festival becoming almost the norm in Genoa, although, as has been seen, he did his best to 'overlay' it with other events. Nevertheless, he appeared almost terrified at the prospect of taking a step too far in local eyes. When the government sought to underline the superiority of the official saint over the Virgin, by rededicating the church of the Annunciation to St Napoleon, Spina spoke out. He saw that local opinion would regard this as a direct confrontation between the government and the Madonna, and the power of the latter among his flock:

> However laudable this might be in the abstract, it seems to me there could be a flaw in the execution. This involves a church that has always, since it was built, been consecrated to the Virgin, and a church which – for exactly the fact of its dedication – has always been very dear to the people – as witnessed by the huge concourse that flocked to it, the day it was reopened.[167]

Spina then proposed a compromise, that either a church converted to secular use could be dedicated to St Napoleon or – and here he perhaps revealed more than he meant – that an altar to St Napoleon be set up in the church of the Annunciation, 'where both the Holy Virgin and St Napoleon could be invoked, together, as is already the practice'. In a rare slip of his pen, Spina let the authorities know that he had effectively sidelined the new festival and attached it quietly to the Assumption. Other clerics blended craft with defiance. It came to light that the whole diocese of Orvieto managed to ignore St Napoleon's Day in 1811, and then the anniversary of the coronation in December, because the acting Vicar-General, Lambruschini, wrote 'printer's error' beside the two dates in the margin of his pastoral letter. This gave his priests the excuse they needed to 'dispense with their celebrations', and it sent Lambruschini to exile in Corsica, where he joined his brother, the bishop.[168]

It was bad enough to be sidelined by the Virgin. In Cornetto, in the Papal states, St Napoleon's Day clashed not only with the feast of the Assumption, but with that of the patron saint of the town, who had been abolished under the Concordat. In 1811 the clergy, *maire* and municipal council, supported by the laity, celebrated the double feast and simply ignored the official saint. This was not the first time this had happened, but it was the last. Alert to the proceedings after incidents in 1809 and 1810, the Gendarmerie entered the churches during Mass, arrested the priests at the altars and hauled them away before the eyes of packed congregations 'who had to be restrained'.[169] Savary condemned the overzealous behaviour of the police, but he did not release the clergy, exiling most of them to Corsica.[170] There were communities which were undeterred by such ruthlessness, just as – in these cases – the French remained unmoved by the prospect of depriving them of normal religious services. In the Umbrian town of Marino in 1812, the Assumption was celebrated with full pomp by the municipal council and clergy with no reference to St Napoleon, an act which got virtually all of them gaoled and saw the churches closed for several weeks. Thirty regular troops were sent to carry out the arrests, at a time when the security forces were fully stretched enforcing conscription and containing banditry in the area.[171] The priorities of both sides were very clear; both took very high risks and paid a very high price for it. Neither flinched from such public, audacious confrontation.

There was a sure sign of having entered the canon of the catalogue of 'most heinous crimes' in Napoleonic Italy, and that was to be accused routinely of something in local denunciations and counter-denunciations. The subject-matter of denunciations is the clearest evidence of what political issues communities and local elites believed the government cared about. Refusal to sing *Te Deums* and celebrate the feast of St Napoleon 'made it', alongside 1799 and opposition to conscription. In a small commune near

Bobbio, in the hills between Genoa and Turin, the *maire* in 1811 accused the curé of just this.[172] The feast of St Napoleon had duly entered Italian life, if not in the way envisaged.

Nothing could have been more public than the opposition to the feast of St Napoleon. It was high drama, in a well-understood context, that none could ignore. Although carried out by the clergy, it would have meant nothing without the presence of the laity, or the sure knowledge that they approved of this defiance, however passively. Confrontation of this kind was a preparation for the nineteenth century; it was the beginning of a phenomenon in modern Italian history, not a set of circumstances connected only to the *epoca francese*. If the unitary state absorbed some of the grosser lessons of all this, after 1860 Church and state alike saw that public celebrations exposed the uneasy nature of their truce for all to see. In 1870 the journal *Civiltà Cattolica* mocked the lacklustre atmosphere of official festivals. The Catholic press, in general, contrasted the power of traditional religious celebrations with the hollowness of those of the state. In 1880 the liberal politician Giorgio Curcio agreed:

> The government has taken a negative approach to amusements … .
> The Catholic Church … has come to the rescue of the vilest classes
> of the people, with festivals and religious processions.[173]

The French occupation was a dress rehearsal for the future as much as a struggle between reaction and revolution.

In the immediate context of Napoleonic repression, the Mass and the Assumption above all became vital elements in strengthening the bonds of community, and the ties between the parish clergy and their flocks, in the most poignant manner imaginable short of martyrdom. The passive, thoroughly non-violent conduct of the clergy ensured the French did not get the chance to grant them this. Thus the French helped to foster exactly that which every revolutionary regime sought to break down: those ties of corporate and communitarian solidarity that stood between the state and the individual citizen. The clergy risked arrest and exile, not for obscure reasons of conscience alone, but to preserve the collective rituals dearest to the people, and the feast of the Virgin was the dearest of all. When the regime honoured the most Christocentric of the surviving High Days, Corpus Christi, by placing a guard of honour on the processed Host, it made a statement. It did so again, if perhaps less deliberately, when it tried to overshadow the Virgin with its own festival. When the clergy rose in defence of the Assumption, it took the road back to populism. When the laity bridled at assaults on the Virgin, but seemingly let the changes to Corpus Christi pass, it confirmed its atavistic allegiances and its relative indifference to the more orthodox aspects of public piety.[174] The confrontation between St Napoleon's Day and the Assumption encapsulated the differences between 'mass' and truly 'popular' culture, as defined by Muchenbled among others: that is, a clash between the genuinely atavistic and a culture aimed at the masses but created by the elite for consumption by the masses.[175] Everyone involved saw this particular confrontation in these terms, however they expressed it. In Napoleonic Italy, the clergy – a very influential part of the elite – made the significant choice of siding with the atavistic, and even reviving it. Independently of each other, and in different ways, the sly Cardinal Archbishop of Genoa and the impoverished *parocci* of the Roman hinterlands embraced popular culture. Carlo Russo has defined two distinct varieties of 'popular religion', akin to the wider categories developed by Muchenbled, warning of the difference between the 'popular' and the 'popularized'.[176] Spina and his ilk sensed this, but their intuitive genius was not to choose between them. Rather they blurred the distinctions and so humiliated the imperial regime. With the arrest of Pius VII in 1809, the time came for the clergy to fight the new regime in its own cause. The changed attitude its members had adopted to popular piety carried people of all classes with it, on the periphery and at the centre. The clergy's battle began in the Papal states, but so much of what had already passed between rulers and ruled in matters of religion meant the Pope had divisions everywhere, hardly bristling with arms, but determined to resist nonetheless.

5

THE CONCORDAT AND
THE ITALIAN CLERGY

The episcopate

The French called awkward bishops many things, indeed several ended in prison, but they almost never accused them of pastoral neglect. Even as Elisa, the Grand Duchess of Tuscany, railed at Paris to rid her of the Archbishop of Pisa – 'who does not hide his hatred for the French … or [his support] for the malign influence of the faction of the Court of Rome: [whose] influence on the clergy of his diocese is deadly' – she admitted that he 'has the qualities and virtues of a good bishop'.[1] Roederer admitted that the late Bishop of Spoleto would be missed on his death in 1812. Although he did little to help with conscription, he gave away his whole official salary in alms.[2] Cerati, the pro-Jesuit Bishop of Piacenza, drew real praise from the ex-Terrorist Nardon on his death in 1806: 'the poor have lost a father, the Church one of her true ministers'.[3] He received this relatively warm obituary from the Minister of Religion on precisely these grounds:

> This Prelate was certainly not French, either by taste or in his principles, but he loved his duty, he respected the [civil] authority and, by a principled conscience, he followed the right path. He feared compromising the Faith, by not obeying the law. I cannot feel the same confidence in the majority of his clergy.[4]

The Minister reported of Cerati to Napoleon:

> He was an endless provider of charity. I have been told he gave virtually all his revenues to the poor. It is said that, in Italy, a bishop can only win respect and carry out his mission well, through generous acts of charity.[5]

To these ends, the local administration – including Nardon, according to the Minister – felt that a wealthy Italian should succeed him. However, buried in this praise is a realization that for a regime determined to stamp out what it perceived as a 'dependency culture' – and Nardon had been very clear that this was especially strong in the Duchies – something quite different was called for. He also admitted that Spina – hardly a model of complaisance to the French – did his duty, as did Turchi's successor in Parma, Caselli, 'for their pastoral letters on conscription'.[6] Damning judgements were rare, such as those delivered by the Prefect of the Arno on Albergotti, the Bishop of the rebellious diocese of Arezzo, in 1809: 'He was led into the episcopate by flattery and the most affected zeal for religion', although the Prefect also added – unwittingly, for it was meant as a slight – that he was one of the founders of a new proselytizing sect in Rome, centred on the Lazzarite and Passionist missionaries.[7]

The Borromean ideal had left a mark on the Italian episcopate that endured into the *epoca francese*. There was much for the French to respect in the generation of Italian bishops they found in charge, despite their 'Roman loyalism', which had been sharpened in the struggles of the 1780s. Throughout the eighteenth century, the appointments made by Rome and the governments of the individual states showed an awareness of the devotion to pastoral duty needed in a time of rapid social change.[8] They were imbued with the model of the French episcopate, and were overwhelmingly aristocratic in background, usually educated at one of the great Jesuit 'Noble Colleges' at Parma, Siena or Bologna.[9] In short, Italian bishops were the sort of men the Napoleonic regime prided itself on being able to work with and 'rally' to itself. They failed. In 1807 – well before the final break with Rome – the Minister of Religion told Napoleon that '[i]n general, Italian precedents do not fare well for long with our principles'.[10] There were only a handful of vacancies in the ranks of the Italian episcopate in the *epoca francese*, but how the French chose to deal with them shows how their policy towards the Church hardened over the years and reveals the extent of the erosion of goodwill between Church and state even before the break with Rome became irreparable.

Nevertheless, there ought to have been some common ground between the Church and the Napoleonic state, particularly in that long struggle for 'the pacification of souls' in the hinterlands. The quest for social control on the periphery and the desire to centre the work of the Church around the episcopate and the parish were the touchstones of the Concordat and the Borromean reforms alike. Indeed, even when the props of Baroque devotion had been battered, the confraternities and regular orders suppressed, and all auxiliary chapels closed by order of the secular power, this shared bond could remain. The Subdelegate for Parma, who acted as caretaker after the departure of Moreau and the arrival of Junot and Nardon, in 1806 advised Nardon that:

> I have heard His Excellency the [late] Cardinal Bishop [Turchi]
> bewail many times, the lack of instruction of the clergy of his
> diocese, except for those of the city of Parma, to whom this
> reproach does not apply. It is absolutely essential to correct this in

the mountain areas, where the peasants are in the most profound ignorance, and where a trained pastor would be a great help, even for the civil administration.[11]

The Bishop of Modena in the Kingdom of Italy felt the same in 1810.[12] Spina bewailed the wildness of the Ligurian valleys – even as he fomented archaism in the cities of the littoral. Following his pastoral visit to the valleys in 1812, Spina told the Minister of Religion:

> As for the inhabitants of the [valley of the] Fontanabuona, who are infamous enough, I have found them a little worse [than of late] … . There is, I believe, something to be desired as regards their private morality.[13]

The Bishop of Biella, in north-eastern Piedmont believed the laity of the periphery was in constant need of episcopal supervision; the *montagnardi* were always one step away from the moral abyss. He took this chance to plead the case for a real alliance between Church and state in this struggle at the inception of French rule in Piedmont:

> [The bishops] have to work in every corner of their dioceses to inspire, to regulate, to remind of, this morality without which peoples fall back into a state of barbarousness, and without which no society can survive for long, even if it be buttressed by good civil laws … . Men will always degrade themselves, and so either they must be recalled to their duty by love, or constrained to do it by authority.[14]

These hopes persisted, although the partnership, even where successful on the surface, contained many nuances in practice, as the Bishop of Vercelli found when he tried to support the state during a tour of the upland parishes of his diocese during the 'war scare' of 1809. Following the murder of two gendarmes in the area, he celebrated the new official *fête* of St Napoleon with considerable ostentation:

> Deeds work better than words. Thus, I made of St Napoleon's day, a *fête* such has never been seen in these mountains. It does well to unnerve these people, and to bind them to their duty, even if through the spectacle of a religious festival. I gathered together the clergy of the neighbouring communes: I led the procession myself: I selected the best preacher for the sermon: musicians were sent for: I ordered fireworks: one hundred National Guards presented arms, so imposing their presence on a crowd of almost 10,000 people who came to the *fête*. It seems the right thing, to me, to hold an

imposing *fête* to soften the spirits and the hearts of these fierce highlanders.[15]

All the outward signs of an alliance between Church and state are on display here. The symbolism, the very occasion itself – the *fête* of St Napoleon, more often a 'flashpoint' in Church–state relations than a source of cooperation – and, above all, the cultural assumptions of the Bishop of Vercelli about the people of the periphery, were all those of the French. Nor is the example of a Piedmontese bishop chosen at random: Vercelli was in the Borromean heartland; it possessed a seminary noted for its Jansenist tendencies.[16] Yet, amidst this apparently viable partnership, the Bishop of Vercelli – probably unwittingly – retained a political outlook that had not shaken off the arbitrational approach to governing the periphery character-istic of the old order – that 'government at one remove' the French were determined to break with. When dealing with the killers of the gendarmes, the Bishop went on:

> I have met with the most important families; I have seen the families of those guilty who have been arrested; I have spoken to everyone; in the end, it seems to me that it is persuasion that wins over people's attitudes, and that, in the long run, makes them follow the law and obey the government. In the meantime, the Criminal Tribunal has not tried to find many of the guilty. I think this prudent. Tomorrow, taking advantage of the moment, I shall harangue the people. It seems to me that we will leave so profound an impression on the hearts of these highlanders, as to last a very long time.[17]

The normal procedure in such cases was to label them 'revolts', to occupy the commune with troops and dispatch those charged with such offences to the Extraordinary Military Tribunals, to avoid exactly the kind of 'indul-gent' conduct suggested by the Bishop, and this is exactly what happened here.[18] The example of this pastoral visit seems to encapsulate the real possi-bilities and the drastic limitations of collaborative 'policing' between Church and state under the Napoleonic regime. Despite their similar perceptions of the masses on the periphery, the Church – even when working within a tradi-tion of subservience to the state in such matters – could not assimilate itself to Napoleonic levels of social control. Thus the gap in understanding between French imperialists and the Italian ruled emerges at its most poignant less in cases of direct conflict than in those muddled attempts at collaboration.

The Piedmontese bishops were, by and large, 'a good lot' to the French; during the *triennio* they were models of consistency in supporting the repres-sion of disorder under successive regimes, to the point that even a besieged patriot went so far as to say at the height of the fighting in 1800 'I fix my attention on the citizen Bishop of Alba, in recognition of the praiseworthy and sensible manner in which he conducted himself in such difficult circumstances'.[19] The French made a clear distinction in Piedmont between a recalcitrant, truly counter-revolutionary lower clergy and the episcopate among whom 'one would search in vain for a Fabrizio Ruffo'.[20] Indeed this first, relatively painless experience of Italian prelates may have lured them into a false sense of security when they first encountered Spina and his like. There was little of significance to divide the role of the episcopal visitation, as outlined by the Bishop of Biella, from that of the new regime, even if it came couched as a complaint about the larger size of the new French diocese:

> It is about visiting an area, it is about travelling, nothing more. The bishop must find out as much as he can; he must examine the conduct of his clergy; he must influence the thoughts of the people; redress opinions; root out superstition, which always reappears; care for their morals; soften the character of the highlanders, especially (and half the people of Piedmont are in the mountains); console the unfortunate; inspire peace and goodwill ... [21]

His complaints about the neo-Jacobin prefects of the early years – 'we are governed by prefects who shudder at the very idea of a priest or a church' – were met, as the character of the Piedmontese prefects moderated in the course of French rule.[22]

The outburst of the Vicar-General of Piacenza, made to Paris in the wake of the 1806 revolt, reveals this truth more starkly, when – bishopless after the death of Cerati – he took upon himself the role of spokesman for a downtrodden flock:

> It is hard to look back on the injustices of Junot's time without pain; it was a time of horror, of terrorism. He fell victim to vainglory, to a disturbed nature, and cared for nothing other than destruction, whose only response to any denunciation of supposed brigands, was to shoot them ... . Those brigand leaders with money or connections got off, and those who were made examples of were, in great number, innocent, because they lacked these means.[23]

The point here is less the accuracy or not of his judgement than the outburst itself. He took a traditional role more openly, in more desperate circumstances – that of defending the people of the periphery against secular injustice, or from the severity of secular justice, depending on the political culture invoked. The Prelate was obviously shocked by the character of Junot's rule and by the power of the new Napoleonic state around him, yet he still spoke out against it to the leaders of that regime – a rare sign of courage at the time – having seen the brusque rejection of a political culture based on arbitration.

The bishops showed themselves to be men of the *ancien régime* in their deeply rooted fear of the moral barbarousness of the periphery, linked in their minds as it was to a latent cauldron of civil disorder, unless checked by the civilizing forces of Church and state. However, this also throws Spina's propensity to court these instincts – through a return to older methods of preaching, encouraging mass devotion to the Virgin and support for the *casacce* – into a startling perspective. It reveals him so driven by opposition to the Concordat that he turned his back on the norms of the *ancien régime* to do so. Nor did Spina make his journey away from the Enlightenment alone. Gazzola, the Bishop of Montefiascone, began the period as a moderate, an open-minded man of the Enlightenment, but became 'a man of the right, who saw masonic conspiracy everywhere'.[24]

The Bishop of Piacenza, Cerati, was hardly a supporter of the French reforms either, and was regarded even by the reactionary, post-Tillot regime as too fond of the Jesuits.[25] His fear of the moral degeneration of the periphery led him, like Turchi in Parma, to throw the Jesuits at the hinterland in the mid-1790s, but in the same spirit he put his clergy to work in the interests of civil peace in the wake of the 1806 revolt. Just before his death, Cerati issued two pastoral letters calling on the rebels to lay down their arms and go home, which the French admitted were highly influential, and he also mobilized the missionary Lazzarite and Reformed Franciscan fathers, thus overriding Moreau's decrees, for what would be their last efforts under the French. The parish clergy rallied: 'The priests of various parishes have concerted [their efforts] to disarm the misguided highlanders'. Several curés were singled out for praise, and the overall judgement given to Paris was that '[g]enerally, the attitude of the clergy is not at all bad'.[26] These efforts should have revealed the utility of the Church to them, in this kind of crisis and in the governance of the periphery in general. Yet they pressed forward with the introduction of the Concordat regardless. The Lazzarites and the Reformed Franciscans went the way of the regular houses, already suppressed to great local opposition. There was a bitter irony about the case of the Lazzarites in particular. They had been locked in a fierce rivalry with the Jesuits in Piacenza during the eighteenth century, and had always been in the vanguard of neo-Jansenist reform. Indeed, Jansenist sympathies were widespread among all the clergy of the town.[27] The French remained blind to this potential. Cerati's successor, Fallot de Beaumont, a Frenchman who was formerly Bishop of Ghent, told the Minister of Religion on his arrival in Piacenza:

> there is it all to do, and it will take a great deal of time and care to introduce the discipline of the French clergy here, I will meet much

opposition ... . Peace must be maintained, the Emperor and the government must be loved, yet all the present usages, however great their antiquity, must be changed.[28]

Collaboration had been there for the asking in 1806, despite the unpopularity of what the French were about, but as early as 1808 it was reported that 'the priests in the mountain parishes of the Piacentino are far from leading conscripts to obedience or fulfilling the intentions of the government'.[29] His experience in Piacenza made Fallot de Beaumont cynical about the distinction between centre and periphery, as regards the attitude of his clergy to conscription: 'The attitude of the mountain clergy is the same as that of the clergy of the plain, but their circumstances are utterly different'. The mountain clergy did not have to worry what they said or did not say on the subject, as their flocks simply avoided it whatever. The clergy of the *pianura* had no choice but to preach the will of the government, which was easily enforced. This led not only to their loss of standing among their flocks 'who say the curés ought not to involve themselves in such matters', but to the disruption of worship:

> the young men no longer show themselves in church, since they have started being watched by the gendarmes, and even the women are now afraid to be found in them.[30]

This is a rare, searingly honest glimpse of the disruption conscription could bring to routine devotion in an area where it was strong. It is also a powerful example of the deep-rooted difficulties of creating a partnership between Church and state in the circumstances of Napoleonic Italy, made all the more poignant by the fact that this took place at the centre, and as a direct result of the state being able to impose itself, not the reverse.

During the tense days of 1809, the French no longer felt able to trust the clergy of the region. The talk now was of 'turbulent priests' who were being watched closely,[31] and the ex-Franciscans, still living illegally as a group, were accused – falsely, as it turned out – of having a cache of arms hidden in case of an Austrian advance. Nardon had defended them, but also noted that they were still highly regarded by all classes of society and that their attitude was wholly different from that displayed in 1806.[32] Some priests were actually arrested in 1809 for pro-Austrian opinions; one, Bruschi, spent two years in Fenestrelles and, on his release, was not allowed back to Piacenza, which was considered too dangerous to harbour him by 1811.[33] No progress had been made in Piacenza; quite the reverse: a window had been closed in a volatile area. The French had deliberately placed 'one of their own' here exactly because of its history of rebellion and 'the great influence held by the clergy over public opinion in this region', but they had manifestly failed to 'enlighten the mass of the faithful, and to attach them imperceptibly to France'.[34] Nevertheless, it was a policy they expanded rather than abandoned.

This policy began at the beginning, in the new Piedmontese departments, with the dispatch of the Bishop of Amiens to organize their religious affairs. He subsequently remained, as Bishop of Casale, after the see was translated from Alessandria. His brief was to 'Gallicanize' Piedmont, and from the outset he stressed the need to introduce the Concordat in full, and quickly, in which task he was backed to the hilt by Menou.[35] They did so ruthlessly. While Pius VII stood aside, the regular houses were suppressed and the Piedmontese dioceses were reduced from seventeen to eight; Napoleon had originally wanted only six: one per department, on the French model.[36] This left the Archbishop of Turin, Burzone del Signore, hampered in his cautious but clear attempts to rally his bishops around him to bridle the work of Amiens. He fought back with one of the first clear examples of liturgical resistance the French faced, when he concluded a pastoral letter to his arch-diocese in June 1804 – most of which was a panegyric to Napoleon – with the phrase '[i]ssued nevertheless under the orders of His Majesty the Emperor Napoleon, as we are mandated by his sovereign letters, on which we have modelled the tenor of our own'.[37] Following his refusal to attend the imperial coronation a few months later, Burzone had his resignation forced from him. Thus the Concordat was in force and its chief critic ousted, but there should have been warning signs for the French in this apparent triumph. Burzone was not a traditionalist, in the Curial sense, indeed he had a deeply Jansenist background, having been Bishop of Vercelli and a product of its seminary; he was of a legal family, and hardly a fanatic.[38] The intransigent nature of the French reforms had been too much for him nonetheless. His successor, Giacinto Della Torre, then Bishop of Acqui, was shortlisted by the Minister of Religion to Napoleon thus:

> This is the candidate who is the least imposing as a prelate, but who conducted himself well for France during the times of trouble [the *triennio*], and who has even issued homilies and pastoral letters in favour of the French.[39]

Della Torre strove to protect those of his clergy considered 'dangerous' by the government, and worked well with Prospero Balbo to enhance the standing of the Church in the University of Turin.[40] Nevertheless, the rela-tive passivity of the Piedmontese dioceses under the French was due in great part to his role as a Napoleonic 'courtier': his collaboration was probably from conviction; he was pleased to be freed from Roman control.[41] The French were not so fortunate elsewhere.

In 1804 the appointment of a reliable Italian prelate to the diocese of Parma, to replace Turchi, also proved successful initially. Carlo Francesco Caselli was Piedmontese by birth, and a regular of the Servi di Maria, who rose to be first secretary of the Order in Rome and then held a high post with the Inquisition. He impressed Pius VII in the negotiations for the Concordat with his sharp eye for detail. Until the seizure of Rome, he worked well with the regime, his appointment a product of the brief 'honeymoon period' between the Papacy and Napoleon. However, he turned against the regime at the *Concile Nationale* in 1811, putting himself at the head of the Curial opposition.[42]

The reasoning behind the appointment of a French prelate to Piacenza, and some of its consequences, have already been discussed, but the arrival of a Frenchman in that particular diocese reveals how traumatic the revolt of 1806 had been for the regime, however easily, in military terms, it had crushed open rebellion. The Minister of Religion made Fallot's role very clear to him from the outset, and it was not that of a conventional 'good shepherd' whose first duty was to his flock:

> You will speak to me, in general terms, of the differences that exist between your circumscription and those of the neighboring bishops. I hope you will send me confidential details of these … I must know all the nuances that go to constitute the whole. You are too good an administrator not to share my concerns here, or to leave me uninformed of either public or confidential matters, as well as of your personal opinion, which carries great weight with me.[43]

It was hardly a role his predecessor would have tolerated, or of which his own Vicar-General approved. Things had come a long way from the days of Cerati, 'the great almoner'.

The French made two more appointments to Italian sees, the first in the Piedmontese diocese of Asti in 1809 and the second – after the refusal of Pius VII to sanction such appointments – to the great Archdiocese of Florence. Both ended in tears. Asti had always been regarded as a problem; its bishop, the Piedmontese aristocrat Gattinara, was deeply distrusted by the French administrators and the local patriots, because of the leading role he had taken in the royalist counter-revolution during the *triennio* and the first years of French rule.[44] In 1810 the sub-prefect warned that 'the chapter is infected by Ultramontane ideas' under the leadership of Carlevaris, the Vicar-General, over whom Gattinara had lost all control. Borghese, the Governor-General of Turin, agreed, saying the new bishop 'ought to be of the right outlook, in order to control those priests'. Thus the Minister of Religion requested that the new bishop be sent immediately, without waiting for a Papal bull, and that Carlevaris be 'removed'.[45]

The choice fell on Dejean de St Saveur, the Vicar-General of Mende, then over sixty and described by the Bishop of Casale as 'having the great misfortune, especially for a public man, of having a hideous face' and of having been 'aged by the experience of the Revolution'.[46] Dejean arrived in Asti without a bull and, following the rupture with Rome later that year, he never received one. His new chapter simply refused to recognize him. Dejean was hardly a 'radical priest', having served as Vicar-General of Narbonne under that most worldly of *ancien régime* 'politico' prelates, Dillon, who lived most of the year in Paris in a highly secular style, while Dejean ran the diocese.[47] He had made his name helping Dillon to manage the Estates of Languedoc, where they had worked to preserve clerical privileges as a condition for support for other reforming initiatives.[48] None of this served him well in Asti, and he emerged from the experience a dedicated Bonapartist. The Vicar-General was eventually sent to Fenestrelles, along with two other canons who continued to refuse to acknowledge Dejean. It took the personal intervention of the Archbishop of Turin to get the rest of the chapter to submit formally to Dejean. This included even the new Vicar-General he had himself appointed, Dani, who submitted only after assurances were given that he would avoid arrest, something the Minister of Religion had reservations about.[49] Dejean paid dearly for this after 1814. He felt the combined wrath of the restored Court and Pius VII, who agreed he should be deported to France, which he was.[50] Dani played a key role in this, according to D'Azeglio, the Piedmontese ambassador in Rome:

I have received from Dani himself an original paper by M. Dejean, which proves the violence used against the former and legitimate Vicar-General-Capitular, which is enough to demonstrate his guilt ... [51]

The whole incident was a failure. It was 'resolved only by ruthless intimidation', and was not forgotten by those concerned, despite the defiant, militant Gallican attitude taken in Paris:

This example of making recourse to the Metropolitan will, in itself, serve very well as proof that where there are problems with a chapter over a vacant see, it is not to the Pope, but to the Metropolitan that the chapter must turn.[52]

Events in Florence were to prove this assessment to be, at the very least, premature.

For all the problems Dejean encountered, Asti was a small see under a loyal Metropolitan, and the work of the diocese managed to continue. It was different when the French imposed D'Osmond, the Bishop of Ghent, on the Metropolitan See of Florence. On the death of the incumbent in 1810, the feud with Pius VII was at its height. D'Osmond was a moderate man, who had overcome initial resistance to his status as a French outsider in a large Belgian diocese, and won many friends there, before his translation to Florence.[53] It was all damned from the start, however, as he not only arrived without a bull, but had no prospect of one with Pius VII imprisoned in Savona.[54] The lesson the French seemed to have absorbed from the experience of Asti was to 'knock out' high-level opponents of the new Archbishop as quickly as possible. When the chapter organized itself to oppose the entry of D'Osmond into the Duomo, Elisa had the two ringleaders, Mancini and Barrera, arrested and ordered them sent to Fenestrelles. That D'Osmond was able to enter 'his' Cathedral in pomp softened her to the extent that she suspended their deportation:

> but my opinion of these two clerics has not changed. By deferring their punishment, I merely propose to choose the moment when this measure [deportation to Fenestrelles] will have the desired effect. I regard Barrera, particularly, as an intriguer who should be got away from Florence as soon as I can do so without provoking new protests from the chapter.[55]

The Minister of Religion wanted this supplemented by the forced resignation of the Vicar-General, Corboli, thereby leaving D'Osmond in sole administrative control of the archdiocese. Corboli's failing was not that of opposition, but of weakness and being dominated by the influence of the 'rebels'.[56] This was a powerful underestimation of clerical solidarity. The chapter met under the supervision of the Director-General of Police on Christmas Eve 1810, and still unanimously refused to accept D'Osmond because he had no Papal bull.[57] The Prefect suspected – rightly – that they were in direct contact with the Pope,[58] but it was their *esprit du corps* that struck him most in this early phase of the conflict, and led him to the revealing outburst that the chapter 'has, in substance, the same characteristics as the monastic houses, and merits the same fate' – that is, abolition.[59] During all this, the news that the chapter had sent Mancini and Barrera to meet D'Osmond at Piacenza, telling him not to enter Florence, had reached the public and was being discussed in the *caffè*.[60] The chapter backed down after the arrests, but the French were wrong to take this as a sign of victory or to assume, as they did initially, that the Duomo was empty because the public was not interested.[61]

The Minister of the 3e arrondissement of Police-Générale was even more mistaken when he told the Prefect

> I like to believe that the clergy of Florence [who are] still guided by the spirit of their former ruler, Grand Duke Leopold, will not set an example of opposition in this business.[62]

A year later, the Director-General of Police informed him of what Degerando had already known seven years earlier: that most of the Tuscan bishops were always opposed to the Leopoldine reforms; that they had worked hard to undo them ever since; that they did all they could to get the Inquisition re-established before 1808; that 'their pretext was to save the holy faith and their secret goal was to make a sacrifice of the Jacobins and the Jansenists'; and they had not changed. Their addresses of loyalty to the Emperor were nothing but tactical ploys.[63] A few weeks later, he was even more scathing about the Florentines:

> But I will tell you confidentially, [that] in spite of his fine qualities, M. D'Osmond will never have great influence in Florence unless he has his bull: His lively, sharp and likeable character contrasts too much with the rigidity and false piety of his predecessors.[64]

In another example of cultural disparagement, the Director-General asserted the incompatibility of the 'Florentine character' with the superior – and emblematic – virtues of the French.

Nonetheless, there was a great deal of hard experience to support his more empirical assessments. Although the Bishop of Pisa was openly opposed to D'Osmond from the outset, Grosiberti, in Grossetto and his chapter, adhered quickly to the new Metropolitan.[65] However, in November, when D'Osmond invited Grosiberti to celebrate the anniversary of the imperial coronation, he resigned rather than do so.[66] D'Osmond and the secular arm struck hard and fast: Grosiberti was sent to Fenestrelles, where he was treated with exceptional harshness and kept in solitary confinement, which even the Director-General thought excessive and 'unfortunate' for D'Osmond's public image. Nevertheless, the example made of him was deemed necessary,

> and it has beaten all the ecclesiastical opposition here into silence. The malcontents may protest to their consciences, but they obey outwardly. Governments need nothing more. And I dare say that this change in the Florentine clergy is due, in part, to the firmness with which I met their first attempts at resistance.[67]

In the course of 1812 the Bishop of Fiesole followed Grosiberto into custody, this time in Parma, and the French police boasted of the 'timid shadow' to which they had reduced Chigi-Zondadari, the 'fanatical but silent' Archbishop of Siena, among others. Corboli, too, 'was going through the motions demanded of him'.[68] Even this proved wrong. Corboli had emerged as a rallying point for the opposition in the chapter, drawing strongly on the fact that Pius VII had renewed him as Vicar on the death of D'Osmond's predecessor and had told the chapter to turn to him, rather than the Archbishop, as the official head of the diocese. Corboli also had a 'good past', being sacked under Peter-Leopold and brought back after Peter-Leopold's departure.[69] Throughout his tenure, the members of the chapter simply boycotted and ignored D'Osmond; only more threats from Elisa made Corboli lead them to him, for a very formal, stilted visit in April 1813.[70] Corboli died of a fever in December 1813, but the damage was already done.[71]

From a very early stage, once the chapter was stifled, resistance to D'Osmond shifted to the parishes. Many curés simply refused to receive visitations from him, or made it clear they did not want to.[72] As early as March 1811 D'Osmond complained that the clergy of Pievani refused to read his Easter message 'because they do not recognize my jurisdiction ... they have drawn together, in a little conventicle'.[73] He wanted the firmest action possible taken against them, and fully supported their deportation to Corsica in May.[74] That summer the curé of Londa, Nuzzi, preached openly against D'Osmond and the whole Concordat, refused to say the prayers for the Emperor and told his congregation the sad tale of a priest who had been excommunicated for so doing; he too went to Corsica.[75]. The Prefect warned Elisa that these were not isolated incidents[76] and this pattern was, indeed, repeated throughout the archdiocese until the end of French rule. In April 1812 eight priests in Empoli refused to make an unambiguous declaration of loyalty to D'Osmond, and said they took their advice from Corboli. In they end, they were forced to obey.[77] A month earlier, Canon Baldi of Florence went to Fenestrelles for refusing to recognize D'Osmond, even as the routine administrative head of the archbishopric.[78] That is, a year on and after severe examples of French ruthlessness, the clergy at all levels, and outwith Florence, remained defiant.

Florentine society found other, subtler ways to ignore D'Osmond and the Concordat. The secular clergy gravitated to the religious foundation of the Vincenzoguerra of San Firenze, which was not banned under the Concordat, where 'fanaticism reigns', according to D'Osmond, although he seemed to fear them and did not want direct action taken against them, which was not his usual reaction.[79] Police-Générale disagreed, because these priests were teaching the catechism to the children of the leading families of Tuscany and acting as confessors to the elite.[80] None of the twenty-nine curés of the city visited D'Osmond, and the police admitted that it was the former 'House of San Firenze that set the tone'.[81] Few of the great Florentine families attended the cathedral, or brought their children to be baptized or for their first communion. It reached embarrassing heights even within the new, official social 'pecking order' of Elisa's court. In 1812 her new Chamberlain, Capponi, had his new daughter baptized with the usual fanfare of a Florentine patrician in the Bapitistry of San Giovanni. However, he did so by private arrangement with a priest known to be anti-D'Osmond. 'The Capponis are as anti-French as they are prominent', remarked the Director-General, 'and it has had a very bad influence on the town'.[82] This was signalled as part of a general and growing resistance by 1813:

They don't bring themselves to recognize the curés named by the Archbishop, and desert their churches completely. The curés in charge already openly refuse to let them take possession [of their curés], that they cannot do so 'in good conscience' ... . The number of curés appointed by the Archbishop grows daily, and misinformation spreads through the countryside, because of their impunity, so the evil spreads. It seems to me that action is essential now, if more severe punishment is not to come later.[83]

Lay violence soon reared up. A curé appointed to the town of Vespasiano by D'Osmond had his presbytery attacked by stone-throwing mobs and he had to flee back to Florence. A year earlier, the police had spoken of 'this sort of catholic anarchy that is surely typified by the archbishopric of Florence'.[84] Events of the kind that followed the publication of the Civil Constitution of the Clergy in France in 1790 were re-enacted in Tuscany, a quarter of a century later. The main difference was probably that the Napoleonic regime was readier to resort to brute force than the 'atheistical' revolutionaries.

Much of the resistance to D'Osmond stemmed directly from the breach with Rome, and the forms it took mirrored the behaviour of the Roman clergy, but initially it was the work of the Tuscans themselves, and often pre-dated resistance in the Papal states. Nevertheless, Tuscan resistance came to be bolstered by events further south. Florence was a disaster, but it was only a foretaste of what was to come. It was probably fortunate for the French that no other sees became vacant in these years, for the experience of D'Osmond was a lesson in how important the episcopate was to the new regime. Desperation set in when resistance sprang up at parish level, however. Political problems of this kind only compounded the other difficulties of parish life the French inherited from the *ancien régime*.

Of the French bishops in Italy, D'Osmond simply withdrew with the troops in 1814, abandoning his see; Fallot was translated to a see in the interior in 1813. The former became Bishop of Nancy; the latter of Bourges in 1813. The bishops of Casale and Asti tried to stay on, but were pressured into leaving by the combined efforts of the restored monarchy and the Holy See.[85]

The parish clergy

In a report of 1806, the Ministry of Religion concluded that low numbers of secular clergy were a problem throughout the empire. No state money had been provided for the 1804 project to establish a seminary in each diocese, and the number of livings had actually fallen below the 36,000 left intact in 1791 – to just over 33,000 – despite the massive annexations that had taken place thereafter. The suppression of collegial and privately endowed benefices – 'in which the faithful found great support' – had created a gap. No less than 60,000 more priests were needed, while 8,000 more vicars were required 'in towns of a certain importance'.[86] None of these proposals were ever entertained by Paris for the urban areas of the Italian *départements réunis*; only for the periphery did French officials speak in the same vein as this challenging report.

Everywhere they looked in Italy, the French thought they saw superstition and ignorance. They also encountered great complexity, nowhere more so than in the parochial life of the Church. This complexity was shared by the centre and the periphery in all the ex-states that formed the *départements réunis*, for nowhere were the structures of religious life easily compatible with the logical simplicity and uniformity prescribed by the Concordat. The French policy of one diocese per department was seldom achieved, but to Italians the results seemed ruthless enough. The example of the Piedmontese dioceses was a message of intent. Reductions were sought later in the Duchies of Parma and Piacenza – where the four dioceses were meant to be reduced to two (still two per department in this case) – and later, with considerable ruthlessness, in the Roman departments. The most common argument put forward for the conservation of a see came from the periphery, based on topography, but Paris had its unswerving answer to hand. It was formulated best by the Ministry of Religion in 1806, drawing on its experience in Piedmont, Liguria and the Duchies. To the 'topographical' argument, Paris replied that the whole concept of a departmental *chef lieu* was that it was easily accessible to all parts of its department, thus being the place from which bishops could reach their curés most easily. For this same reason, bishops should deal with only one prefect, and they should be as close to each other as possible, because – in a frank admission – experience taught that there were always many disputes to be resolved between them should a prefect have to deal with several bishops, and *vice versa*. Thus a bishop should be under the nose of one prefect, and not able to play one off against another.[87]

One diocese per department was awkward enough for the Italian Church, but the mosaic of devotional worship below it belonged to another world for a system which recognized only the curé and his subordinates as its providers. Even they were not to be trusted, however. Curés were best kept isolated in their own parishes, under their bishops, and the French disliked even those aspects of reforming legislation they found, as in Tuscany where the Synod of Pistoia had authorized regular meetings of *parocci*. Although there was no attempt to ban them, the Ministry of Police warned that of Religion that there was to be 'nothing secret' about them, adding that 'this kind of gathering raises doubts about the advantages to be gained [from its existence] in the current situation'.[88] The Concordat had no place for the regular orders or the confraternities; it confined worship to Sundays and brooked very little outside interference in the work of the parish. It abolished all private benefices and the tithe, making the parish clergy wholly dependent on their state salaries or private income. This was a true revolution, at least in intent, something even Trent did not confront. However, the transfer from the *ancien régime* to the Concordat proved almost impossible in many cases, and the curés were the chief victims of this, especially in poorer areas. The Vicar-General of the diocese of Casale told the Prefect of Genoa in 1810 that the transfer simply had not been made over most of the diocese. Most curés did not have incomes from the bishop and relied entirely on their parishioners, something the Concordat simply did not assume. It was geared to replacing episcopal income with a state salary; where this had not happened – and it was widespread – the parish clergy were left with nothing.[89] There were similar complaints that year from the Bishop of Piacenza about the plight of his mountain parishes.[90] This was equally true over the highland areas of the Kingdom of Italy, where the parish clergy depended on local support to supplement thin landed revenues, and whose personnel – while drawn from all ranks of society – came increasingly from the poorest sections of the peasantry, nobility and artisans.[91] In the Apennine hinterland district of Alpi Apuane, above Reggio-Emiliano in the Kingdom of Italy, parochial patrimonies saw no improvement as a result of the Concordat; the revenues of the rural confraternities yielded no profits, as originally they had only sufficed to maintain their own masses and administer their properties. The clergy remained in the debt of their flocks.[92] Clearly, in the poorest parishes of some of the poorest parts of the periphery, the Concordat had made a difficult situation worse, and not really only in the initial stages of French rule. In Tuscany, however, these difficulties seem to have been largely avoided, thanks to the heritage of the Leopoldine reforms, which provided for the upkeep of churches and of their priests from diocesan funds. The problem here arose from the transfer of these responsibilities from the bishop to the parish committees, the *fabriques*.[93] It was administrative, rather than structural, in origin, as both Church and state admitted.[94]

On the periphery, the French found a scattered, overstretched Church, starved of both material and human resources, greatly dependent on the missions and the preaching skills of itinerant regulars, and riven by the lay factions that dominated its isolated parochial outposts. In the cities, they found an ecclesiastical structure 'deeply interwoven with the economy and society of the *ancien régime*', while

> the local Church remained atomized, incapable of overcoming the strong, internal resistance of the city, where, within a limited area, institutions could be harnessed by particular interests.[95]

The French had to challenge the wealth and influence of the confraternities in urban centres, not just in the context of social control, but in the cause of putting the curé and the parish at the centre of parish life. It was a battle against pluralism, in town and country, mountain and plain, that others had lost before them.

The periphery

Just as their relations with the episcopate reveal the limits and strains of collaboration between willing partners, so their relationship with the parish clergy was generally marked by tolerance stretched to its limits. However much they distrusted, and even feared, the *parocci*, the French still preferred them to the regulars or the members of the lay confraternities, and strove to concentrate all forms of religious life around the parish. The terms of the Concordat actually restrained the French, because it made them utterly dependent on the parish priests, although it was also arguably that aspect of the Concordat that brought the religious policies of the new regime closest to those of Trent. On the periphery, the Napoleonic quest for tighter hierarchical control and a stronger external presence in these communities, often revealed that Trent had only partially succeeded in replacing the earlier role of the priest as part of his community, sharing its collective prejudices and priorities, with a representative of the intellectual dictatorship of the Church hierarchy.[96]

The upheavals of the *triennio* often weakened episcopal control in the hinterlands, the important place of religion in counter-revolution not withstanding. The vastly different responses of the Piedmontese episcopate and its subordinates, especially in the highland parishes, meant the French never extended their confidence in the bishops to the *parocci*. In 1801 Jourdan was chafing at the bit to get at them:

> in general, the clergy of Piedmont are pronounced enemies of the French government … . As long as [it] continues to close its eyes to the criminal conduct of the priests … public tranquillity will always be threatened, the people of the countryside … will always be disposed to take up arms against us … the bulk of the country's people has a blind confidence in their priests and, thanks to their perfidious suggestions and outright lies, they … see in every Frenchman only an enemy.[97]

However, the French were constrained to endure them. The attitude – and the discourse – initiated by Jourdan spread among his colleagues as the empire expanded; the hatred of the French police for the Italian *parocci* is almost a commonplace in their correspondence. Moreau de St-Méry lashed out against the clergy almost instinctively at the first news of the revolt of the Piacentino in December 1805: 'It is known to me, personally, that the men of the cloth have incited this disobedience'.[98] At the height of the 1809 revolt in the Veneto, Napoleon himself ordered Eugène to arrest the Bishop of Udine for treason and to have him shot, orders which the Viceroy managed to contain by a brief detention.[99] Yet a sense of realism emerged in quieter times. According to the Director-General of Police in Florence, in 1809:

> I do not doubt that various priests do not distinguish themselves by seditious conniving and through alarmist sermons. In these circumstances, the police must act with a certain latitude. It is probably more important keep the government at a distance from any appearance of religious persecution, but it is also essential to repress the audacity of troublemakers and fanatics.[100]

The clergy of the periphery were feared as much as their flocks, even when French rule had become secure. As with the *parocci* of the highland zones of the Kingdom of Italy, however poor, they were invested with tremendous influence in their communities and, during the *triennio*, they had used it to drive the counter-revolution, usually escaping episcopal control.[101] By the time that control began to reassert itself, Church and state were at odds over the captivity of Pius VII. D'Auzers saw the priests of the Ligurian valleys as an integral part of their communities, made all the more dangerous by their role as intermediaries with the centre:

> This ferocious mountain country, lacking main roads, is very backward in terms of its civilization. The priests do well from this ignorance in misleading the people. They use superstition and fanaticism to great effect ... . It is certain they have had word about the Pope. They circulate ... all the seditious writings from Rome, giving them a dangerous character.[102]

D'Auzers stressed how isolated and thinly spread were the forces of order in these valleys, making a hostile clergy all the more dangerous. He wanted examples made, even of the Bishop of Sarazzana, but another school of thought believed the clergy of such areas could only push their flocks the way they wanted to go. The incarnation of the government's nightmare was probably Biggio, the curé of Orrero in the notorious valley of the Fontanabuona in Liguria. He was avowedly anti-French, lived openly with the mother of his child and defied Spina's reprimands. Biggio preached openly against conscription. He was also rich and immensely influential:

> He spends his night in the cabarets, and goes about the valley armed with a musket and a knife. Through his wealth, his character and his alliances with the leading troublemakers of the Fontanabuona, his spiritual ministry from the pulpit and the

confessional, he has made himself influential and formidable, to the point where no one dares denounce him or confront him.[103]

Biggio was less pre-Trent, than pre-Constance. This was where the Counter Reformation and the counter-revolution parted company, and the case of Biggio brought D'Auzers and Spina into a relatively rare but powerful alliance. It took D'Auzers almost two years to convince Paris to arrest him, and gaol him in Parma, but Spina was able in the interim to confine him in a retreat.[104] Where it was a case of gross clerical indiscipline – and the Apennine parishes seem to have had their fair share – Spina and D'Auzers always worked together, along with the local authorities, as in the case of the curé of Levaggi, who took up with the wife of a parishioner.[105] When a similar case arose in the Piacentino in 1813, they combined again to have the priest Boselli of Montechiarugolo arrested. Boselli had links with a family of known counter-revolutionaries, and was now known as a drunken, violent womanizer, although he was released after an interview with the Prefect.[106] In such cases, the old problems of simply governing the periphery bound all the authorities together. Whether Spina was a true counter-revolutionary or not, the mores of Trent took precedence over politics, at least in the hinterland. The cold comfort D'Auzers could draw from this was that at least Spina did not manipulate such men, even if no one else did either.

The kind of rigid internal discipline and powerful intellectual leadership mustered by Corboli in the cities and plains of the archbishopric of Florence, could not be replicated in the dioceses of the periphery, for better or for worse. The one great constant was Easter, however. This was, perhaps, the most lasting, pervasive victory Trent had won over the course of the early modern period, and it haunted the French. It was a lesson they learnt early. Jourdan told Fouché in 1802:

> the Easter season ... is the time when priests exercise their greatest influence over the people through the confessional and, in general, [the priests] are loyal to the King of Sardinia. This is the second year I have noted that people are at their most volatile at this time.[107]

At the other end of the period, and of the *départements réunis*, Roederer in Umbria told Paris to forget any immediate hopes for many laymen to serve in local government, for:

> we are approaching that dread period for the full deployment of the power of the clergy, Easter ... . We are in a country where no one, whatever his rank or wealth, neglects his devotional duties; there is

no one who does not make a show of communicating at Easter, for fear of losing the confidence and respect he enjoys.[108]

The point in this context is less the universal importance of Easter, in both centre and periphery, than the truly seasonal nature of clerical influence in the latter, and that the French had learnt to see it as malign.

Civilian and clerical officials were often less damning than the police about the lower clergy of the periphery, but they were never foolhardy enough to hope for much. Rolland in the Apennines said in 1809 that

> One cannot say that the clergy of this department are motivated by an excellent spirit, but it is not true that they show a bad one either.[109]

Six years earlier, Bressy, the Jansenist ex-priest and sub-prefect of Saluzzo in Piedmont, remarked

> I would not assert that all the curés are loyal to the present government, for that would not be the case, only that they are peaceable men, that they are the friends of peace.[110]

This was about as enthusiastic as French discourse ever became on the subject, but there was real, if rare, common ground. The petition of Nenci, the *parocco* of Bettolle in Tuscany, shows that, before the Concordat was introduced, there were parish clergy ready to support a strong state. Nenci organized a petition of the most important property owners of his commune, demanding that the new government use force against 'several individuals of the village, whose honesty there is every reason to doubt', and duly supplied a list of them. 'They have little or no religion', he added,

> They live far from the holy sacraments, from any pious instruction, and – even though they are all adults – they have never been admitted to Holy Communion.

They were all thieves.[111] The Governor of Siena supported this, and wanted troops sent to the area.[112] Quite apart from a laudable and none too common support for the French in the restoration of order, Nenci's zeal also showed him to be very much a part of his community, perhaps too much so. Yet here too were grounds for a good working relationship with the new state, even if the connection made between godlessness and lawlessness was alien to most gendarmes. The Tuscan clergy reported to the *Buon Governo* fairly regularly under the *ancien régime*; it can only be remarked in a general way, that such information does not seem to be present under the French police – and the simultaneous breach with Rome – after 1809.

Beyond the habitual refrain of the police against 'fanatical, superstitious enemies of the government' – of the threat of counter-revolution – were also many more mundane cases revealing a highland clergy that had escaped ecclesiastical discipline. The numbers are impossible to evaluate, nor is there any evidence on a scale to suggest such things were common, but their presence shows a persistence of problems common under the *ancien régime*. In 1805 the new French Bishop of Casale noted the extremes he found in the poor mountain parishes of his diocese, where the *desservants* in charge of isolated hill chapels came to see themselves as independent of the curés to whom they were subordinate, while in other parishes they did not have the means or standing to do their jobs properly.[113] The portrait of Salvi, the curé of the Tuscan village of Sovicilla, reveals anything but a Tridentine model. He came to the attention of the new regime in 1810, when he was accused of attacking the *greffier* of the justice of the peace with a cutlass, and had already been in trouble trying to get a friend exempted from conscription and an abortion for a girl he may or may not have made pregnant.[114] None of the charges were proved, but what emerges is more a local notable than the Tridentine professional found at the regional centre, Siena:[115]

> he has made himself the landlord of several farms around the commune, he has opened his own pharmacy, and also dabbles in surgery and medicine. In these ways, he has made himself influential in the area, and has excercised his influence for many years; it extends to all sorts of things, even as far as contravening the authority of the *maire*, the justice of the peace and the other officials in the commune … . His activities have always led him to be thought of as the protector of his parishioners, and during his clashes with the *maire*, he has been able to get many certificates out of the people of his parish, in which these imbeciles attest that the *maire* tried to assassinate Salvi.[116]

This kind of interest in modern science and medicine was hardly what the Ministry of Religion had in mind in its calls for a better educated clergy. There was no question in anyone's mind that he was an awkward *chef populaire*, even when the authorities agreed he was probably innocent. It was his power in the commune that made both the Prefect and the Vicar-General of Siena want him moved elsewhere.[117] However, he was a known supporter of the French, 'who does not mix much with monks or priestly cliques'. Paris ruled that he was to stay, for political reasons, and that his political loyalty should be used to better effect by the local authorities.[118]

Even where there was real consensus, it was often impossible to act upon. Spina returned from his pastoral visitation to the hinterlands in 1812 more satisfied than he had hoped with the level of education of his clergy, but as unhappy as the French that 'so many of them serve as secretaries to the *maires* … which must distract them greatly from the duties of their vocation'.[119] Neither the secular nor the sacred arm could reverse this in the early nineteenth century, but there was a shared preoccupation.

There were serious criminal cases involving the parish clergy from time to time, and the French did not often shirk their duty to protect the public. Even in the vilest, however, there were significant problems. In 1812 the authorities were all agreed that there was an indisputable case of serious child abuse against a canon of Velletri in the ex-Papal states. However, the canon, Giorgi, was also one of only a handful of local clergy to have taken the Oath of Loyalty to the regime, leading the Procureur-Impériale to reflect that 'the publicity would be a triumph for the refractories, as well as a social scandal'.[120] Paris shied away from a public trial and ordered Giorgi dealt with under Haute Police, which also coincided with the wishes of the family.[121] Another case from the Roman departments reveals much deeper complications for the French, however. Ferdinando Cerelli, a priest from the isolated village of Ceprano, was accused in 1812 of poisoning his nephew with opium. The Procureur noted that 'as it was a question involving a priest, the hall was full of his supporters', but the real problem went deeper:

> I am in a difficult position as to where to stand in this unfortunate business, which also, perhaps, has to do with the status of the accused, and with the old view that such a person cannot be judged by laymen … . It is one of those problems that one dares not admit, even when it is as obvious as it is probable.[122]

There were exceptions to this, however. In 1807 several parishes in the Piacentino made use of the new French legislation to drag their curés before the courts, not because they had done anything wrong, but to give evidence in delicate family cases, one of which involved the reputation of a young girl. The Bishop did not like their involvement in this sort of thing and, worried that it would compromise their position of leadership in their communities, asked Paris to keep them out of court.[123] Nothing was simple or easy, in the relations between Church and state.

The French feared and often hated the parish clergy of the periphery, but they also had a commitment to help them materially. Everywhere they looked in Italy, they found a poor, over-extended clergy in the hinterlands, quite different from the superfluity of priests in the lowlands and the urban centres. It is a sign of the suspicion, frustration and open hatred of the clergy by the police that they alone made no distinction between centre and periphery in this matter. They called for a reduction in their numbers everywhere. Lagarde, the Director-General in Florence, demanded first a reduction in the number of dioceses from twenty-two to three – one per department, on the French model – and then of curés to one per justice of the peace, which would reduce those of Florence from twenty-nine to six.[124] In Rome, Norvins raged: 'To reduce the number of priests, is to reduce the opposition, the influence of bad advice and the hot-headedness that ruins families'.[125] The number of parishes in the Piacentino was reduced severely – and very promptly – after the 1806 revolt.[126] Yet parallel to this ran the official policy, laid down in Paris, that these same secular clergy were 'the true and respectable organs of Religion ... . The government knows no others'.[127] The irony is underlined further when this attitude is juxtaposed to the arguments for small parishes and dioceses, made by the Bishop of Biella in 1802, that 'if dioceses became too extended, the bishops will not be able to oversee them alone', and that is why the monarchy deliberately kept them small.[128]

Dejean de St Saveur, the Bishop of the Piedmontese diocese of Asti, probably epitomized the embattled French position in Italy. He had little love for his flock but during the reorganization of 1810, although fully supporting the government in reducing the 'over served' parishes of the plain, he fought to keep the small, numerous parishes of the foothills, as did his colleague in Saluzzo, a native Piedmontese.[129] However, well before the revolt of the Piacentino demonized the highland *parocci* in official eyes, an official in Piacenza acknowledged not just the difference in wealth between the parishes of the highlands and the *pianura*, but that

> The plurality of the mountain parishes only serves to reveal a picture of the most afflicting distress. This means that very capable, worthy men, who should be filling the vacant parishes [of the highlands] leave the field clear for men who are very mediocre, and incapable of serving the needs of the state. These low incomes destroy the ability of the curé to help his parishioners, in times of trouble or need, which is the only way to win their affection or confidence.[130]

This represents a very clear formulation of what guided the policies of the ministries of the Interior and Religion. A number of cases of indiscipline reached Fallot from the Piacentino over the years that confirmed this view of the low quality of the parish clergy there, including that of Corazza, the curé of Carmaglia, who lived openly in his crumbling manse with his three sons and their mother. Tournon drew attention to the understaffed, over-worked provincial clergy of the Roman countryside, where a superfluity of bishoprics did not mean a numerous parish clergy: there were only 582 curés in the two Roman departments, most of them poor, while the lower clergy

> who help serve the churches are in an even worse state. Thus the most active section of the clergy, that which bore the burden of the work of the Gospel, gives it up as soon as it can provide for itself.[131]

These concerns are reflected in two reports drawn up for the Prefect of Genoa in 1810 and 1811, both of which reveal the poverty of the secular arm of the Church in the north-western Apennines. The first was *Observations on the Planned Reorganization of the Parishes of the Diocese of Casale and Its 444 Parishes*.[132] The Diocese of Casale spanned the Apennines and the plain of the Po, but the report focused on the mountain parishes, most of which were in the suppressed dioceses of Tortona and Bobbio – over 200 – an area of difficult terrain and few means of communication, where

> the people of the hamlets and small settlements would be left without the spiritual support of religion, or of Christian moral teaching, should they have their curé or vicar removed.

The report pointed directly to the dilemma facing both Church and state in such an area: the need to retain parishes in remote areas had to be weighed against their poor livings, which 'diminished the dignity of the curé'. The report especially disliked the dependence of many curés on local charity or on income derived from their parishioners, in keeping as much with the preoccupations of Borromeo as with those of the National Assembly. To this end, the government had already shifted some of the revenues from 'over-endowed' parishes to the poorer ones. It was not enough, however, and the report concluded by proposing a 'triple order' of clergy, which would 'convert' many of the smaller curés into vicaries (for areas under 250 souls) and dependent chapels (for those under 800), leaving true curés for centres of over 800 souls. Even then, it warned, money would be tight. The findings of this report were applicable elsewhere along the Apennine chain. To an extent, its conclusions echo the pleas of the Bishop of Montalcino in Tuscany, who sought more vicars for his mountainous, rugged diocese, rather than more cures, for those already in existence were too poor to support a single priest. He was concerned that the vicars were so poorly paid that they had to earn their livings saying masses on High Days, leaving the curés virtually unaided most of the time.[133] The parish priest of Marradi in Tuscany told Menou that he had a poor parish and many priests to pay who had to support themselves by saying masses. He hoped the new government would find other ways to pay them, presumably with the properties and revenues of the suppressed monasteries.[134] The ground for collaboration in this field was workable, if not actually clear.

The problem of poor pay and resultant clerical greed was one of the few issues where the state could ally with the laity against their priests. In 1812 the sub-prefect of the mountain arrondissement of Novi informed his superiors of complaints against the curés [who] demand vast sums for the administration of the sacraments, and who propose to raise them, since the government has assigned them fixed salaries.[135]

If Biggio and his ilk were authority's idea of the 'nightmare curé', a parishioner's model was Mosconi, from the remote parish of Sozzola in the diocese of Pontremolì, which bordered Tuscany, Liguria and the Piacentino. He encapsulated the problems foreseen in the official studies. Ignoring the Edict of 8 June 1810, which abolished the tithe – and of which he later pleaded ignorance[136] – he declared at the altar that those who did not pay the tithe were excommunicates, and used the confessional and the refusal of absolution to make his point.[137] It took two Directors-General of Police and three bishops to bring him to heel.

The second report, *Repairs to Churches and Presbyteries* from 1811, was devoted to the diocese of Casale and showed the literal shambles much of the rural Church was in. Eighty-five parishes either had no presbytery at all, or ones that were in ruins. Many also had dilapidated churches.[138] The hard evidence of the poverty of the Church was all too obvious, as was the inability of even so powerful a regime as the Napoleonic empire, to meet the challenge.[139] A similar report for the Tuscan dioceses by the Prefect of the Arno in January 1811, drew careful distinctions between centre and periphery, mountain and plain, as well as hinting at his growing hostility to the bishops.[140] The expansionist demands of the Bishop of Fiesole – shortly to be imprisoned – were staunchly rebuffed by the Prefect. Fiesole had twenty parishes for only 6,580 souls,

> which proves the uselessness of the proposed increase ... . This observation can apply to almost all the communes of this department, from which Your Excellency can judge the need for a new parochial organization.

The exception that proves the rule was in the hill commune of Figlino, where poor communications led the Prefect to support the Bishop's hopes for expansion, limited to more dependent chapels rather than full cures. He took the same line with the Bishop of Arezzo – hardly a friend – in fighting to conserve small parishes in the commune Bibbimma, 'which is cut off from Arezzo for many months of the year', while stamping on his plans for expansion in the larger towns. He recommended the closure of several churches in Arezzo itself, where there was a parish church for every 720 souls, 'which gives us the scandalous spectacle of deserted temples'. In the Alpine bishopric of Ivrea, of the nine parishes abolished in 1810, three were in the towns; the cures 'created to meet the real needs of the people ... in mountains cut through with torrents' were conserved.[141] The state could and did listen in these circumstances.

'Au début les montagnes' was a curse on the Church, just as much as on the state. Here should have been common, if inhospitable, ground between the Borromean mission and that of the new regime. Indeed, some prelates were glad to see the end of many *ancien régime* restrictions on their jurisdictions. The Bishop of Vercelli lambasted the negligence and obstructive behaviour of lay patrons of parishes in his former bishopric of Biella with the same bile as any secular prince. His flock told him repeatedly that they would have had the means to revive their parishes if the lay patrons either did their duty or renounced their feudal prerogatives.[142] This was one prayer the French answered, at least. In the main, however, the French reforms were compromised by natural obstacles and the resources it took to challenge them. The mountain did not move for the last emperor of the west, any more than for the great saint of Milan.

However, the terms of the Concordat, and the rigid manner in which the French stuck to them, made their task harder – and more resented by the faithful of the hinterlands – than it need otherwise have been. The new regime simply refused to recognize the complexity of the Church on the periphery, or why it needed to be thus. This attitude is already evident in the decision to suppress the missions, an 'addition' to the terms of the Concordat the French need not have adopted. The real problem on the periphery was its insistence on the parish as the sole, as opposed to the dominant, force in religious life. Local observers resented this assault on tradition, but they also believed it unworkable. It was an issue that roused the periphery to petition the centre, and the profusion of evidence it generated meant the new rulers could not plead ignorance. The rebels of the Piacentino included in their complaints the abolition of three regular houses in the Val di Trebbia. Other protests came in more supplicant – but emphatic – form. In 1808, and again in 1810, the people of Giara in the Alpine foothills north of Biella petitioned for the restoration of their parish church; they were now far from their parish church and too poor to support its costs, compared to their old church, 'being for the most part day labourers, *mezzadri* and artisans'.[143] This was not the voice of the urban, often well-heeled confraternities, or of the regular orders, but the genuine cry of popular piety. A flood of similar petitions came to the Prefect of Genoa in 1810, in the hope that the projected reorganization of the parishes would mean expansion, not the contraction usually favoured by the regime. Most resembled that of Giara. The people of Sturla-Marina in the hills outside Genoa argued from poverty and topography, [144] as did those of the parish of Santa Maria di Grenacolo in the hills on the other side of the city.[145] The former even offered to rent the Church from the authorities at their own expense, if only the department would pay the priest a small sum to augment their own alms, a request that showed both strong popular piety and a complete misconception of French policy over clerical pay. Two years later, the mountain parish of San Bartolemeo degli Armeni even won the support of Spina – to no avail – who promised to appoint and pay the auxiliary chaplain himself, if the church were reopened, as it was needed in winter.[146]

Some petitions show a remarkable mixture of ignorance and innocence, about Trent as much as the new regime. The *maire* of San Fructuoso told the Prefect of Genoa that his people had petitioned him to reopen a chapel outside the town:

> it used to be very advantageous for my commune in the years when several solemn festivals were held [at the church]; where great crowds came to enjoy the clean air of the place, and thus a lot of wine and meat were sold in the inns of the commune. This made an appreciable addition to my *octroi*, and I can at least lay before you the prayers of my *administrés*.[147]

The struggle may have been even greater than many contemporaries imagined. Interim periods between occupation and annexation are often revealing of this huge gap in perception in such matters. In January 1808, on the eve of the French occupation of Tuscany, the people of the villages of Bardani and Giannini petitioned Menou

> to be able to gather together, in good faith, and as they have practised up to now, the voluntary devotions of the people, in the Oratory of San Niccolao, and to celebrate Mass there, on the saint's day.

The naîveté of these isolated communities is predictable, but a devotional world utterly at odds with the Concordat emerges from their doomed petitions. Even more striking was the advice of the Tuscan equivalent of the Ministry of Religion, the *Regio Diritto*, to agree to this 'general orders not withstanding', because the villages were remote from their parish church.[148] In the same year, the *parocco* of Tizzana in the diocese of Pistoia petitioned the *Buon Governo* that the sacred furnishings and ornaments of an oratory in his parish had been stolen 'by the thieves who continue to infest our countryside'. He hoped the oratory could be refurbished with funds confiscated from the suppressed religious houses.[149] High and low, centre and periphery, missed the point. Eleven parishes of Genoa extra-muros petitioned to save their auxiliary hill and field chapels in the autumn of 1810 and, however hamfisted their 'political' approach to the regime, they all went to the considerable trouble of putting their addresses in French.[150] It was a matter of some concern.

In 1808 the Prefect of the Po welcomed

the closure of several churches, which only mar the impact of religion; it will produce great good in the small communes where these
rivalries between annexes and chapels lead to discord and
disorder.[151]

Loysel, a man of republican stamp, showed a canny grasp of the nature of
many local problems by pointing to this aspect of parish organization; he
saw the point of so many dependent chapels and so was able to reach
beyond the administrative reasons, based on topography, on which petitions
usually dwelt. Rival clans had, over the centuries, simply avoided each other
by persuading the ecclesiastical authorities to give them their own chapels
away from a parish church dominated by their rivals.[152] Even so, Loysel
failed to grasp Borromeo's insight that such peace could not be made from
within communities. That was what the missions were for, but the French
had abolished them; the only way to make the Mass central to the faithful
was to let them hold it where they wanted, as long as it was in a consecrated
space. To save the Mass, to enforce communion, rural parishes fragmented
in this way, just as those of the cities and towns were cut through with the
oratories of the confraternities. Even though he perceived the great problem
in this form, Loysel rejected a wealth of received experience about how to
cope with it. This kind of compromise was not in the nature of the regime.

The use of such places to express the collective strength of communities
worried the new regime, a phobia carried over the Alps. Hill and field
chapels were a step away – often literally – from the dread grottoes of the
madonnas. They were the physical space where archaic piety met counter-
revolution, at least for the French police. In 1809 the Prefect of Genoa
lambasted the 'innumerable' unauthorized *feste* taking place in closed
chapels all over Liguria: 'they lead only to unrest, and I don't think they
should be tolerated'.[153] D'Auzers had a more sinister view of them:

> the oratories and chapels spread over the countryside, or along the
> roads, which are useless for worship, are dilapidated and often serve
> as shelter for brigands … the first category that must be closed are
> all those more than a kilometre from rural communes, because they
> are too difficult to watch, even if they do have enough funds for
> their upkeep.[154]

In 1810 a priest in Arezzo used private connections to get permission from
the imprisoned Pope to open several domestic chapels. Although the government took a dim view of this, it only demanded his arrest when it became
clear they were all in rural areas.[155] Once closed, such chapels could turn
into focal points for even more archaic forms of devotion. The phenomenon
of 'power through neglect' so widespread in images of Marian devotion,
soon found parallels in other forms, as the consequences of French policy

began to be felt. In the hills outside Rome in 1811, a hermit reoccupied a suppressed field chapel and set up on its altar – 'with a kind of ceremony' – a wooden crucifix which had been torn down from the exterior of the chapel and had only its arms left. Warned that 'the common people, and the women especially, came running in crowds to adore the arms of the crucifix', the police broke up the crowd, arrested the hermit, and deported him back to Piedmont, his place of origin. When asked why he had set up the crucifix, he replied that 'he had been forced to cede to the will of the people'.[156]

Taken together, the relationship between the Church hierarchy and the Napoleonic state as it developed on the periphery was fraught with problems, but there were at least signs that the 'civilizing mission' discerned by both might serve as the foundation of a working compromise. Both were often prepared to risk the ire of the laity, the better to control them. Incompatibility was never far from the surface, but in practice it could be held in check. It was not the same at the centre, in the great cities and the lowlands.

The centre

On the periphery, the French faced a problem that was literally as old as the hills, as well as problems thrown up by the political traumas of the *triennio*. They faced a different set of obstacles in urban and lowland areas. In direct contrast to the periphery, they believed there were too many clergy in the great cities and lowland plains of Italy, an attitude which made its way into the consciousness of the laity and the local authorities, if sometimes in exaggerated form. Just as the people of Emploi in Tuscany interpreted the French penchant for abolishing High Days as a sure sign they would cancel Christmas, so during the reorganization of the Church in 1810 the *maire* of Voghera, on the border between Piedmont and Liguria, wrote with trembling hand to Paris, expressing local fears that his sizeable town would be reduced to only one parish and one church.[157] The difference was that the *maire* and his *administrés* had long experience of the French, and they were absolutely right. There was only one proper parish church in this town of 8,000; all the rest were oratories of confraternities or held by the regular orders. In 1812 Voghera still had but one church.[158]

The Prefect of the Arno in 1811 was very clear that twenty-nine parishes were enough for Florence, a town of over 72,000. Pisa also followed this pattern. In 1784, when Ricci and Peter-Leopold tried and failed to change this, there were eighty-two places of worship for a population of 7,468 souls, a ratio of 1:91. All was not as it seemed, however, for only fourteen of them were parish churches; the rest had belonged to the confraternities, the regular orders or were private oratories.[159] This is what the French believed to be sufficient.[160] Parma had thirty parishes for 34,000 people, eight of which depended on the regular houses and were without support after their abolition, together with the Cathedral Chapter and four collegial churches. Only one parish in the town was considered by the French to have a reasonable revenue; most of the ninety-four clergy attached to them were in private benefices, shortly to be abolished under the Concordat. It was further noted that canons were paid almost twice as much as parish priests, and that one third of revenue designated for their pay did not reach them, but went for 'public service', meaning charity.[161] These were among the privileges and practices, clawed back by Turchi after the fall of Du Tillot, that Moreau de St-Méry said he most detested in his unpublished history of the Duchies. They underpinned a venal, useless consistory and starved the parishes of revenue in the interests of holding the idle poor in awe and superstition of the Bishop.[162]

The French perceived the persistence of *ancien régime* problems quickly enough – 'the fragmentation of "associative" religious life [the confraternities and oratories] to the detriment of the parish nucleus', and the subordination of the parish churches to the regulars[163] – but they did not think of expanding the parish network, only of cutting away 'the competition'. They were not concerned with rectifying the problems of the traditional parish structure to meet the demographic shifts of the late eighteenth century. What drew their attention was the correlation of existing resources to the numbers of clergy employed; there was never a question of expanding numbers. The French were ruthless with the Roman dioceses, twenty out of thirty-seven were abolished in the 'first wave', before yet more of their incumbents refused to take the oath. The rationale was that they were too small, some no bigger than a French parish.[164] This accomplished, even the loyal and the relatively exalted were not safe from this imperative. A report to the Minister of Religion noted a few months later that '[t]he number of canons who have taken the Oath in the suppressed chapters greatly exceeds the number of prebends in those chapters still conserved'.[165] Tournon noted the superfluity of clergy in Rome as compared to the rest of the department: 407 secular clerics, compared to 582 curés and 1,474 vicars for the rest of the Papal states. Rome had eighty-one parishes, only thirty-three of which were 'proper' cures, but this figure was still capable of being reduced.[166]

When it came to dealing with Church property the French deemed redundant, their ruthlessness could be breathtaking. They could get their comeuppance, too, as in 1803 when they blew up the cathedral of Alessandria, the second largest city in Piedmont, which was losing its see to Casale and so did not need one anymore. When a prominent local Jacobin was hit by a stone from the blast, and killed, the local clergy turned it into a miracle, a sign of divine wrath, and refused to absolve him or bury him.[167] Tournon was sensitive to the importance of actual buildings and their contents to the Romans, although he still despised the devotional culture behind them:

Although numerous, [the churches] scarcely suffice for the religious services which the Romans are so used to. Each neighbourhood, each street, has one or several churches where the local is used to fulfilling his devotions. There is not a church without a miraculous image, a tomb, a tradition, that does not make it venerable in their eyes. The faithful would be hurt, public opinion would be shocked, if the number of these places of worship was to be limited.[168]

Nonetheless, Tournon saw a clear division between those churches of artistic and historical interest, and those of interest to 'purely local observance'. Only the former merited reopening, and only then if others were closed in recompense. Fortunately for the service of parishes, Tournon believed that many parish churches were more artistically important than the oratories. French aesthetic taste would dictate the fate of Rome, even when its Prefect showed an awareness of local devotional culture rare among the occupiers. His Emperor thought twenty parishes enough for the capital of Christendom, out of the existing eighty.[169] Yet even Napoleon did not formulate policy with as much ruthless clarity – or ill-disguised sarcasm – as the Director of the Domain of the department of the Reno in the Kingdom of Italy. The requests of the Vicar-General to reopen ex-regular churches for parish use met with this reply:

The Vicar flatters himself in being able to conserve the churches already allocated to him without the obligation to renounce others, and he bases this presumptuousness on the need for them revealed by the throngs of people who attend the open churches. I would observe to him, that the existing churches already cost the government the allotted sums, and he would do well to indicate which churches he would close in recompense.[170]

The French never developed a coherent strategy for the city of Genoa, but the closure of all the churches and chapels of the regulars, and most of the oratories, left huge gaps in parish administration. It also exposed the gap in wealth and resources between the parishes and the 'associative' and regular arms of devotion. The Prefect saw this as a means to further the deeper policy at the heart of it all, by pilfering the wealth of the regular houses, their churches and the private oratories, thus

surrounding the curés – who are the only true ministers – with all the attention, all the pomp and all the magnificence that the celebration of the holy mysteries deserves.[171]

The curé and parish of San Vincenzo wanted to transfer the parish church from their own church – 'so small, so airless [and] very inconvenient for the inhabitants' – to the church of the Consolation, formerly belonging to the Dominicans and now vacant.[172] The French encouraged this exchange, but did not think in terms of expansion in Genoa any more than in Tuscany. Although the Prefect was favourable to reopening the ex-Capuchin church of the Annunciation as a parish church in 1811, it was on condition that the existing parish church of San Carlo closed, and he demanded its amalgamation with three other parishes. The Vicar-General objected, to no avail, that were the parishes merged to include 4,000 souls, then both churches would be needed.[173] Rural topography made a readier impression on the regime than did urban demography.

'The parish as vulture' was one of the few potent weapons the regime had in winning acceptance for the many changes it tried to impose on religious life. In 1808 the Tuscan bishops seem to have cooperated with the French to prevent some priests speaking out against the sale of the property and the harvests of the suppressed regular houses, partly by appealing to the benefits that might accrue to the parishes as a result.[174] Indeed, in 1811 D'Osmond reported a flood of requests from parishes for church furnishings and holy objects confiscated from the monasteries. Bells were particularly sought after, and parishes were willing to pay the costs of their delivery. He advised the government against selling off organs to private individuals or destroying them; instead they should be reserved for parish use.[175] Paris agreed, but left it to the prefects to decide which churches would benefit.[176]

'The parish as vulture' could have an obvious, if confused, appeal in poor rural parishes. Even in urban centres the line between government policy and the sensibilities of its *administrés* could be thin, however. The opposition to the loss of the oratories of the confraternities has already been seen, but even where such closures were finally accepted, other unacceptable faces of popular devotion could emerge. Following the closure of all the oratories and confraternities in Voghera by 1811, the *maire* told the sub-prefect that 'the universal desire' of the town was to have the church of San Giuseppe reopened as the parish church. It stood in the main *piazza*, with a new steeple built in 1806, with a clock in it, and a beautiful façade. This, in itself, is striking evidence of the wealth and enthusiasm of the lay brothers who had so recently paid for it. But there was more. The church lodged three paintings of saints revered by the local people, together with an altar set up in 1810 to the patron saint of the town, San Bovus, whose relics were solemnly paraded through the town each year.[177] The gap between rulers and ruled becomes breathtaking in the face of such petitions, a sign that devotional practices of this kind were not only popular, but still believed acceptable, even in middle-sized towns. When the Vicar-General of Casale petitioned for the reopening of an oratory in Brignano, an isolated mountain parish with 600 scattered souls, he showed a far greater awareness of the way to the regime's heart. He played on topography alone, stressing that the oratory had served as an auxiliary chapel in the past and that

[a] great number of the inhabitants would not only lose frequent [access to] the Mass, they would also be deprived of spiritual support in case of sickness, without the facility of the said oratory.

He ended by emphasizing that all that was wanted was the reopening of the building, not the refounding of its confraternity, and he got his way.[178]

Maintaining the service of the parishes, urban or rural, was a maxim the French held to, even in the darkest corners of resistance. At the height of the crisis over the Oath, Tournon used this argument in vain to dissuade the many non-juring clergy from abandoning their parishes.[179] He had backing in Paris, where the Minister of Religion told Miollis that the only spiritual function non-juring priests could perform was saying Mass.[180] Stripped of their incomes, set for exile and even gaol, this exception to their lot was very revealing of the dilemma in which the regime had placed itself. Even Roederer in Umbria, probably the most ferocious of the prefects, drew back from this prospect:

[It is] infinitely preferable to have refractories at the head of the parishes, than to deprive the people of the Mass, given that the refractories would not give in anyway, and that the closure of the churches would create a dreadful way to raise the people in revolt.[181]

Yet no one came closer to destroying this maxim than the French themselves, through their own policies.

The imposition of the Oath on the Roman and Tuscan clergy was the single greatest example of this, but there were other trends at work within the regime, which ran against the restructuring of the parish clergy. The Sub-Prefect of Genoa responded thus to the request to take Holy Orders of four well-qualified boys in 1805:

I cannot keep silent about the large quantity of ministers of religion; this arrondissement is full of them. Measures must be taken to ensure that a great many young men do not assume this condition … . [T]heir ministry is, effectively, useless, because of the multiplicity of benefices, which forces them to find other ways to get the people to support them. They are a burden on the people, and superstition alone allows them to carry on.[182]

This is as revealing of official prejudices, as of indigenous 'superstition'. It is also something that is and is not true. The assumption that there were too many vocations runs against the history of the Church in early modern Italy.[183] Yet it also touches on the problem Ricci tried to confront in Pisa a quarter of a century earlier. Indeed, when asked to produce a report on who he considered best among the Tuscan clergy, Tardy, the Vice-President of the *Corps Législatif*, said that not only were there more able men among the regulars than the seculars, but that this was due to the massive number of benefices in private, usually noble, hands. They were passed on to

> the sons of their servants, who, for the most part, have no learning, no aptitude nor any vocation for the clerical condition. They embrace it with the sole end of obtaining the revenues which serve, at once, as a pension for the services rendered by the father, and a clerical title for the son. This problem has filled the Tuscan clergy with rankly stupid priests – lazy, poorly trained and utterly unable to fulfil the work of the Holy Mystery.[184]

Comments of this kind are hard to quantify; they are impenetrably subjective. Nevertheless, the Leopoldine heritage did not indispose the French to the Tuscan clergy. Tardy, like so many others, came away bitterly disappointed by Tuscan realities, but he was not without local support. The Bishop of Chiusi and Piena rejoiced that the Concordat had abolished private benefices and given him the power himself to redistribute the revenues of the eight canoneries of Pienza nominated by the descendants of Pius II, who usually had no aptitude for them.[185] Nevertheless, his plans to fill the vacancies by a public examination were scotched by Paris, for the intention was to abolish them completely.[186]

Whatever evaluation is put on the problem of recruitment to the parish clergy, the best solution would not appear to be turning away good candidates, but something in the Sub-Prefect balked at the prospect of the 'best and the brightest' entering the Church. The government was even equivocal about the one remaining seminary in Rome itself. A report to the Consultà in 1810 predicted that it would soon collapse without government help. There were now only forty-seven students, most of whom were 'aspirants to the priesthood', with only two in orders.[187] Two years later, although the Minister of Religion said that 'the first see of Catholicism cannot be threatened with the loss of its seminary', he would only save what was left, not expand it. Paris ordered part of the building turned into a *lycée*, with the rump to continue as a seminary.[188] Parma's seminary had all but collapsed by 1806. It had twenty-five students, but all the teaching was done by the university, soon to be abolished; although recommendations were made for it to be reformed and aided,[189] it was closed with the university.[190] Savary was of the stated opinion that no more priests should be ordained in the Italian departments until 1820; some of the present 'surplus' could be sent to parishes in the interior.[191]

The French *idée fixe* of an overstaffed urban Church was contested by the Italian clergy everywhere from the outset of French rule. The impact of the dissolution of the regular orders on parish life was made worse by the stipulations of the Concordat that 'foreign clergy' were not permitted to work in the empire, nor were clergy from the imperial departments to do so in the Kingdoms of Italy or Naples. Many prelates echoed the outspoken Archbishop of Pisa, when in 1808 he protested about their imminent expulsion on the eve of the annexation of Tuscany:

> the foreign priests working in this diocese, all upstanding subjects and of exemplary conduct, must be allowed to continue in their work by the government, it being impossible to replace them, given the scant number of diocesan clergy.[192]

Cardinal Fesch himself intervened to no avail for the Dominican friars and sisters in Parma and Piacenza, who had been deliberately encouraged to come from elsewhere by the Duke, 'people who have given their youth and their labours to the service of the Sovereign'.[193] Typically, Spina turned this to the advantage of his diocese in an act more subversive, if less ostentatious, than the defiance of his colleague in Pisa. The Edict of 1 September 1810 banned all clergy 'sent home from abroad' from serving anywhere in the empire unless they took the Oath. Spina simply ignored it, assigning them to parishes as auxiliaries where they were celebrating Mass, hearing confessions and teaching the catechism. He simply used a 'loophole' that – unlike in Tuscany and the Papal states – the Ligurian clergy had never been asked to take the Oath. The Police Commissioner of Genoa hoped that a reduction in the number of urban parishes would make it easier to recruit only loyal, juring priests, without jeopardizing their pastoral work.[194]

An even greater challenge faced the new regime, wherever Tridentine discipline had become a reality. It was finally expressed in Article 49 of the *Vues sur l'organisation du Culte Catholique*, drawn up by the Ministry of Religion as a guide for the new Concordat of 1813, but embedded in Gallican thinking since 1789. It declared that curés should be 'worthy, by their morals and intelligence, to be teachers of the people' but in the same breath declared that

> being salaried public officials ... their interest will be intimately connected to that of the state. Their *esprit du corps* will disappear; priests will become valued members of society.[195]

The fundamental clash with the Borromean ideal was unavoidable, but the French were right to wish to dismantle collective clerical discipline, for it became a powerful weapon against them. Corboli had shown this in the Metropolitan See of Florence, and many of his clergy, high and low, went to prison as a result. As was evident in the support they gave the new regime over the sale of the properties of the regulars, the Tuscan episcopate could turn the tap of resistance on and off to a considerable degree, if only because they knew how to appeal to their clergy: They were obeyed because they were believed. It could – and did – go the other way as the effects of the Concordat began to be felt. There would be more to come in Rome. In his memoirs, Tournon admitted a connection between Tridentine discipline and the assertion of 'conscience', so despised by all revolutionary regimes, from 1790 onwards:

> This sacrifice was made to an abstraction; this abnegation of their own convictions (for they all admitted that there was nothing criminal in the oath itself) in the face of the orders left by the Pope, had something imposing about it that inspired respect.[196]

Tournon did not flinch from his duty either. At the time, rather than in the memoirs written under the restoration, it was at best the respect of one professional for another. It took discipline, as well as conscience, to withstand the blandishments of the French, as well as their threats: these priests lost their livings immediately, unlike those previously arrested in Tuscany.

When the French felt under pressure, they lashed out at the clergy if they showed themselves disobedient. In the fraught days after the revolt of the Piacentino, following the refusal of a priest to bury a French official, Junot thundered at the Bishop of Borgo San Donnino to 'police the conduct of the clergy of your diocese', but in a very different cause to that of Borromeo:

> [Priests] can forgive or not forgive in the confessional, but they are not the judges of people's consciences. God alone has that right, and it is right that you make them appreciate that they have no temporal power.[197]

In the heat of a crisis, this was the face of Bonapartist theology, and it had nothing in common with Trent.

The French disliked the very sight of a numerous clergy; it was a bad sign, for there was far more to French attitudes than finances or the deployment of resources. In 1805 the Piedmontese bishops, including Amiens, Paris's own commissioner for Church affairs in the new departments, asked that twenty-six of the fifty-four collegial and abbatial chapters of Piedmont be retained. The Minister of Religion refused; all fifty-four were suppressed, 'so that ecclesiastics will not be so numerous in the future'.[198] Moreau de St-Méry and Nardon had grave differences over the future of Parma, but they had identical views on the clergy of the city: to begin with there were too many, and they earned their living in useless ways, by saying masses, thus encouraging the conservation of too many High Days. Above all, the presence of 'numerous celibate men introduces the corruption of morals', to the extent that Moreau wanted the churches closed before dark 'to stop them being the rendezvous of the debauched'.[199] Nardon's deputy lashed out in 1806 that

> You would probably be revolted to know that young creatures of eight or ten are sold into prostitution ... the state must attack this propensity for licence at its source ... . The number of priests must be reduced.[200]

These objections were not administrative in origin.

The relationship between the French and the secular clergy was, unsurprisingly, very complex, but the French had the dubious talent of reducing it to its stark essentials, a process fostered by the rigidity of the Concordat. In most cases where compromise was both possible and sought, it came 'from the bottom up' – from the Italian clergy, usually and significantly at local level and on the periphery. A pattern emerges in these dealings and, while not universal, it is dominant in the relationship between ruler and ruled: Italian *parocci*, and occasionally their superiors, sought to draw from the system imposed on them by the Concordat what help they could in the struggle against poverty and the world of 'nuestras Indías' many still perceived around them. There was seldom any question of the regime giving in to them over local customs or traditions. It was seldom a 'two-way street', for where the French might give way – usually over reopening an isolated oratory – it was for the imperatives of their own policy, not out of deference to local tradition, as shrewder petitioners soon learned. 'Integration', as defined by Nathan Watchel – the voluntary incorporation of foreign elements into the indigenous system – was not unknown in the relationship between the French and the secular clergy, at least on the periphery, but it occurred only at the behest of the conquerors. Moreover, it took place within the framework of an official policy that corresponds deeply to Watchel's definition of 'assimilation' – the elimination of indigenous traditions when overwhelmed by foreign rule.[201] This, almost without exception, is what the French serving 'on the ground' in Italy wanted to see, and that is how they usually interpreted the application of the Concordat, although it usually emerges more starkly in an urban context than in the hinterlands.

Those in the 'front line' of the empire often swept aside the differences between the piety of the centre and that of the periphery, even if they acknowledged their existence. For the Sub-Prefect of Pisa in 1813, it would all be a cloak for revolt as it had been in 1799. Regional differences were real, but that was not the point. Should the enemy arrive,

> nothing could contain the populace of the towns, to whom religion would serve as a pretext, [while among] the ignorant bands who inhabit the countryside, respect for this same religion tips into fanaticism.[202]

The only valid division for some imperial officials was between the vicious cynicism of the centre and the barbarousness of the periphery. It applied to religion, as to most other things.

There is at least a grain of truth in some of the cynicism. The Italian prelates especially led the French a merry dance. Although Giacinto in Turin proved a loyal collaborator and Caselli 'turned' only at the end – though to great effect, it is true – others played the sort of game that Paris often missed, but that drove the French in Italy to distraction. The Roman Cardinals and overtly defiant bishops like those of Pisa and Fiesole could easily be packed off to prison. Spina in Genoa and – to a lesser degree – Chigi-Zondadari in Siena were harder to pin down. Faced with ruthless arrests and exiles, they played a game careful enough to dupe those outside their areas, but defiant enough to draw the bile of the French with whom they dealt. Chigi-Zondadari was the less overt of the two. He had, indeed, been cowed by the French police early on, not least – as Lagarde proudly admitted – because they played ruthlessly on his dire financial straits when raising the spectre of exile.[203] Despite this, the widespread use of *biglietti* was not even uncovered in his diocese until 1812. If he helped smooth the way over the closure of the regular houses, he did nothing to dampen the fires of anti-Semitism in the residence of his see. He 'blessed' Tournon's marriage in Paris in 1810, but got out of actually performing the cere-mony.[204] Spina's conduct was the more dramatic and enraging, but only to those with local knowledge of what he was about. He had accepted the Concordat in Liguria in 1806 without waiting for Papal approval.[205] Nor did Spina martyr himself at the *Concile* in 1811, and he advised caution and conciliation throughout the years of the French occupation. He sided with Maury and Fesch at the *Concile* and accompanied Caprara to Savona to try to convince Pius to accept the extension of the Concordat to the Papal states, and is said to have been received 'without emotion'.[206] One historian sees him – reasonably from this perspective – as the 'Emperor's man'. [207] D'Auzers and his subordinates would have laughed at such an assessment. Pacca – the 'oracle' of the Roman interpretation of the clash with Napoleon – is utterly silent on Spina at this time. Arguably he did more than any other single prelate not only to thwart the French in particular, but to set Italian Catholicism on a new path. His many activities in this field may rightly be called 'subversive', not only in that they undermined the integra-tion of the Concordat in Liguria, but because they broke with the eighteenth-century disdain for popular devotion. At the centre at least – in an urban context, if hardly in the hinterlands of the Fontanabuona – Spina was setting the Church on a new course under the well-informed and not wholly uncomprehending Gallic noses around him. Spina stands at the threshold of the Marian, populist revival that culminated in the promulga-tion of the doctrine of the Immaculate Conception in 1854. His actions in Genoa helped initiate that 'linking of the Virgin of the Grotto and the

Virgin of the Immaculate Conception [which] epitomized the alliance between the Vatican and the faithful' discerned by Ruth Harris at its high point at Lourdes in the mid-nineteenth century.[208]

Spina was, in a very real sense, 'the morning star' of the nineteenth-century Catholic revival, and for this very reason he was on dangerous ground, less in his subtle war with French secularism than in the old struggle against religious archaism. When Spina invoked Marianism, the Vatican had yet to formulate the doctrine of the Immaculate Conception, its own sanitized response to the cult of the Virgin.[209] Spina did not have this apparatus behind – or indeed, above – him when he took the populist path during the *epoca francese*. He could not impose the Immaculate Conception on archaic Marianism, nor subsume it into a 'safe', Romantic sentimentalism that did not yet exist. This made his course of action all the bolder and more dangerous, for Spina, unlike his nineteenth-century successors, had to ride the tiger of popular religiosity with only his own episcopal, essentially Tridentine authority to hold it in check. This was probably why he chose to confine this dangerous alliance with populism to 'the centre', to the cities and the Riviera. The untamed archaism of the periphery was still too potent, raw and, above all, independent to be treated with anything other than Tridentine severity at this stage of the Catholic revival. Spina was too close to the reality of 'nuestras Indías' to have truck with the later sentimentalism bestowed on such communities by Lasserre and the proponents of Lourdes later in the century.[210]

This was why, despite his other antics, Spina could still win praise from the Minister of Religion, who bracketed him with Caselli in a report to Napoleon in 1807 as having distinguished himself 'in his pastoral instructions concerning conscription, and other various things that are of interest to the government'. This was accurate: if the government's concern was the hinterland, where conscription was the main issue, then Spina 'played the game'. It was different elsewhere. The same report asserted that:

> Religion is monarchical. It is disposed to obey, it stifles the spirit of independence, it normalizes family feeling, together with all the peaceable, sociable virtues. Its good effects are recognizable in the countryside.[211]

It is the last sentence that matters. By following his own predispositions on the periphery, Spina masked from Paris the real 'counter-revolution' he was working in Genoa and the towns of the littoral. The stifled spirit of independence and the 'peaceable' virtues were not evident to French eyes in the streets of Genoa on High Days, even if the 'sociable' virtues were alive and well for those carrying the *casacce* and the priests – often foreign or non-juring – who blessed them. As the old ways persisted on the periphery, they were being nursed back to life at the centre. If the official totem of the parish Mass on Sunday were to survive – the new *Pax* for a new empire and a new age – there was only so much the French could do against the secular arm. It was different for the regulars.

The regular clergy

The Napoleonic regime did not like the regular clergy, male or female. It did not see their worth, foresaw no useful place for them in society, and so swept them away. They were perceived as dangerous, as well as useless; Napoleon called the friars of Lombardy 'the Papal police'.[212] With rare exceptions – for those involved in nursing, for example – the French had one solution: the abolition of all regular communities and orders. Thus the new regime treated this large sector of the Church as a monolith, in the direct tradition of the framers of the Civil Constitution of the Clergy of 1790, nor would this change from the annexation of Piedmont to the seizure of Rome. Among the French, champions of the regulars are few and far between. They were hated for many reasons, but hated they were. As in 1790, with the findings of the *Commission des Réguliers* easily to hand,[213] the imperial regime had a wealth of information, culled by its own officials and unsolicited in origin, about the many, complex and varied roles played by the regular clergy in Italian society, at the centre and on the periphery. It swept them all aside and remained firmly on the course laid down in 1790.

There was very little, even in the tumultuous relationship between Church and state in late eighteenth-century Italy, to prepare either the regular clergy or the laity as a whole for French policy. None of the reforming initiatives of the late eighteenth century had been as sweeping, or as ruthless, as the Concordat. In Lombardy, Joseph did indeed abolish many regular houses, but he did not ban entire orders or stamp out the regulars *en masse*.[214] Nor did Peter-Leopold in Tuscany, whose main concern was to detach the regular orders from direct obedience to Rome.[215] In Parma, Du Tillot closed a number of houses and introduced new legislation on *mainmorte* to prevent the extension of Church properties, largely aimed at the regulars.[216] Only the expulsion and dissolution of the Jesuits came close to matching the terms of the Concordat in scope. There were examples of direct imitation of the French among some of the patriot regimes of the *triennio*, but the pattern was not universal: In Lombardy, where Joseph II's reforms had left the regular orders weakened, the Cispadane Republic set about confiscating their remaining properties, supported by strong, if latent, currents of Jansenism. However, by 1799 their work was far from complete.[217] The Ligurian patriots attempted to abolish the religious corporations in 1797,[218] although by the following year they settled for closing only some houses and expelling foreigners.[219] However, in Puglia elements within the regular clergy were active supporters of the Republic and as a result became targets of counter-revolution in 1799.[220] Quite apart from the avowedly reactionary regimes in the Papal states, Tuscany and Parma, republican governments took a much more moderate stance after the trauma of *Novanatanove* than they had before it. In Liguria there was no attempt to renew the radical legislation of 1797, and the French found a very unreformed Church when they annexed it in 1805, despite five years of nominally 'patriot' rule.[221] There were few Piedmontese patriots intent on the destruction of the regulars, as borne out by the proposals of the short-lived Ecclesiastical Commission of the Provisional Government in 1800. Its Jansenist leanings notwithstanding, the Commission made no attempt to abolish the regular orders *en masse*, although it did close a significant number of individual houses.[222] The Italian patriots seemed to have learned something in the course of the *triennio*. For all their ingrained fear and contempt for the Church and its influence on the masses, the *giacobini* in office immediately after Marengo showed many signs of moderating their stance, particularly as regarded the regulars.

In contrast, the Napoleonic regime, so often depicted as the conservative saviour of the Church in these years, retained the much more militant stance of the Revolution and never wavered from it. Even before formal, full annexation to the empire, the French showed their hand. In Piedmont, as early as 1802, Jourdan put a stop to any more novices being received into the Piedmontese houses, and also forbade them receiving any regulars sent to them from elsewhere by their Generals. He reserved a particular contempt for the mendicant orders, in 1802 demanding they be stopped from begging and suppressed as quickly as possible, given the poverty of the region just after the war.[223] Part of his reasoning was their growing poverty following the failure of the government to provide pensions for them.[224] At one point, Jourdan begged the government either to let him send them home with pensions – arguing that their families would not accept them otherwise – or even to allow them to reassemble in communities. Jourdan was, to say the least, anti-clerical, but he concluded that 'Justice and political reality demand some prompt, workable decision'.[225] The incompetence of the regime in paying ex-regulars the pensions they were promised continued from beginning to end. Janet was so slow about it in Rome, Tournon remarked in his memoirs, that had he done so the confiscations might have cost the government more than it was worth.[226] When the money did arrive, it was often not enough. Even the Prefect of Genoa and Cardinal Spina managed to agree on this in 1810. They remarked that as the numbers increased with the advance of the empire, the level of the pension fell: while the ex-regulars of Piedmont and the Duchies received, when their pension was paid, 600 francs and 500 francs per month respectively for men and women, those in Liguria received a maximum of 416 francs and 469 francs respectively – often less if they were under fifty. The Ministry of Religion never revised these levels; its policy was to choke off the numbers of regulars before the suppressions took place.[227]

In Parma, prior to the introduction of the Concordat in 1806, Moreau de St-Méry had 'frozen' the regular houses. The ten male houses of the city were no longer allowed to receive novices at all after 1805; the twenty-one female houses could only take novices on appeal to Paris, nor could a novice take vows without the approval of the Minister of Religion, which was never accorded.[228] Even when the French themselves demanded exceptions to this rule, they did not treat those spared well. In 1805 Napoleon himself asked the Sisters of Charity in Turin to reassemble in order to staff the hospices of Turin, Asti and Alessandria. They replied that it was impossible, for 'the congregation is losing members daily, because the high demands of their work are shortening their lives'.[229] As the breach with Rome grew, even this kind of concession disappeared from official policy. The Imperial Decree of 13 September 1810 spelled out starkly the end of all monastic life, male and female, in the Ligurian and Piedmontese departments.[230] It took the rarely seen concerted efforts of Spina and the Prefect of Genoa to save the Sisters of Refuge, the main source of charitable nursing in the whole of Liguria, but the Daughters of the Visitation – whom they had saved in 1807 – did not escape the 'next round' of 1810–11.[231]

Even the assumptions of many patriots were in for a shock. In 1808 the President of the Tuscan *Buon Governo*, who served the French well, believed that they would go no further than forbidding future vocations, assuming 'it would not be inconvenient to allow those who have already taken orders to continue to live outside secular society'.[232] He obviously had no prior knowledge of the stark statement that came from on high – 'As for Liguria and the states of Parma and Piacenza, there are still houses to be suppressed'[233] – at the definitive 'reunion' of the churches of Piedmont, Liguria and the Duchies to the Gallican Church.

The regime had no illusions about the popularity of the regulars when it actually came to closing down their houses and churches, and – literally – carting them away. The suppressions in Parma and Piacenza in 1805 were carried out at four in the morning, without the knowledge of the bishops, nor was any warning given to the regulars themselves.[234] Nor could the local authorities be depended upon, especially when the regulars simply ignored prior orders. Most non-Tuscan regulars did not seem to respond to the first orders, producing the emphatic response from the *Buon Governo* that 'all foreign clergy must leave' early in 1808.[235] The Tuscan regulars went quietly – in the end. Nevertheless the police noted, in the same breath, signs of profound passive protest among the laity, even as they mocked the culture behind them:

> The people have been superstitious, but never disorderly. They show respect for the stupidest things. There is a well in the Carmelite church in Florence. When the monks left it, a crowd came with little

vases to carry some away, as if it had miraculous qualities. The well was dry in two hours.[236]

The peaceful nature of such events should not detract from their intensity. Italy may not have been Aragon; the Carmelites of Florence went their way obediently, rather than fighting street-by-street as did their brothers in Zaragossa that same year, but the love they inspired among the laity was no less great for being gentle. These quiet scenes were not to be counted on, however.

Napoleon ordered 10,000 troops into the Roman departments expressly to oversee the closure of the regular houses, and wanted it done in a fort-night,[237] orders which terrified the Consultà.[238] His reasoning was clear, ruthless and cynical. He knew the regulars would oppose this and proposed to turn it to his advantage. It was a way to cow the secular arm:

> It highly probable that when the curés see that the rebellion of the senior branch of the Church [the regulars] has obliged [its members] to leave their country, and led to the confiscation and sale of their properties, they will not want to expose themselves or their communes to a similar fate.[239]

It was a huge task, as these comprised 519 communities containing 5,852 people.[240] The Consultà tried to plan the suppression of the Roman regulars with care, at least for their properties. Janet and Tournon drew up detailed inventories, although Tournon had doubts about the honesty of some of those employed.[241]

Indeed, he drew Janet's attention to the fact that some of the personnel employed enjoyed their work rather too much. Narni and Donnat, Janet's assistants, broke into the convent of Santa Margarita with excessive force

> which could only trouble and frighten the sisters … . This conduct is as indecent as it is scandalous, and is far removed from the princi-ples of moderation and gentleness to be expected of employees charged with the abolition of the convents; it can only worsen public opinion.[242]

There were thefts and scandals throughout the operations, as the regulars tried to conceal their art treasures and the French broke down doors to get at them. It culminated in what were little more than raids on six convents, on the night of 14–15 June 1810. The arrival of the commissioners caused something like blind panic, although prior notice had been given. Dal Pozzo remarked in his report:

A general alarm ensued, a terror among the nuns who did not know which way to turn; there was general confusion, looting took place, and many of the nuns took flight.

Tournon felt malicious rumours had been 'fed' to the nuns. Although the result of the incident saw Janet stripped of his remit to carry out the closures, Dal Pozzo and Tournon saw a well-organized plot in it all. The nuns wanted to be forced out by troops – as they had to be – and made a point of wearing 'ridiculous clothes that brought undue attention to themselves' as they left. For all Tournon's later attempts in his memoirs to portray himself as a friend of the regulars,[243] at the time he concurred with Dal Pozzo that the nuns were 'quelques femmes bavardes' in league with troublemakers.[244]

There were certainly Mothers Superior who showed more defiance than the male abbots and priors. The Mother Superior of a convent in Cento, near Bologna, lambasted the Prefect of the Reno:

> What a fatal blow against Humanity, Signore Prefect! Closing the convent where we hoped to pass the rest of our days in peace! We are forever, nevertheless, the adored of God's justice, and there is not with me one member of this community who will abandon Him, or fail to obey His superior orders, to keep the Rule and lead a retired life![245]

Nuns did, indeed, fight back. Tournon had no doubt of this, telling Police-Générale that, had the Oath been asked of them in his department, 'we would have met with even greater resistance than among the men'. Things were bad enough, however, for they were falling ever deeper into poverty, 'which makes an even worse impression because of the great interest their sex inspires'.[246] They could be tenacious. The convent of Monte Castrelli in Umbria was suppressed in June 1811, but over two years later Roederer found that fourteen of the nuns had reunited in the same building and under the same Mother Superior, as if nothing had happened, except that they were now politicized, 'inculcating the youth of the area with anti-government principles, and forming a very suspect group'.[247] If the French feared the reaction to the closure of the male houses, they were walking on eggs when it came to the convents.

There were two main prongs of the Concordat: the closure of all houses and the deportation of all 'foreign' ex-regulars back to their places of origin. The effects of the closures were felt in those communities where they took place. The ramifications of the deportations affected the clergy directly, but also diffused the impact of their plight across the length and breadth of the *départements réunis*.

On the periphery, the French often saw the monasteries as oppressive, feudal landowners, channelling the wealth of the countryside into their own coffers and generally holding back the progress of the areas they dominated. Moreau de St-Méry dispatched a factfinding mission into the Apennine valleys in 1805 – prior to the revolt – and its conclusions bolstered these views. There was no denying the poverty of the area, which in turn made the region so lawless. It was reported that a major cause of this in the Valdarda were the heavy dues levied by the monastery there.[248] The author of the report was the notorious Captain Antonio Boccia, later discredited for his brutal and incompetent handling of the suppression of the revolt. Nevertheless, the French themselves collected evidence quite to the contrary of Boccia's report: among the demands of the rebels of 1806 in the Piacentino were calls for the restoration of the regular houses in the Val di Trebbia. In Tuscany, the Prefect of the Arno amassed evidence in 1810 that gave him pause for thought. The difference between centre and periphery was clear to him, and he took it as his starting point. Although he had no mercy in store for the urban or lowland communities of regulars, in the Apennine valleys he pointed directly to the pivotal role of the six monasteries found there, even if he did not hesitate to advise their closure:

> Their revenues are distributed in the area, thus spreading a kind of prosperity around these isolated places, and increasing production through favouring land clearance … . To close these religious houses, at present, [would mean that] the mountains would revert to wasteland, these disadvantaged places would become deserts.[249]

There was no question in his mind, even in the face of this evidence, that they might be spared in their traditional form, for this would leave the people of the valleys 'as superstitious as they would be poor without them'. It would be very dangerous to make any exceptions to the policy of abolition. The Prefect proposed to staff them with those regulars too old go out into the world – those over seventy – and, after having nationalized the property, to turn these ex-monasteries into hospices for travellers and the old and infirm of the locality, 'which would win the loyalty of these people for the government'. This was an acknowledgement of the wider point that regulars often served those areas the secular clergy could not reach, as well as admitting the dangers involved in the assault on what both the National Assembly and Joseph II before it had labelled 'useless institutions'. The Prefect added a comment very revealing of his own attitude to the different role of the regulars on the periphery and at the centre. He felt it was far better for the government to put all regulars over seventy in these isolated houses, rather than let them live in urban centres where it would be easy for them to regroup, unpoliced, in their old communities:

These houses would soon become centres of intrigue, of seditious projects, havens for subversive writers and secret agents, who would torment [people's] consciences, and sow discord and unrest.[250]

The regulars are depicted as intelligent and cunning; their ability to influence urban populations, as well as the isolated peasantry of the valleys, is taken for granted. Above all, there is a clearly stated desire that those who could not be secularized, simply be got out of sight. All this would come back to haunt the French, and this policy would be undone by other aspects of the dissolution of the regulars.

Tournon pointed out that the Cordeliers house in the woods of Fonte Colombo in the hills near Rieti would be a real loss to the hill communities, as it served as a hospice, and the Minori Osservanti of that area had proved themselves useful in preaching peace and obedience to the government among the peasantry. Nevertheless, he told Janet that it would be dangerous to make exceptions. He ignored all petitions for exemption from the suppression.[251]

Closed, isolated communities of regulars often seemed better aware of the preoccupations of their new masters than the *maires* and notables of many provincial centres. The *Procuratore* of the Tuscan Hermits is one such. There were four hermitages, all in remote Apennine valleys, and in his petition to the *Buon Governo* in 1808 he stressed the economic importance of their forestry industry for the people of the area and its technical sophistication, as well as the spiritual work they did among the indigent population of the periphery. All this was normal enough. However, the *Procuratore* was also at pains to stress their work as conservationists: while all the secular landlords had destroyed their forests through ignorance and greed, the skills of the Hermits had preserved the only sizeable forests in the region, the conclusion being that they alone were to be trusted with this precious resource.[252] This revealed a remarkable grasp of the regime's concern with protecting forests, both in the public interest and as a military resource.[253] It still did them no good.

Whereas the abbeys and monasteries of the periphery were detested for their power and wealth, the mendicant orders in urban centres were loathed for their own poverty – as Tournon revealed so clearly in his comments about the Passionists of Rome – as well as for the alms they themselves diverted from the poor. Some archaic customs made traditions of almsgiving to the regulars. In Genoa in 1810 the *maire* informed the Prefect that 'from time immemorial' the mendicant orders in the city entered the timber markets, by the docks, and 'spontaneously received a piece of this combustible wood, from buyers and sellers alike'.[254] Moreau noted that the ravages of the war increased the begging of the mendicant orders in Parma, making of their poverty 'something mystical' in popular eyes.[255]

When their refusal to take the Oath forced many into further poverty, as their government pensions were withheld, the power of this mythic status emerged on a massive scale – to the consternation of the regime. Roederer in Umbria was among their worst enemies, but he readily admitted that the poor were supporting the ex-regulars without pensions.[256] The combination of bungled pensions throughout the *départements réunis* and the principled stand taken over the Oath by many regulars in Tuscany and the Papal states created a nightmare for the regime; in the latter case, the Oath made their poverty a clearly political issue, undisguised by bureaucratic incompetence. The Sub-Prefect of Perugia believed French policy was reinforcing exactly the kind of influences the Concordat was meant to eradicate. It reinvigorated exactly those regulars whom the French most detested: the mendicants and the Capuchins – the specialists in urban missionary proselytizing – in particular. By 1810 it was all made worse by deportation:

> The refractory Capuchins, who are very numerous, are the most dangerous. Those who have no other sources live by alms, spread over the countryside, and sow their maxims.[257]

Two years later, his superior, Roederer, admitted they held the advantage over him:

> The confidence the people have in these individuals cannot be imagined, or the influence that they wield; they are not unaware of this, and that is what makes them so very arrogant.[258]

In a report of 1811 on who among the regulars had taken the Oath, Roederer noted sarcastically that contemplative orders, like the Conventicali Minori, who held property were more inclined to do so; 109 out of 159 gave in, 'the habit of prosperity seemed to have moved them in the face of poverty'. The Augustinians did much the same. In some respects, the level of refusal in such orders is actually quite striking, given what they stood to lose. The mendicant orders, the Capuchins above all, were a different matter.[259] Roederer admitted, if in a somewhat backhanded manner, that there was more to this resistance than Papal directives:

> This Order never held property, and a great many of them only became refractories to avoid the reproach of betraying their vows that they must own nothing [by accepting a pension]. Moreover, they are used to begging, they live that way, in any case, and they have the added advantage of having become objects of respect and pity, which makes their circumstances seem touching, at least initially.[260]

His exasperation reached its height after almost four years of this when, in 1813, he ordered his *maires* to tell all the non-juring regulars that, if they were found begging or without some visible means of support, they would become the first inmates of the department's new *dépôt de mendicité* and put to work like other beggars.[261] This surely represents the nadir of French policy towards the regulars. Arguably, it is also one of the most emphatic 'results' won in European history for a campaign of passive resistance. None of the mendicant friars in the Archdiocese of Bologna had accepted the parish posts they were offered in 1810. The Vicar-General admitted that the best among them were determined to defy the law and to continue preaching wherever they were asked, moving from parish to parish as invited.[262] They defied not only the law, but the whole new order founded on the strangle-hold of the parish, and it was the 'best and the bravest' who took this path. Confrontation with the new regime threw these orders back on their austere roots, and they were not found out of character. However, in the context of the Concordat, there is another aspect to the resistance of the mendicants. Just as the sisters of Bologna defied the regime for the freedom to be clois-tered, so the mendicants held out for freedom of movement. This was a struggle for personal liberty, as well as for tradition.

The French came to fear the charity dispensed by the regulars, not just to despise the alms they received. A study of poverty and public charity in *ancien régime* Parma concludes that the Church

> had assumed the task of responding to the demands of the social services ... . The will of the Church, of individual clerics or of private charity, was the origin of all forms of assistance in the city.[263]

This was soon revealed to the men most set on destroying this network and the powerful social control they felt went with it. The successive administra-tors of Parma – Moreau, Junot and Nardon – all reviled the regular clergy, but the cold figures of Nardon's report of 1806 show the varied and useful roles they played in the life of the city. All the nuns taught young girls; the Capuchins served the prisons and the hospital; the Benedictines gave boys under eighteen a free education; the Raccolti worked, free of charge, in the French military hospital.[264] None were spared. Nor were the foreign regu-lars allowed to stay to continue their parish work, despite the intervention of Fesch. In Bologna in the Kingdom of Italy, the Vicar-General berated the civil authorities about the disruption caused to parish work by the suppres-sion of the regulars. The loss of so many of their churches was bad enough, but he 'played the big card' when he said the administration of the sacra-ments was now suffering.[265]

The closure of the convents angered the laity for more than humanitarian reasons. Petitions and protests from all over the *départements réunis* revealed the central and often unique role played by the female orders in educating girls. The *maire* and the Sub-Prefect of Voghera petitioned vigorously to save the seven Augstinian sisters of the town, who were its sole source of female education. The *maire* had a daughter with them, and he spoke from both his heart and his wallet in telling his superiors that the girls of the town would now either go without an education 'or their fathers will be forced to give them an education in other towns at very great cost'.[266] However, Paris was adamant that they could not do so as a community.[267] At the other end of the *départements réunis*, Tournon informed Paris that '[t]hey miss the convents greatly, for in many areas most families saw them as useful for the education of their daughters'.[268] It was no different in the Kingdom of Italy. The 'Instructions for the Execution of the Royal Decree of 25 April 1810' reminded prefects that those female houses spared in the first suppressions of 1805 because their educational work were only having their fate 'postponed'.[269] The Director-General of Police in Florence warned Paris that the *Conservatori*, the famed Tuscan girls' schools so admired by Napoleon, would have to close – which they did – before the government's plans for their expansion could go ahead, because they were staffed by nuns.[270]

Regulars were not allowed to stay where they were unless they were natives, not of the new imperial departments as a whole, but of the former *ancien régime* state in question. It was a policy the regime pursued doggedly, for there were periodic 'mopping up operations'. The year 1810 saw not only the order given in the new Roman departments for 'all secular priests and all regulars (of both sexes) in Rome to return to their native countries', but also the deportation of any regulars left in Piedmont either to their place of origin or somewhere appropriate, as determined by the bishops and prefects.[271] The feelings of those about to be expelled can be glimpsed from the petition of Francesco Antonio Carme, a Piedmontese-born friar, due to be deported 'home' from Tuscany in 1808:

> I have been attacked, as so many others, by the government's decree for all foreigners to leave Tuscany in a few days … . Forced to look elsewhere for an uncertain resting place … . I have a humble request: In Piedmont, I embraced a condition consecrated by the Faith that was once respected by the laws of that country. At the age of eighteen, the Revolution chased me out, without any provision for my well-being. I found a refuge in Tuscany, where I could live according to my vocation … . Now, as I begin to recover my health, I am to be chased from here, in danger of a sudden death.[272]

For many regulars, male and female, the gradual process of annexation meant that they were expelled more than once. Many Ligurian nuns in Piedmontese convents were deported home in 1803, penniless, to families that could not support them, and were taken into convents in Genoa. But, like Frà Carme, the Revolution caught up with them when their houses were abolished following the French annexation of Liguria in 1806. Many were found begging on the streets, a fact Spina was quick to report to his new masters.[273] In 1810 the *maire* of Genoa received a desperate letter from his counterpart in the Roman hill town of Todi, where several nuns of Genovese origin were stranded without their pension following the suppression of the Roman houses. The *maire* of Genoa reminded him, sadly, that they could get their pensions only in Genoa; he could not send the money elsewhere.[274] This was the least of French worries, once the likes of Frà Carme got home, assuming, that is, that they still had homes to return to. By 1812 Miollis lamented the whole policy, and held up the example of three ex-regulars, sent home from Tuscany to Gradoli in the Papal states, where

> they abuse the simplicity of the local people and exercise a strong influence on the other clergy, turning them against taking the Oath, persuading them that it is impious to do so, and inspiring a hatred in everyone against those who do their duty.[275]

This was not an isolated case. No less than the Commandant of the Tuscan Gendarmerie took it upon himself to report Torello Galestri, a former Vicar-General of the Capuchins, newly deported home from Rome to Montalcino. Galestri represents the two worst consequences of the French policies of secularization and deportation. On the one hand:

> [H]e exercises a dangerous influence on consciences through the confessional [having become a secularized parish priest] announcing that he will not grant absolution to those who have bought goods belonging to the religious houses from the government.

This followed an attempt to re-enter secular society, as it were. While working as a schoolmaster, he seduced two women and had to flee Montalcino for a remote parish.[276] A crumb of comfort offered by this case, may have been the proof it offered that irreligion and Jacobinism did not have a monopoly on immorality. Clerics like Galestri had their place in the French eighteenth-century canon of anti-clerical stereotypes, as *Thérèse Philosophe* reminded its wide readership. The regime might well have pondered which was the worst option, in such cases, but it did not. The regulars, unless literally unfit to walk, were released into society.

The regime had two hopes for the ex-regulars. Many, especially within the Church, hoped they could be absorbed into the secular arm to fill the huge gaps in its ranks. There was some official encouragement for this, but with conditions, as has been seen in the case of the ex-missionaries. They were welcome as parish clergy, but not as predicators, where many bishops felt their services were most needed. Spina's views on this subject are already known, but he was not alone. The suppression of the regulars destroyed a long tradition of Easter devotion throughout Italy. In February 1808 the invitations to the Capuchins and the Minori Riformatori to preach in the Tuscan dioceses were issued for the last time until 1814.[277] In 1809 the Bishop of Sarazana in Liguria informed the government that the Easter preaching had always been done by the regulars – parish clergy simply did not have the time, and usually were not good at it – and here, unlike Tuscany, they were usually invited to do so by the local authorities. He pleaded with Paris to let this continue, but to no avail.[278] Bravely, he told Paris:

> The absence of the Easter predication has damaged the spiritual well-being of the souls of the faithful, for, in every era, it has been through it alone that good Catholics have been made ready to receive the Grace of God, and to prepare themselves for Easter. These preachers were the true helpers of the curés in the vineyard of the Lord.[279]

In response to a general circular in 1813, the bishops were unanimous in blaming the absence of good orators on the dissolution of those orders which had specialized in producing them.[280] The Bishop of Civita Castellana in the Papal states put it in context:

> in the past, I could rely on outsiders and regulars, who understood how to do it; but they are no more today, and it is hard work to blend this with the work of running a diocese.[281]

It was an art and a tradition the French wanted destroyed. Even those absorbed into the secular clergy were forbidden to predicate at Easter if they had ever been missionaries.[282] Yet the French wanted them in the secular arm. In Umbria, Roederer deployed in parishes those ex-regulars who took the Oath, if only to fill the gaps created by the many curés who refused to take it.[283] These were desperate measures in the midst of a crisis, but in his report on Tuscany in 1809 Tardy hoped as many ex-regulars as possible could be redeployed in this way, simply because they were 'better material' than most seculars.[284] This is, perhaps, the best evidence – however subjective – that there were still many regulars with real vocations in this region. By contrast, the French remained hostile to clerical educational institutions, male as well as female. A host of pleas to save a number of Tuscan academies – many of which had been retained by Peter-Leopold – were ignored.[285]

Clearly, although there was a perceived need and a real role for ex-regulars in the Gallican Church, it was well prescribed around the central role of the parish and the availability of the Mass. It could backfire. The presence of such men could actually reinforce practices the parish clergy were meant to stamp out. The Gendarmerie in the Kingdom of Italy reported that as late as 1811, in many parishes on High Days, ex-regulars now in secular orders went about 'with baskets and purses, collecting alms in the name of the Holy Sacrament and the Madonna'.[286]

The other path was into the lay world. There, too, trouble lurked, perhaps less for the ex-regulars than for the authorities and the society which had to come to terms with their new status. The French had a vision of liberating many men and women from lives of denial forced upon them by a superstitious, decadent culture, and there is some evidence to support this, but there were others, such as one Martino of Montefiascone in Tuscany, who proved real menaces. After the dissolution of his order, Martino went to live with his brother, a peasant smallholder, where he raped his niece with considerable violence and then threatened the whole family. Here no one attempted a cover up, and the authorities worked together to get him arrested under Haute Police. The Vicar-General said he had always been violent and irreligious, even as a monk.[287] Such cases illustrate the irony pointed out by the Bishop of Montefiascone that men in holy orders could always have been detained indefinitely in safe retreats by the Ordinand. However, since the regular houses no longer existed, he could no longer help the police in this way; he had several disorderly clerics on his hands and could do little.[288] His remarks are a reminder of how central the Church had been to social control, and even to practical policing, under the *ancien régime*. The Concordat was part of a wider policy to increase the direct presence of the secular state in society, and to tighten its grip, but remarks of this kind also indicate the gap French policy could create before attempts were made to fill it. With Martino, as in so many similar cases, Haute Police saved the situation.

It did not take cases as dramatic as these to show the regime its dogmatic views on the regular clergy had created a widespread, if deeply personal and atomized, crisis in society. Tournon remarked, in a general but profound tone, that 'many families have had great problems with the return among them of relatives with whom they have nothing in common'.[289] Nevertheless, the search for a new life, a complete break with the past, was frowned on by the society around the ex-regulars. The case of Magdalina Brighenti, a Florentine nun, illustrates the clash between French prejudices about the coercive character of vocations and Tuscan mores. Although in orders since 1799, Brighenti had never adapted to convent life and eventually got Papal permission to live at home, although her vows were not dissolved. She took her chance, under the new regime, but the local authorities were frightened by the prospects:

> She has been with a servant named Bianchi for some time. The news of this marriage caused a big storm in Florence, to the point that the Prefect asked both me and the *maire* not only to avoid the publication of the marriage, but even the marriage itself.[290]

Paris stood by Brighenti's rights and its policy, but the response of the Prefect – Fauchet, a republican 'of the old school' – shows how high feelings could run over these things. When an ex-monk, Recco, wanted to marry in Genoa in 1808, Spina told the *maire* that even a civil ceremony was out of the question as 'he is still bound by clerical ties'.[291] The Prefect and Paris made short work of Spina on this occasion,[292] but that Spina 'stuck out his neck' in so direct a manner – probably knowing he would lose – is a sign of the depth of feeling surrounding the case. Miollis revealed an interesting set of French attitudes to this sort of thing, and to religion in general, in his reaction to the case of a an ex-regular in Viterbo. Pansieroni, now a priest, was still saying Mass while living openly with a woman, despite an interdiction from the Vicar-General. Miollis, an old soldier and something of a roué himself, put it all down to jealousy and animosity on the part of the Vicar-General and doubted the justice of the interdiction. There was no question of Miollis intervening in his private life.[293] Ominously, perhaps, Miollis reported his joy that the Spanish Jesuits resident in Rome 'have set a fine example of cooperation with the government', for all but the elderly had married.[294] The irony was lost on one so dechristianized.

After 1814 several Piedmontese cases came to light that lend credence to French claims that the regular orders had harboured unwilling inmates. By 1817 the ex-Dominican Nicola Tedeschi was a successful lawyer in Tortona, conducting an affair with a married woman who had separated from her husband. Under the restored monarchy, his father could at least cut him out of his will.[295] Miollis would have paid no attention. Seen another way, many French prejudices were not always unfounded. Even the restored Savoyards recognized this, post-1814. Their ambassador fought the Holy See hard to 'calm the worries of the secularized regulars' that they would be able to keep their pensions and not be reintegrated to their old houses, a fear among those who had become secular priests as well as those now laymen. Rome gave the decisions to the bishops in 1818, and Turin feared this would produce trouble.[296] Yet, in the course of their protracted debates with the Holy See, the Piedmontese also pressed the cases of many ex-regulars who wanted to re-enter orders, if possible. The restored regime in Turin, for all its avowed reactionary nature, was capable of trying to sift through the traumas caused by what its ambassador, Barbaroux, termed 'too general a secularization'. This never dawned on successive revolutionary governments any more than it did on the restored Papacy after 1814.

When faced with supporting alien and often indigent relatives or seeing them embrace the world in one way or another, there is no doubt what Italian society preferred. The problems of reintegrating individual family members at the fireside must be set in the wider context of the sacrifices, in terms of alms given and respect paid, for the non-juring ex-regulars, who had pensions waiting for them in the imperial coffers. Family disruption must be weighed in the scales beside the efforts of laypeople of all social classes, and of the regulars themselves, to refound communities in full defiance of the law. There was no doubt what collective culture dictated over the path the ex-regulars must take: there was nothing 'ex-' about them. French policy allowed another act to be played out in a timeless struggle between the unconventional individual and a society with a dominant cultural ethos. The confrontation proved this ethos was not that of the intrusive, imperial regime, which was always on the side of the marginal individual. Here, as in so many other cases, the gap between rulers and ruled was yawning.

In his memoirs Tournon blamed the policy behind the suppression of the regular orders on pure official greed,[297] but the sources – some under his own signature – shout back something far deeper and more complex. The French were not content to seize the properties of the regulars and deport them 'home'. They tracked their progress as carefully as they could to thwart their attempts to enter the service of the elite as tutors or chaplains, and to prevent them regrouping – technically now as private individuals – in communities. This policy was aimed at every social class, high and low. The politics of religious culture among the upper classes, rather than the culture itself, was the dominant concern of the regime. Savary had a particular suspicion of the household staffs of the great Italian families, a loosely controlled section of the clergy that absorbed many ex-regulars during the French occupation:

> Every household of any standing in the former states of Piedmont, Genoa and the Duchy of Parma had one or several clerics (*abbés*) in its pay, entitled 'secretary', 'Intendant of monies', 'revenue collector', 'librarian' etc. ... . This class is, without doubt, the most dangerous, because it regards itself as independent of the government, from which it has nothing to hope, and from which it has nothing to fear, as it clings to the households of the rich and the big landowners. It passes on disruptive news that stirs up opposition and unrest among the highest echelons of society, and thus it seeps down to all social classes.[298]

There are many examples of exactly this. Private chapels abounded in Umbria during the occupation, despite official distaste and suspicion. The rich, influential Oddi family retained one such, and used it as a refuge for non-jurors, regular and secular alike. The Sub-Prefect of Perugia had no doubt about which feelings this sprang from, nor whence they led:

> The mistress of this house would rather give up something [namely her money] to hear Mass from a refractory cleric, who in her opinion ought to be considered like one of the saints of the primitive Church, who fled to the catacombs to avoid persecution.[299]

This is, of course, a story as old as the Revolution. Nevertheless, in the light of the regime's own rhetoric on early Church history, the irony is stunning. The French did not leave these nooks and crannies in the ecclesiastical fabric alone for long. An Imperial Decree of 22 December 1812 ordered the closure of all private and domestic oratories and chapels, prompting the Prefect of Genoa to confess to the *maire*: 'I can't hide from myself that this task will involve some difficulties'.[300]

The example of the Piedmontese aristocracy in the assisting the exiled Roman clergy was not unique. Police-Générale drew attention to an ex-Passionist in Cornetto, who was acting discreetly as a confessor to the wives of the local nobility, and was doing so in private houses in violation of the law.[301] Even at the height of French rule, some noble families went still further, helping communities virtually to reform in only slightly altered guise. The authorities usually dwelt on the overtly political aspects of such cases. The priory of Teompone, near Vercelli in Piedmont, was under the patronage of the Count Corte-Mozzè and, particularly, of his wife. They founded it in 1805 as a refuge for ex-regulars, and it became almost a place of local pilgrimage; their chief work was ministering to the local sick. The case came to light through allegations – which the Bishop said were false – that the priory had celebrated the Austrian declaration of war in 1809. Nothing could be proved, but the police were more disposed to listen to the ex-Jacobin *maire* and the curé, who wanted the benefice for his parish, than to the Bishop.[302] Even those in government pay could be behind these communities. A group of ex-regulars in Spoleto, judged dangerous by the authorities, had been supported after their initial suppression by an official of the State Domain.[303]

Nuns were popular recipients of aristocratic and bourgeois patronage too, even in the teeth of the law. Norvins was almost colic at the thought of the help given by leading Roman families to support clandestine convents after the suppression:

> these gatherings take place every day … . It is in these dangerous reunions, conducted by fanatical priests, that the nobles and the leisured classes assemble, who are their protectors and providers; it all contributes to opposition to the government.[304]

Women supported other women against French policy, aristocrats championed the cause of poor and rich nuns alike. A dramatic – and temporarily successful – example of this was when the former Princess of Parma, daughter of the late Duke, took up residence with the threatened Ursulines at their house in the city. Her actions saved them until 1810. Napoleon allowed them to keep their properties and to wear their habits, but only within the convent. Even this gallant Bourbon lady could not win them back the right to receive new novices, however.[305]

Their ex-confessors also stiffened female resistance to the Concordat. The nuns of the suppressed convent of the Annunciation in Arezzo used their confessor, Sansoni, as an envoy to the wealthy families of the town, thus providing them with the patronage they needed to keep them together clandestinely. He also 'exhorted them not to accept the state pensions they were offered'.[306] The authorities were determined to break up these gatherings. No less an official than the Director-General of Police for the Kingdom of Italy looked into a group of nuns in Bologna who were violating the suppression, still wearing the habit in private and living a cloistered life. They seem to have been supported by a wealthy merchant, Nusconi.[307] Thus support for ex-nuns was not confined to the nobility, the poor or other clergy. The wealthy urban bourgeoisie – the 'centre' personified – was also actively a part of this kind of passive resistance. In this case, Milan developed a skilful compromise of allowing communities of four or less nuns, if without habits. The Prefect said they 'stood up for themselves' and asserted that they had led blameless lives. They also made the thinly veiled threat of the impact it all would have on public opinion:

> Deprived of support, they would find it wherever it was offered, and they would be welcomed elsewhere, because of their ancient, good name. Disorders might develop were they abandoned, in response to this bad behaviour.[308]

The cloistered sisters were no less politically astute than their harassers. They stressed their 'otherness'; there was no appeal to utility but rather the assertion that their holiness, the uniqueness of their example was, of itself, deeply valued by their culture and would be defended. But they went a step further, and took on the regime on its own ground, for the sisters asserted that their seclusion was wholly voluntary. They flung Diderot back in the face of his public: this was a direct challenge to the commitment of the Napoleonic state to freedom of conscience. Seen another way, there is a trace of what Nathan Watchel calls 'integration' at work.[309] In the shattered peace of the cloister, these sisters were making the transition from defending *ancien régime* privilege to insisting on a very post-revolutionary freedom of association. It was not quite the path the new regime had hoped integration would take, however.

In the case of nuns, and of the habit, there was something deeper at work in the official mind than purely political considerations. There seems to have been an element in some French officials that enjoyed disrupting the life of the female cloister. The scenes in Rome, which Dal Pozzo reported on with less than a bleeding heart for the sisters, were not unique; they had precedents. During the suppressions in Parma in 1805, the Benedictine house at San Giovanni – the largest convent outside the city – was subjected to a 'night raid'. The locks of the gate were shot open and the stores were ransacked, leaving the nuns without provisions for a week and reliant on charity.[310] Such happenings may have been the residue of the Army of Italy's connection to the *armées révolutionnaires*, but it ran higher as well as deeper. A real scandal connected to the convent of the Conservazione in Chiavari in Liguria brought out these prejudices in D'Auzers. A prominent family, the Rorgoli, placed one of their daughters, still a minor, in the convent under the protection of her aunt, a nun. With the help of another nun, the chaplain of the convent seduced the girl, who was then kidnapped and taken to Pisa, where the authorities intervened. There followed a conspiracy of silence between the family and the convent, which got the case thrown out of court. It provoked this from D'Auzers:

> I have already had cause to assert that in this area, where superstition and religious fanaticism are very strong, many people will try to hide this kind of horror if they can, in order to save a priest or, even more, a nun. It is impossible that those in the convent had no knowledge of this deed ... I have reason to believe the same nun and priest attempted something similar with another girl, aged only fourteen ... . This sort of thing is all too common.[311]

The genuinely sordid nature of this case brought out a prejudice in D'Auzers, hardly a man with a 'dechristianizing' background. There are echoes of Diderot, mixed into the justified rage of a decent man. As the last female houses were, in 1810, facing another round of 'reorganization', they could expect no support from the police. The Prefect of the Arno said convents 'were nothing other than perpetual prisons where the victims of the cupidity or the fanaticism of their fathers were locked up'. If so, there were a great many bad fathers about. The convents of Prato in the 1780s may have had fewer vocations than in the seventeenth century, but they were still overpopulated.[312] Fauchet then asserted that, of the 3,600 remaining nuns in Tuscany, only 155 'wanted to renounce the world', a figure easily disproved by the scale of subsequent passive resistance to the closure of their houses.[313]

Intriguingly, the French developed an almost pathological obsession with the appearance of the habit. It took two forms. The first stemmed directly from the overt defiance of the law involved, but there was something deeper lurking behind it. The 'Instructions for the Execution of the Royal Decree of 25 April 1810' in the Kingdom of Italy were very precise about the timetable for the disappearance of the regular habits: men had twenty days in which to abandon theirs, women had two months, 'and no more'; they were also to cease to wear all other 'distinctive ornaments' of their orders. There were payments towards new civilian clothes. Nuns were forbidden to go out in their habits after these specified periods, even if they belonged to communities that were to be spared.[314] Soon afterwards the *podestà* of a small commune wrote to the prefect in Bologna, saying that the brothers of the small Capuchin house in his commune simply could not comply within twenty days. The reply was that, although the schoolmaster among them would not be deported 'home', it was 'vital to the good administration of the parish' that they abandon their habits.[315] The defiance of the nuns at Imola drove the authorities almost hysterical. They were first reported by the Gendarmerie as still going about openly in their habits in October 1811, 'an intolerable state of affairs'. However, on closer investigation, the Vicar-General uncovered a far more subtle form of passive resistance: they were all dressed the same, exactly, and in the same colour as their old habits, but the clothes themselves were not their habits. The Prefect ordered the Gendarmerie to stop them wearing these clothes, habits or not, on threat of 'political and rigorous measures'.[316] A year after the great revolt in this region, these reactions appear, to say the least, exaggerated. It was yet another example of a handful of women irking the new, powerful state – and with considerable skill. The second reaction is, perhaps, the more revealing of imperial intentions. There was a marked unease about the reappearance of the habit where it was almost no more, as in Piedmont. Lameth, the Prefect in Turin, complained in 1810 that the Piedmontese ex-mendicants returning 'home' from Rome were still in their habits. Quite apart from their begging and becoming a focus of public sympathy because of their poverty, '[monastic] robes have not been seen up here for a long time'. Their reappearance was not a good idea.[317] Two years later, the Sub-Prefect of Pinerolo made the same comment when non-jurors from Rome were exiled to his *chef lieu*.[318]

These reactions reveal something of the true revolutionary nature of what the French were about in their quest to reform the Italian Church. A Roman priest deported to Corsica spoke of it all as 'a vast plan aimed at the total control of the Church in its two components, the political and the spiritual'.[319] Their obsession with the destruction of the outward signs of the monastic, communal life – and, in the face of the evidence, the word is not too strong – indicate just how vast this plan was. There was to be a complete break with a very significant part of the past. People were meant to forget, and the regime was going to make sure they did by removing the visible proof. The imperial regimes in Milan and Paris hoped to oversee a process akin to that of the first years of the reign of Elizabeth in England, according to Eamon Duffy's analysis, that even 'where no ... dramatic repudiation of popery occurred, time did what ideological confrontation could not'. Duffy concludes his great study thus:

> By the end of the 1570s ... a generation was growing up which knew nothing else ... which did not look back to the Catholic past as their own, but another country, another world.[320]

There were signs that this might be happening in Piedmont; there were even more that this was what the new regime wanted. The question of habits, in particular, and of the whole treatment of the regular orders throughout the French occupation points in the direction Duffy has described. In 1810 the Director-General of Police in Milan warned the Prefect of Bologna that the regulars expelled from the Papal states would be crossing his department in great numbers. Vigilance was needed, as they 'attract too much popular compassion', and those still in their habits were to be kept moving by the shortest route possible, preferably at night.[321] After having sent them on their way, Tournon wrote from Rome with relief and a premature sense of triumph that 'Not one person is left in the department dressed in a monastic habit'.[322] This was seen as a turning point.

These hopes for a real transformation in Italian culture foundered on more than military defeat, however. Well before war cut short Napoleonic rule in Italy, the signs of opposition were already clear. It is impossible to predict whether the signs of secularization present in Piedmontese society would have spread with time, or whether Italy would have gone the way of Tudor England. What can be said, through the case of the regulars, is that opposition to the Concordat existed among all classes and in all places. Above all, it centred on the will of the regular clergy themselves to resist the French as best they could: passively, but as a body. The new order could not shatter their collective discipline. Men and women were everywhere seen to defy the government. This discipline could work for the regime. In Siena on 15 October 1810 the regular clergy of the diocese agreed *en masse* to take the Oath. They did so, they declared, because Napoleon was one secular ruler, replacing another, and the Church had a duty to obey; they also did so 'to preserve public peace'.[323] It was a warning, more than a surrender. When the breach with Rome reached its height with the occupation of the Papal states, this discipline was turned against the French. The regulars had already set the necessary example. Soon, it embraced a whole state in a massive campaign of passive resistance to French rule.

The laity appealed to tradition against the Concordat; the petitions of *maires*, confraternities and communities stemmed from the disruption of established practice and worked back from local needs to traditional customs. In contrast, the regular clergy, significantly the more aware of the prejudices of their new masters, appealed directly to utility, generally eschewing tradition *per se*. There were also signs that the more vulnerable sectors of the Church – the nuns and the mendicant orders – were turning the discourse of the liberal state against itself, with couched appeals to personal liberty. When it seized the Papal states, however, the imperial regime faced a new form of opposition that enabled all the others to rally around it: opposition to the Concordat here – and nowhere else – appealed to legitimacy, political and spiritual. The arguments deployed by Chigi-Zondadari to his regulars in Siena, only a few months before, became worthless in a Roman context. Pius did not command this opposition because he was head of state; he was very clear about this. He could and did command as head of state, however. No other deposed Italian leader could evoke this type of obedience from both clergy and people, legitimately and without inherent contradiction. Pius VII could, and did. The impact this made on the form and scope of passive resistance to French rule was as dramatic as it was crucial. Everywhere else opposition had been real, deeply felt and, within the parameters of the possible, hard fought. Nevertheless, it had been atomized and fragmented in ways all too typical of counter-revolution. This was not so in the Papal states, for here many strands of resistance to imperial rule came together.

6

THE ROMAN CLERGY AND
THE CRISIS OF THE OATH

When Pius VII finally excommunicated Napoleon with the bull of June 1809, it was not as a shocked, spontaneous reaction to his arrest or the invasion of his country. Tensions of a profoundly religious nature had been building between the French and the Holy See since at least 1805. This was the culmination of a process, not the beginning of a new quarrel. Nor was its nature diplomatic or even narrowly ecclesiastical. It was not really about forcing Rome into the blockade, the seizure of the Papal states, the Pope's arrest or even the installation of bishops, although this is how Napoleon sought to disguise it, both before and after the arrest of Pius in 1809.[1]

Rome had felt, with some justification, that it held a stronger hand in negotiating the Concordat for the Italian Republic than in negotiating that for France. Napoleon, too, knew he was dealing with a society where the Church still held a pre-eminent position, the Josephine reforms not withstanding. The Papacy engaged in protracted negotiations between 1802 and 1804, extracting several concessions it perceived as crucial at the time. With considerable reluctance, Napoleon accorded the bishops more control over the curriculum of their seminaries; the divorce laws were stricter than under the French Concordat; although the Oath of loyalty was imposed, Rome won in return the exemption of the clergy from military service. Above all, Napoleon backed down over the proposed abolition of ten sees in Lombardy, Modena and the Legations, and, paramount in the eyes of the Curia at this point, Catholicism was declared the official state religion. The Italian Republic, unlike the French empire, was not a secular state. Napoleon swallowed hard. Melzi, his Vice-President, tried to fight back with a decree issued just after the signature of the Concordat in January 1804, which asserted the supremacy of the state over the Church, thus destroying the notion of the Concordat as a compromise, because he demanded that the state set the fundamental boundaries between the secular and spiritual spheres. Melzi had been a close collaborator of Joseph II and saw the French Concordat as closer to the Josephine model. When Napoleon forced him to back down in June 1804, it almost led to Melzi's resignation. Pius VII now felt that the tide was turning in favour of the Church and assumed that, in an Italian context, the terms of neither Concordat would be enforced to the letter. These hopes were dashed by two decrees in 1805, which effectively renewed the principles set out by Melzi. The Civil Code was extended to the Italian Republic in full, thus negating the concessions won over divorce and civil marriage, while the regular orders were suppressed entirely, so dashing Pius's assumption that the Concordat would not be enforced in full. Church–state relations were thus permanently poisoned in the new Kingdom of Italy, but in a wider context Rome now saw that its real enemy was the Civil Code and the ruthless, incalculable introduction of legislation outwith the terms of any Concordat Rome might negotiate with Napoleon. In 1801 Napoleon had imposed the 'Organic Articles' unilaterally in the face of Roman protests.[2] Henceforth, it was clear he would behave no differently outside 'old France'. Concessions like the recognition of Catholicism as the state religion, or even the conservation of threatened dioceses, were now seen as the empty window-dressing they were.[3] In 1806 Napoleon replied to Pius's protests against its extension beyond the limits agreed in 1802, that the Concordat and the Code were the embodiment 'of the political system inspired by Providence itself.'[4] Napoleon did not refer to 'Divine Providence'. The battle lines were starkly drawn.

In August 1806, when Napoleon extended the Concordat and the Civil Code to the newly conquered territories – Liguria, the Duchies of Parma and Piacenza, Lucca, and also to most of the former Venetian Republic, the bulk of whose territories had recently been ceded to the Kingdom of Italy by Austria – the College of Cardinals warned:

> in each of His Majesty's conquests is seen the ruin of many reli-
> gious institutions and the norms of the Church … . These are our
> feelings, which you can regard as our Testament, and we are ready,
> if we must, to sign it with our blood … . Happy are those who
> suffer persecution for justice.[5]

A month later, Pius created a special team of theologians to assemble a bull to condemn 'all the ills that prevail in France and Italy, contrary to Doctrine and to good standards'.[6] In May 1808 Pius denounced religious toleration, as embodied in the Concordat, as 'nothing but a pretext for the lay power to insinuate itself into spiritual affairs'. Equality accorded to different religious beliefs, he concluded, could only damage the Catholic faith.[7]

In 1809 this belief that the quarrel was profoundly religious and touched the heart of the faith was unambiguously expressed in Pius's denunciation of Napoleon:

> The true sin committed by the French government does not concern
> our temporal authority. Such aggressions and usurpations, however
> unjust, arise in the course of history. The illegality of the claims of

the Emperor on our territories are unjust and absurd, the result of overwhelming force, and they will be clearly recognized for what they may be by the temporal powers of Europe ... [but] such enterprises cannot be attributed solely to political or military reasons ... . We have soon recognized that this business goes much farther than military or temporal forward planning ... . [The French] would put in place of the Holy form of government left us by Christ ... a new order of things ... which are criminal sacrilege against the liberty and holy doctrines of the Church, which have been introduced now into our own provinces, as they have been in every other place under the power of this regime.[8]

Pius dwelt far more on the damage done to the Italian Church as a whole, than on the seizure of his own domains. The Concordat had been introduced into Italy 'in a wholly arbitrary and perverse manner'; the 'holiest form of government, that left to us by Jesus Christ' had been replaced by

a Code which is not only opposed to the Holy canons, but to the very precepts of the Gospel; it has introduced a new order which tends to identify sects and superstition with the Catholic Church.

That the confrontation took place in 1809 – after the invasion of Rome – and not in 1806, can occlude its profound social and cultural nature, but the signs were there. They are often buried by the empirical manner in which Pius chose to argue against his powerful opponent between the creation of the Concordat in 1802 and 1806. The Concordat itself had been a hard-fought series of negotiations, and the simultaneous annexation of Piedmont to France meant that Rome was not allowed time to settle. As early as 1803 the French and Rome were locked in dispute over the number of dioceses for the new Piedmontese departments, in negotiations the French ambassador to Rome described as bitter. Rome gave way only because the regime threatened to confiscate Church property in Piedmont. Pius was deeply aware that there was no theological justification for the unprecedented abolition of so many dioceses at once. The ambassador made two prophetic observations at this early date. The first was personal. Pius was 'religious, heart and soul ... he is a holy man, of good character ... a pure soul'. The second was that Pius objected to far more than the loss of so many bishops: he also objected to the loss of so many parish priests and the regulars, 'workers in the vineyard of the Lord'.[9] The following year, Pius raised doubts about the ability of the Piedmontese bishops to receive the Légion d'honneur, a normal award for bishops and prefects. He feared that this oath bound them to support the divorce laws and the concepts of liberty and equality, which were against Church doctrine. He also feared that 'defending the laws of the Republic' might imply legitimizing the Terror. The matter was resolved in this instance, but the signs of unease were clear.[10] In 1805 Pius wrote directly to Napoleon to protest about the abolition of the regular orders in Parma and Piacenza.[11] Each of these specific incidents outlines the issues around which the ultimate clash took shape. The sweeping aggression of the Concordat, in an Italian context, emerges in these early reactions to the reduction of the secular arm and the suppression of the regulars. Opposition to the extension of an essentially civil oath to Italian clergy was a sign not just of dislike of oaths of this kind, but betrayed an increasingly tangible dislike of the whole ethos of the secular French state. Napoleon's response was to hasten the implementation of the Concordat in all the new territories.

The annexation of Lucca to the empire in 1806 came close to lighting the fuse of the conflict. The Archbishops of Genoa and Parma went their own way in 1806, accepting the Concordat in return for avoiding the Oath. Their colleague in Lucca turned to Rome for guidance, however. Here Napoleon and Elisa sought to impose the Italian Concordat, with its insistence on the Oath. Pius told the clergy of Lucca to refuse it and avoid association with the new regime. Although Pius admitted they dare not oppose the suppression of the regulars, 'submission by force of circumstance must not be seen to equate with submission to injustice'. Therefore to take the Oath was unthinkable, and Pius had not acquiesced to it in the *départements réunis*. Elisa wanted to force the issue, but Napoleon drew away from direct confrontation simply because of his military preoccupations. The most immediately important result was that the clergy of Liguria, Parma and Piacenza, and the ex-Venetian states, were not asked to take the Oath. The clergy of Lucca were offered the French, as opposed to the Italian Concordat, and so the issue of the Oath was avoided. In the words of one historian, 'hostilities were postponed'.[12]

The uneasy truce soon fell apart over the nomination of bishops, but there were some signs that the French could have mistaken – at least from Paris – as sprigs of hope. Luigi Ruffo, the Archbishop of Naples, refused to swear loyalty to Joseph and fled to Rome, but there was little widespread imitation of this among the lower clergy. Nor did Rome's refusal to recognize Joseph unconditionally prevent the transfer of power.[13] Maury was persuaded at this time to leave the small Roman see of Montefiascone – which he held as sinecure for his work in the Curia – for that of Paris. This was taken as a sign by many of where real power lay, and of Napoleon's continuing ability to separate power politics from specifically religious questions.[14] In 1806 overt acts of defiance by the upper clergy were the exception, not the rule. Force had prevailed and, as soon as circumstances allowed, there was good reason to feel it would do so again. In the wake of the successful military campaigns stretching from Jena to Wagram, the regime ignored the many undercurrents of unrest in Italy; when it was at last ready to resume, the war began with the skirmish at Lucca three years before. The victory of Lucca would prove, however, in the war against the Church to be the equivalent of Baylen in Spain in 1808. A long, if non-violent, guerrilla awaited the French. In 1806 in Lucca, Pius did not have to test the loyalty of the faithful or his 'troops'. By 1809, after his arrest and deportation, he had to renew the call. Both the clergy and laity of his states responded *en masse*.

The Oath and the clergy of the Papal states

The French knew exactly the ultimate fate of the regular orders; whatever the price of the confrontation, and whether they took the Oath or not, they were to disappear. The fate of the secular clergy could never be so straight-forward. The Roman bishops resisted the Oath staunchly and were supported by their canons; Napoleon's reply was to arrest and exile them to France, and then sequester their properties. The Cathedral Chapter of Spoleto was reduced to a single canon in 1810.[15] This was more than an act of spite, however. Their resistance was foreseen and the ruthless treatment accorded the prelates was part of a well-planned policy to overawe the parish clergy, whose cooperation with the regime was deemed essential by Paris. In June 1810, Napoleon dictated a note in the Council of State, ordering the Oath not be imposed on the *parocci* of the new Roman depart-ments until more troops arrived and the regular orders had been abolished – and until the properties of the non-juring bishops had been sequestered:

> It is highly probable that, when the curés see that the rebellion of their superiors has ended in their exile, and has entailed the confis-cation and sale of their properties, that they will not want to expose themselves or their communes to similar goings-on.[16]

It was manifestly clear from the start what refusal to comply would mean. Arrest, exile and poverty befell the good and the great first, not last, in Napoleonic strategy. The enemy was found, brought to battle and suffered maximum damage. If the new regime did not hesitate to deport and impoverish fourteen princes of the Church, the *parocci* had nothing to expect but worse. All subsequent resistance to the Oath must be set in this context.[17]

Nevertheless, there were some initial signs that this might be working. Norvins felt that resistance to the Oath diminished the further an area was from Rome.[18] The periphery – whether in Umbria or on the Neapolitan border, as in Frosinone – was the best place to expect support.[19] In July 1810 it was reported that most of the curés of the mountain communes in Umbria had taken the Oath,[20] whereas only six had done so in the city of Rome; the rest were deported, leaving only their vicars and auxiliary clergy to cope.[21] However, a year later the Sub-Prefect of Perugia said that while this was still the case in the parishes around the city, it was no longer so in the hinterland where the clergy had, initially, taken the Oath.[22] By December 1810, 225 cures were vacant in the department of Trasimène – over 30 per cent – and it was impossible to find enough juring clergy to fill them. Norvins was looking for signs of a regionalized pattern of support and opposition, as had emerged in France, but the facts refused to correspond to the known model. Very quickly it became clear that the French were faced by something very generalized in character. When the Prefect tried to insist that all new curés take the Oath, he was told by the Vicar-General of Spoleto that they would be filled by supplicant priests, not curés, to avoid confrontation. When the Prefect protested to Paris, Police-Générale decided to accept the lesser of two evils. The response was telling:

> It is to be feared that worship will become clandestine, taking place in the catacombs, in country barns, and in the woods, with rocks for altars. That is where the hotheads can get to work, and political feelings can re-ignite and spread.[23]

The official vision of hell was the Church in the wilderness, and by 1810 there was no longer any doubt that it could do well in Italy. For all that, imperial policy insisted on the Oath in these territories, from beginning to end, thus playing directly into the hands of the Church. It was soon generally admitted that the periphery was impossible to control and that, as opposition to the Oath grew, it could become the 'danger zone'. Nor was it long in coming.

The ramifications of the Oath to the Civil Constitution of 1791 could have alerted the French to the dangers of insisting on oaths of so public a nature. Claude Langlois has argued convincingly that one of the most dangerous aspects of the Oath was the way in which it nationalized the conflict between Church and state, extending it both territorially to every parish and beyond the arena of clergy and bureaucrats to involve 'the totality of the *Nation*'.[24] The crisis over the Oath produced a rare example of a 'national crisis' in pre-unification Italy, a formidable – if wholly ironic – achievement by the regime so often lauded as the forebear of the Unitary state.

Even so, this must be weighed against the relative success the regime had in persuading thousands of *émigré* priests to return to France, prior to the ratification of the Concordat in 1801,[25] and take a revised Oath pledging obedience to the government, as opposed to loyalty to the Constitution as in 1791. The imposition of the oath in France had, at least, produced a complex mosaic that was only intelligible in highly nuanced regional terms and corresponded to no previous phenomenal patterns. There had been significant pockets of success in the long term, when tested against the forces of counter-revolution.[26] The experience of the Cisalpine Republic during the *triennio* mirrored closely that of the 1790s in France, giving no clear signal that the 1801 settlement would have a different impact when applied to Italy. In both these instances, the Church proved very divided over the Oath, with no clear focus for opposition. In France, by the time a clear Papal line emerged, the die had been cast for many jurors; later, in the Cisalpine Republic, no leadership emerged at all.[27] In 1806, by not imposing the revised Oath that was now incorporated into the Concordat as Article 6, the regime at last seemed to have begun to withdraw from the revolutionary policy of oath-taking, bound up with notions of transparency. The model for ruthlessness was now the Kingdom of Italy, where the Oath was strictly enforced, not France.[28] Events in Lucca seemed to confirm this trend in imperial policy, but it was a false dawn. The most telling lesson, with the benefit of hindsight, was the hardening of the Papacy over the Oath. Henceforth, there was no ambiguity in the clergy's duty to refuse it, for excommunication awaited those who did.

There were two forms of resistance to the Oath: outright refusal or retraction at a later date. Both were usually dramatic and public, if in different ways. The French soon faced widespread retractions, a phenomenon they should have been alert to. As early as 1793 many Parisian regulars had retracted the Oath to the Civil Constitution[29] and, although the real impact of retractions by secular priests in France was only about 6 per cent in reality, contemporaries were struck by a wave of perceived retractions in 1791.[30] As early as 1801 the regime forbade retractions by juring priests, even before the Concordat was ratified.[31] The Roman phase of opposition-by-retraction began at the top with the Bishop of Tivoli, one of only six original juring bishops. He retracted his Oath before a full congregation at the high altar on St Peter's Day – to reinforce the obligatory nature of the act – after apologizing to his flock for the embarrassment he had caused them by taking it.[32] He 'fell into the arms of the gendarmes', as one historian has put it, before being carted off to Alessandria to join the original non-jurors.[33] He set a trend. The canons of the provincial towns of Canepina, Cori and Subiaco followed the lead of Tivoli, saying from the altar that they had been tricked into taking the Oath, 'retracted it gloriously' and posted a notice to that effect on the Church doors as they were marched away to exile 'surrounded by gendarmes'.[34] In 1811 the canons of Velletri retracted their oaths in time for Easter, and then offered to take them again 'as a gesture of goodwill', but did not hand in their official retractions. By the end of the year, they and several more were finally gaoled for refusing to celebrate the holiday for Austerlitz.[35] The Mass, especially on a High Day, became a moment of drama and tension in a very real sense, as many juring clergy chose these circumstances in which to retract the Oath.

Neither did it die out quickly. In Civitavecchia in 1813 the two most prominent priests in the town retracted their oaths during Holy Week, and so were able to say Mass before full congregations and hear numerous confessions as non-jurors. The price was arrest at the altar by the omnipresent Gendarmerie on Easter Sunday, followed by deportation to Corsica.[36] The tendency of recalcitrant clergy to court state violence at the climax of the Mass was already apparent elsewhere over the singing of *Te Deums*. Now, with the Pope and most of the Curia in captivity, it sometimes reached new heights. Perhaps there was more even than martyrdom present in these acts. They might mark something of a return to a pre-Tridentine conception of the Mass as a public sacrifice, in which occult violence was embedded. Following the thoughts of John Bossy, the late medieval Mass was 'a locus for the extrapolation of social violence', be it from the laity's view of Christ as a sacrificial scapegoat or as expiatory victim. In Napoleonic Italy, the priest first renounced the safety of the Oath, in full knowledge of his fate, partly to atone for the sins of collaboration – individual and collective – but also to expose the latent violence of the new order. At a much deeper level than the regime could ever have suspected, it is arguable that these confrontations served to revivify those atavistic, sacrificial aspects of the Mass that Trent sought to occlude. The direct confrontation between the secular state and the Church, when constructed in this way by the clergy, seems to have set in reverse the process by which 'sacrificial rites may lose their power to convince when systems of public justice supersede private systems of conflict settlement'. [37] These matters had to be public and collective, and admitted no truck with judicial process, and the sacrificial aspect of these acts of resistance seems to be heightened by the absence of violence, coupled with mass support, that surrounded them. The comment of a historian of the *Kulturkampf* is equally applicable to Napoleonic Italy:

> The image of an embattled Church – wounded, bleeding – constituted a powerful symbol, one that placed a claim on the devout, demanding sacrifice and self-abnegation.[38]

There were many less spectacular but equally significant retractions of the Oath. In 1810 Roederer reported that many who had taken the Oath in Umbria would retract, if they had not already done so, because of the influence of non-jurors who had either avoided deportation through ill health or had returned from exile for the same reason. Their consciences were 'being worked on'.[39] More demoralizing still were the letters written home by exiled priests, particularly because the pensions of those deported were claimed – wrongly and deliberately by the exiled priests – to be higher than the salaries paid by the government to the jurors.[40] Norvins stressed the example of the refusal of the ex-regulars to take it, and their resultant poverty, as a major 'eroding factor' in the resolve of the juring clergy, who saw their opponents supported by alms alone.[41]

The French were correct to see the trouble as starting in Rome, where the clergy refused the Oath almost *en bloc*, but by 1811 Tournon came to feel that hierarchy and clerical discipline, coupled with an acute awareness of both French and Papal policy, was what was truly decisive, rather than the relationship of centre to periphery, although he was aware that Rome gave a clear lead to the surrounding dioceses. He pointed to the initial willingness of ten of the twelve bishops in his own department to take the Oath when it was generally thought to apply only to bishops. However, when it became clear that all canons and curés would also be subject to it, 'opinion began to turn against the Oath': the conduct of the juring bishops came under attack and hence public confidence in the juring priests was undermined. It was made all the worse because 'public opinion made itself felt in such a way that no one knew who was behind it. It never came into the open'. From that moment on, Tournon discerned, the retractions began among the bishops. Of the twelve juring bishops, only seven stayed loyal.[42]

From this point, retraction was overtaken by open refusal to take the Oath, and it stemmed from the line adopted by the bishops. Whether Tournon was correct in thinking the bishops had been pressured into changing their stand by lay public opinion is uncertain, for the majority in the Papal states as a whole were non-jurors from the outset, but his estimation of the power of hierarchy and Tridentine discipline was correct. The capacity of the bishops to lead their *parocci* had at times stood the French in good stead elsewhere in Italy. Now it was turned fully against them. The incontrovertible authority of the bishops over their priests shown here – and in Tuscany – was anything but as evident in France, where cathedral towns and areas of ultramontane traditions were almost the only places where the bishops could influence the lower clergy; in areas penetrated by Jansenism, they were deliberately defied.[43] The different paths taken by the Catholic Reformation in France and Italy are very evident in the Oath crisis. Of the 1,100 canons of the department of Rome, only fourteen took the Oath; in the provinces, retractions followed the opinion of the bishops.[44] Norvins interpreted this in a disparaging light, but he acknowledged the *esprit du corps* evident among the rural canons of the smaller Roman dioceses who did not come from important families and were quite poor. They risked losing their properties and livings, just the same:

> Some have refused the oath in *esprit du corps*, others from ignorance or because they were afraid to contradict the Pope's orders; in the provinces, many have blindly followed the example of their bishops.[45]

Even the most cynical observers sensed that the clergy were far from leaderless, and that they knew their duty.

The first deportations from the rural areas often matched the drama of the first retractions. If anything, they were even more archaic in character.

Tournon described scenes that show, emphatically, the ironic juxtaposition of a Tridentine tradition of clerical obedience to hierarchy, expressed in exactly the manner the secular clergy had combated for so long:

> In several villages, at the moment of deportation of the refractory canons, the local people joined with them, and went from church to church, the canons processing in their bare feet. The pious recounted how the madonnas had turned their eyes to watch, and of how crucifixes had dripped with blood.[46]

Such instances represent a deeper revolution in Italian life than anything wrought by the new regime, at least seen from the perspective of the post-Tridentine Church and the faithful. A powerful alliance was forged between a Tridentine and an atavistic laity, and its catalyst was the Oath.

Universal opposition to the Oath sometimes healed old wounds between the secular clergy and the laity. Under the *ancien régime*, the Papacy had actually tried to reduce the pastoral role of the bishops and parish clergy, partly by subordinating them to the temporal authorities, partly by encouraging extra-parochial and -diocesan spiritual bodies, the confraternities among them.[47] The Police Commissioner of Civitavecchia noted how the popes had built up the lay confraternities as counterweights to overpowerful bishops and clergy, and that they still exercised a strong, malign influence over the Oath. He recommended their suppression, or their subjection to episcopal control,[48] when only a month before he had drawn attention to the role of the flagellant confraternity *Della Morte* in protecting and sustaining non-jurors, as well as ex-regulars.[49] The wider point would seem to be the way in which the aggressive intransigence of French rule brought former rivals together, and that their rivalries were of a cultural and not merely political nature in the past.

The backhanded acknowledgment of this was the swift action taken by the Consultà over what Tournon called 'these ridiculous scenes': the pace was forced and the curés were ordered to take the Oath within the month. By the end of the summer, the majority of parishes were empty, and the Mass only continued to be said and the sacraments available because of a loophole in the Concordat that exempted all parish clergy, save the curés, from the Oath. In April 1811, as Easter loomed, Norvins admitted that one of the greatest impediments to the acceptance of the Oath by laity and clergy alike was 'the bad reputation of those who have taken it'.[50] The work of the Church was also saved by the simple inability of the French to do anything about this kind of mass, passive resistance on the periphery. In May 1811 Roederer admitted that, despite the fact that 100 of the 174 curés of the arrondissement of Spoleto – under his own nose – were now deported or in gaol, almost all the churches were still in service – run either by non-jurors who could not be caught or by ex-regulars who had no right to be serving them: 'You have to close your eyes to this mess; to repress it would only worsen things'. In Foligno, Roederer had 72 vacant cures out of 126 and was resigned to the fact that even juring clergy would refuse to serve there if requested, 'but the churches are always full of the refractories or the auxiliary clergy'. Roederer almost inadvertently pointed out directly the remarkable nature of this state of affairs. He had no doubt that this was not spontaneous; the local communities were not getting along on their own, independent of traditional ecclesiastical authority, as had often been the case in France in the 1790s.[51] Paggi, the Archpriest of Foligno in the absence of the bishop, sent out ambulant priests, all non-jurors, to serve the parishes each Sunday, and he kept them on the move. This was not confined to the Umbrian dioceses. In Corneto, the diocese was in the hands of a priest, Paolucci, said to have been invested verbally with apostolic authority. He confessed in private houses and kept moving, holding services in closed hill chapels to avoid the authorities.[52]

They were doing this without formal pay, because they refused all contact with the civil authorities. The clandestine Church was operating on its own and surviving, 'and I would ask Your Excellency [Police-Générale] to take into consideration the position I find myself in'. Only in the three Umbrian dioceses whose bishops had taken the Oath – Perugia, Città delle Pieve and Città di Castello – had all the curés followed their example, and only there were things normal.[53] As will be seen, the authority of these bishops, however effective in their own dioceses, could not be extended beyond them. Nor could it always be sustained. A report of May 1812 revealed that many rural areas of the diocese of Città di Castello were full of unreliable clergy, whom Roederer wanted replaced.[54]

The French were not above getting rough with the non-juring clergy of the tightly knit communities of the periphery. In the summer of 1811 troops were sent to arrest them in Tolfa, a town noted for its rebellion in 1799. Norvins had no doubt they all deserved exile and set about hunting down those who had escaped him.[55] However, there was little they could do in the face of the highly organized, widespread passive resistance they met in the four Umbrian dioceses of Assisi, Foligno, Amelia and Norcea. The bishops of these dioceses, all marked down for abolition by the French, mounted their opposition to the new regime in a manner that drew together all the strands of spiritual, passive resistance the French had encountered in Italy to date.

The forms and methods this resistance took form almost a microcosm of all those aspects of the Catholic faith, short of violence, the Church could turn against the state. However, they were also able to introduce an element unique to the circumstances of the Papal states, the appeal to civil servants and laymen in general of the question of sovereign legitimacy. Pius's own words leave little doubt that the motives for resisting the French were, essentially, spiritual, and so were the tactics of his bishops. Yet for all the ramshackle weakness of his state, Pius had a hold over his subjects possessed by few other Italian rulers. When the French seized the temporal states, Church and state could not coordinate their opposition to the new order: princes were deposed and removed; bishops stayed on, rudderless. In the Papal states, however, Pius was able to order civil, as well as clerical, disobedience, and by the same methods: excommunication for those who took the Oath; refusal of confession and communion to those who served the French. His bishops were also his provincial governors, and could enforce this. In Rome and its environs, they did not stay in place long enough to do so, but it took that bit longer to deal with the periphery and, when Roederer arrived in Umbria, the clergy were ready for him.

Roederer was first struck – and his hand forced – by the ability of the bishops to disrupt local administration, for they summoned a worrying level of lay support. They made the Pope's orders clear, to the point that most municipal officials refused to serve the French or, if they did so, would not take the Oath. All the employees of all the hospitals refused to serve, as they were directly under the bishops and faced excommunication. Roederer was only able to get the mayors to stay on – 'oathless' – by playing on their fears that their places would be taken by 'the worst sort'. Even so, resignations soon followed as Easter approached. Municipal government virtually collapsed over Lent. In April 1810, Roederer admitted:

> It has not been possible to have a meeting of a municipal council anywhere in many dioceses; work is suspended ... the priests are pleased by the number of resignations they receive; in dioceses where the priests are more insistent, whole councils have resigned *en masse*. As the work for conscription approaches, there are many communes where I have no representative of the government.[56]

Talks with the bishops only revealed the depth of their will to resist, and the wealth of means at their disposal. The Bishop of Assisi announced, 'with the greatest *sang froid*', that after considering the matter his conscience did not allow him to admit government employees to communion and absolution, that he had ordered confessors not to absolve them. Then – in an admission of pure defiance – he said he had ordered his *parocci* to omit them from the distribution of the Easter *biglietti* – now, of course, illegal in themselves. He told Roederer that he had made thorough preparations for his imminent deportation. He seems the most forthcoming. The bishop of Foligno told Roederer that, as the civil authority, the communion was none of his business; the bishops of Norcea and Amelia had territories across the border in the Kingdom of Italy, where it was reported they were preaching open revolt and threatening to excommunicate anyone who joined the French against the bandits. This was as close to violence as it ever came and the power of the confession was, of itself, enough to frighten Roederer:

The fire of civil war is fanned in the confessionals; if the government is not allowed to supervise them, if confessors are not made accountable for their conduct, if the government has no powers over a whole group of citizens who are silently undermining its work, this country will be in flames at the first opportunity.[57]

However powerful the reach of the confession, Roederer was wrong about the imminence of a holy war. Resistance remained non-violent from beginning to end, which is probably even more remarkable in an area soaked in banditry and collective resistance to conscription.

Arrest and deportation were swift and inevitable, but Roederer was careful not to give these bishops the platform for spectacular protest afforded the rural canons. He waited until after Easter to avoid open revolt, and arrested them on their return from their pastoral rounds on the first Sunday of Trinity. Fifty troops were sent to Foligno to take the bishop and his canons, but they were not needed. They were all seized in dead of night – 'no one noticed' – and taken to Rome. It was only the beginning of resistance, however, not the end. Roederer assumed the preparations taken by the bishop of Assisi meant the sale of his harvests to provide for himself in exile. He was wrong. On the night he was taken, the bishop gathered together his clergy before the high altar of the cathedral, where he made them swear loyalty to himself and the Pope, and to promise never to take the French Oath. He then laid down a chain of command, and concluded by saying he would rather see a layman in his stead than a juring cleric.[58] He meant it, and so did his clergy. In the months and years ahead, the Vicar-General and the archpriest followed him; by 1813 the diocese was in the hands of a parish priest, Paolucci, who held confession in private houses and whose claims to apostolic authority were widely believed.[59] By the Easter of 1811 it was clear a similar chain of command had been organized in Norcea. By then the diocese was run by a parish priest in the Kingdom of Italy, following the arrest of the Vicar-General, who had kept the bishop in touch with the diocese while he was in Bourg. The bishop himself was moved to Fenestrelles to halt this correspondence.[60]

Resistance – and persistence – of this kind over so long a period was a tribute to the Borromean ideal of clerical discipline and attention to doctrinal purity, as well as to pastoral devotion. Norvins came as close to admiration for this as was possible for him:

This ability to transfer all these apostolic powers prolongs the internal crisis we face. It is very much to be hoped that political circumstances will eventually win over the spiritual leader of the Church to the best interests of the clergy, and help achieve the pacification of his former subjects, because his blind obstinacy has been the only source of the trouble.[61]

All the more striking, this took place in the small, isolated dioceses of the periphery.

However, it would have counted for little without the mass support of the laity of all classes. There were moments when the non-violent nature of resistance appeared a façade in the hands of laymen. In April 1811, Roederer persuaded two of the leading curés of Assisi to take the Oath from him in private but, when the news got out, public opinion forced them to flee the area.[62] Norvins tacitly admitted in 1812 that non-jurors – secular and regular – were still openly saying Mass in the churches of the diocese of Assisi and that they were always better attended than those of the jurors. His only answer to a phenomenon almost as old as the Revolution was to arrest and deport the priest then acting as Vicar-General;[63] the real point was the impotence of the state.

Nor could the presence of a loyal bishop turn the tide. The juring bishop of Città di Castello, Filippo Bechetti, was a rare and prized bird to the regime. Roederer believed him to be the only truly learned bishop in the department; the scion of a noble family of Bologna, he was well read and a noted historian, as well as a theologian.[64] His sermon in favour of the Oath in December 1809 had won over all but two curés of the town.[65] It did not extend to the laity of the rebel dioceses, however. One of the hidden problems of using auxiliary clergy to staff the many vacant cures of the Roman departments was their refusal to do much more than say the Mass and administer extreme unction; they would not usually marry couples or baptize children.[66] The low number of baptisms in Umbria worried Roederer, and he persuaded Bechetti to tour the department and so fill the gap. Over 600 children were baptized on his tour in the summer of 1811, but all of them were from his own diocese; not one child from the four 'rebel dioceses' was brought forward.[67]

The French blamed many things for this kind of resistance, usually the continued influence of the Pope, strengthened by the clandestine local correspondence between him and the exiled bishops; they pointed to the presence of the ex-regulars and non-juring seculars; to the ignorance and fanaticism of the people. Almost never, however, did they believe that violent coercion within these communities was behind this 'deaf resistance' that went to the core of family life. The popular nature of this passive resistance was never denied. Indeed, it was openly avowed. The impotent rage of Norvins is manifest when he told Paris in 1813 of the non-juring clergy exiled to Civitavecchia from Umbria:

> These priests confess, despite promising not to confess; they take charge of childrens' education, on the plausible pretext of earning a living; they are always in close touch with the people ... . All attempts at surveillance are futile against the effort of thirty priests who work in the shadows, and of whom half their number would

suffice to corrupt a much larger town than Civitavecchia ... . Every family is with them; the parish churches are empty; the juring clergy have no one to confess.[68]

Three things are important in this outburst beyond the admission of the impotence of the regime in the face of truly popular opposition. One is the sustained nature of the resistance, which began in 1810 and was still powerful in 1813; another is the way in which clerical discipline and determination in exile enabled resistance to spread from the periphery to the urban, lowland centres like Civitavecchia; finally, the magnitude of lay support for this handful of impoverished clerics is striking. All these factors transformed the defiance of these small, mountain dioceses into a much wider problem for the French.

Lay opposition to the Oath transcended class, as well as the divide between centre and periphery. Norvins was terrified by the indirect power wielded over the administration by the non-juring clergy in Rome. Many civil servants who had taken the Oath were protecting the non-jurors, he argued. The civil servants, in their turn, misled Miollis, thus paralyzing French policy. Norvins believed there was a well-coordinated plot centred on one priest, Nicolai, a popular confessor whose influence extended from field guards to the highest levels of the civil service.[69] It is impossible to prove the veracity of Norvins' fears, but two clear points emerge. The French 'on the ground' in Rome had no doubt that the non-jurors had to be deported. It was also debatable which was worse to them: a civil servant who openly defied them and refused to take the Oath, or those supposed 'fifth columnists' who did. There were plenty of examples to choose from.

The most prominent laymen confronted with the Oath were the high magistracy of the Papal states: the 306 *curiali*. In July 1811, fifty of the Roman *curiali* – 'chosen from among the most eminent' – were arrested at night and their property sequestered. Unlike the prelates they served, all but fourteen of them broke down for the sake of their families and took the Oath. The fourteen who refused were exiled to Corsica.[70] An amnesty was granted to all who would take the Oath in November 1811, but the Ministers of Justice and Police-Générale still felt the most recalcitrant should be dealt with harshly. Although they now drew back from deportation and sequestration of property, this was only because these measures would have to go through the courts, whereas internal exile could be done through Haute Police. The Minister of Justice, especially, was incensed by 'the collective defiance of a whole corporation'.[71] The Public Prosecutor of the Imperial Court of Rome thought legislation should be introduced to abolish the legal standing of the *curiali*, reducing them to private citizens. Those among them who were prepared to serve in the new courts were not 'the most esteemed among them' in any case. He also admitted that the most highly thought of were those who held out longest.[72] The French readily admitted that the *curiali* had been broken by the needs of their families, although several from the small Umbrian towns held out longer than most, until April 1812. Two of them were fathers of large families.[73]

Even this stubborn resistance could not match that of the 'Roman priests' deported to Parma, Piacenza, Bologna, Piedmont and Corsica. This diaspora turned a case of limited – if widespread – resistance in two departments into a much wider problem.

The Roman diaspora

The clergy exiled to Civitavecchia – the Roman Cardinals, bishops and canons – were but the vanguard of the mass deportations that followed the mass refusals of the Oath. Indeed, deportation soon came to embrace just supporting the non-jurors. In a monumental administrative blunder, Vicars-General were not required to take the Oath. As a result, many became effective leaders of resistance in the dioceses, but this did not save them from deportation. Corsica became the gaol of last resort for the most troublesome among the clergy, of whom there were more and more, according to the authorities, as the years went by. By 1811 200 had been sent there. Parma, Piacenza, Bologna and Alessandria – in the diocese of Casale – were all under reliable bishops; they are also notoriously the coldest cities in Italy in winter. By 1811 there were over 700 priests in these centres, with a further 350 in Civitavecchia.[74] This does not count the many priests who returned home from exile, through old age and ill health, to stiffen local resistance to the Oath.

The gross miscalculation by the authorities of placing them in groups only provided further proof of the strength of hierarchy and discipline among the secular clergy, at least matching that of the regulars. The Police Commissioner of Civitavecchia spotted the potential for this from the outset. He believed the canons now to be deported to the north would miss their families and incomes, but would hold fast if kept together. Only if separated from each other, and got out of the large urban centres they were now in, could they be pressured into taking the Oath.[75] He spoke from experience, but was not heeded. The police noted this – and lamented it – when they tried to break them down. Nardon was made aware of the power of hierarchy in these makeshift communities. He noted in January 1811 that

> those invested with various ecclesiastical dignities and the canons of the cathedrals have the most power and influence among them; the others only follow their lead.

He felt the solution was to exile the 'officer class' to Corsica.[76] It did not work. After the first such deportation that month, he called the remaining priests together – without success. This shook him, for it revealed that there were other sources of support than hierarchy. When the leaders had gone, there was still the laity. He concluded that they had to be cut off from the people of the city as far as possible, and that they could work great mischief if they were not.[77] The upshot was that one hundred more of them were sent to Corsica.[78] The Prefect of Bologna also came to believe that only by virtually incarcerating the Roman priests could they be separated from the considerable support they got in the city.[79] In 1813, D'Auzers also thought hierarchy a powerful source of their solidarity, creating a 'systematic opposition'.[80] By then whatever had held them together had been subjected to considerable strain. Their own experience of the 1791 oath should have alerted Paris to the folly of this policy. As Timothy Tackett has noted of the pattern of resistance to the revolutionary oath:

> For the priests themselves, faced with the dilemma of the oath, the presence of other clerics in the community created a context of support and emulation, reinforcing their sense of hierarchy and strengthening their resolve to act in uniformity against the oath.[81]

Napoleonic policy actually created such communities where they had not existed before. The failure to learn from experience, as well as from the reports of its own officials, is staggering.

Administrative bungling often left them deprived of their pensions and of proper accommodation or provisions, which reinforced their *esprit du corps* in the face of adversity. Their arrival in such numbers terrified the local authorities, both in practical terms and for deeper reasons. The Sub-Prefect of Piacenza wrote, alarmed, to Nardon in July 1810:

> The unforeseen arrival of so many of these clerics ... demands my special attention, and it has driven me to ask for special instructions ... . [I]t is urgent to give me orders about these priests. They say they have been given nothing for their journey; many of them have no means of support ... . The clergy of this area is not generally well disposed to us, and it would be better not to let them get close these men; politics dictates that they ought to be sent elsewhere.[82]

At the outset Paris agreed in the case of Piacenza. The Minister of Public Worship did not want them to stay in Piacenza,[83] His colleague in Parma did not want them to stay either; one hundred could be put up in the closed college of Santa Caterina – a deep irony, to say the least – but this was all the town could cope with.[84] The bishop agreed, adding ominously that, it being beyond him to cope with the predicted – and realized – number of 400, 'I can think of nothing else to do, at the moment, than to hand them over to the charity of the faithful'.[85] Stay they did, however. The brief attempt to lodge them with families was scotched by Paris in no uncertain terms,[86] and they found themselves in those former priories and convents of the two towns that were too dilapidated to be sold.[87] The 'overflow' from Parma and Piacenza was directed to Bologna.[88] When they got there, numbering 127, the mayor made it clear to the prefect that he could cope with no more and hoped that the rumour of a total influx of 200 was wrong.[89] It was not.[90] Most were housed in the derelict former convent of the Annunciation and accorded meagre daily rations of bread.[91] Those exiled to Corsica – the most obdurate in saying Mass and hearing confessions – were finally gaoled in the remote fortress of Sestri and put on bread and water for their defiance.[92] At times it is the casual remarks made in the course of routine administration that are the most revealing. The first time the clergy in Parma and Piacenza received their pensions on time was in December 1810.[93] These facts reveal that many of the letters written home boasting of higher pensions and better treatment than the stipends accorded the juring clergy were pure lies, if skilful propaganda.

The Roman clergy certainly had high-ranking, wealthy men within it, but the majority were of modest means. They needed their pensions, and lost a great deal by their refusal to take the Oath. French policy took account of differences in personal wealth, placing the Roman clergy into three categories: the poorest got 40 francs per month; the next, 20 francs per month; the wealthiest, nothing. In January 1811 the Vicar-General of Parma reported that only four of the 175 clergy still there after a big deportation to Corsica got no pension, thirty-nine were in the middle category and fifty got the full pension, as and when it came. The remaining eighty-two, the clear majority, received only the standard minimum pension.[94] Of the 200 in Bologna, there was more private wealth, at least according to the French. There, thirty-nine got no pension, sixty-six were in the middle category and ninety-five received the full allowance. Many of those on pensions of 20 francs petitioned for full allowances, and the civil authorities – in their places of exile and at home – almost invariably supported them. Their petitions also reveal how straitened were their circumstances, how much their extended families depended on them and, above all, how principled was the stand they had taken. Even Roederer could be moved by such requests. In 1811 he supported a deported priest in Parma, who had been accorded nothing, in his claims for a full pension; he had been obliged to sell his properties to pay his debts and for his journey.[95] Nardon – the 'host prefect' of Vicenzo Clarioni, a parish priest in Rome who was ill and had no support other than his family – supported Clarioni's claims to get a full (rather than half) pension.[96] 'Back home' the mayor of Poggio, in department Rome, supported the petition of his deported curé, painting a picture of a modest cleric:

He has some land here, which forms his patrimony, from which he draws income in cash and kind from his *coloni*, but all the local problems, added to the passing of time, have left almost nothing for his own support, which has left him in real poverty … . He had to neglect his affairs to see to the cure of souls, something he always did with distinction, never meddling in secular affairs.[97]

The mayor of Rieti asked for help for his curé, exiled first to Piacenza, then to Bologna, who had only his benefice to support him. The mayor of Bastia, near Assisi, pleaded for Don Antonio Ciar, also in Bologna, that he was of a poor family himself and had had to support them from his benefice.[98] The mayor of Valentano, near Viterbo, stressed that Felice Damiani, a canon, had several nephews who had been dependent on him, and he had had nothing to support them with but his benefice. He had been given no pension, because it was good benefice.[99] This kind of support also shows the esteem in which most of the exiled clergy were held in their communes.

Nor did their plight leave the laity around them unmoved. Help came to them in very practical ways, and they paid for it in traditional form, often by saying masses for money, which was illegal on two counts: as an act in itself and because non-juring clergy were not allowed to exercise their offices in public. Bologna is the gastronomic capital of Italy, and its inhabitants responded in kind for the masses they craved from the Roman clergy. Even the Roman priests admitted, under police pressure, that they could not afford the daily supplements of soup, wine, a piece of fruit and three potatoes from their own incomes. People crowded into their quarters to hear them, even around the barred windows. Milan's response was to withdraw even the daily bread ration from all those who could not prove destitution.[100] In Parma, formerly the seat of a great university and the Jesuit college of Santa Caterina, several prominent local families sought to employ Roman priests as tutors for their children – an example followed in Piacenza, notably by the Scotti family, whose fiefs had stood at the heart of the 1806 revolt in the Piacentino. Paris moved swiftly to stop this. Police-Générale belatedly came to share the fears voiced by the Sub-Prefect of Piacenza in 1810 that these priests had corrupted the whole town.[101]

Finally, and most importantly, they became heroes and celebrities wherever they went and among all classes of people. In this way, the example of resistance forged in the Papal states, often in the smallest and most remote dioceses, was carried to these large urban centres. Now 'the desert' was no longer the preserve of the mendicant orders, its 'normal' inhabitants. Princes of the Church and Roman canons with the fattest livings in Italy took their place in their cramped quarters, alongside poor *parocci* from the Umbrian hinterland, under the gaze of urban northerners who now had first-hand knowledge of their resistance. Before their experience is analysed, it should be stressed that all these men went quietly, as had the regulars before them; no one attempted to avoid his fate. There were no 'deserters' among them, whatever the hardships or dangers of their forced marches. In September

1810 five priests from Rome reached Parma, having made the journey without even their small travelling allowances. They had been robbed by bandits outside Viterbo, not far from Rome: 'They lost everything, and their health has also suffered considerably'.[102] Nor did they ever deviate from strict personal discipline. The civil authorities were unanimous in agreement that the personal conduct of all these priests – without exception – was above reproach. Personal immorality was completely absent from their ranks. People craved their spiritual services, as has been seen. These men were invested by Pius with the powers of papal legates, able to set up an altar and administer all the sacraments, wherever they found themselves and without the permission of the resident bishop. They did so. In Piacenza they spent the winter of 1810–11 in a gutted, windowless ex-convent, which was filled to bursting on Christmas Eve, as the snow poured through the roof. The major noble families attended and the laity were led there by their curés.[103] Fifty of them were soon exiled to Corsica, the first group reaching La Spezia on the Ligurian coast on 20 February. The police sent them there under a Gendarmerie escort, at night to avoid La Spezia, and then by sea to the naval base at Varignano to avoid passing through several small villages along the coast. This secrecy followed the warm welcome given them by the mayor of Pontremolì earlier in their journey, which the French did not want repeated.[104] The French knew all too well what they were about. Increasingly, the regime turned to coercion. Illness had always been regarded as just reason to allow even the most 'opinionated' priests to go home, but in June 1812 Nardon refused this to Mondacci, a curé of Foligno exiled to Piacenza, unless he took the Oath first.[105] This was only a minor case, however, given what was to come.

Finally, it was decided to treat the Roman clergy as common criminals. The Imperial Decree of 4 May 1812 ordered all the deported clergy who refused to take the Oath to be sent to prison and deprived of their allowances.[106] In February 1813 Paris told Milan that the French government would no longer pay priests in Bologna their allowances.[107] When Milan protested that the Italian government would not do so in its stead, Napoleon simply ordered them sent before a military commission to be tried as brigands.[108] By March they had all been sent either to Corsica, or to Alessandria to go on to Fenestrelles.[109] This was the nadir of French ecclesiastical policy in Italy. It was also a great victory for the Roman clergy. In the face of all this, only a handful ever took the Oath. Five did so in Piacenza, and were driven to the brink of nervous collapse by the others by the time the French finally let them go home.[110] More did so in Parma and Bologna, although no figures were kept, and there were reports of retractions when they got home, such as canon Forcella who, on returning to Cornetto as a juror, immediately retracted his oath before the Church of the Penitence.[111] By July 1812, after a conference with them that lasted three and a half hours, the Prefect got twenty-nine to take the Oath; fifty-nine still refused, the

Decree of 4 May not withstanding.[112] Of the 200 sent to Corsica, thirty-three broke down and took the Oath. Seven were canons of Rome, who had been there since 1810; they all did so only after having been sent before a military commission.[113] Twelve took it in Pinerolo by 1812, but it was admitted that they did so only after their own funds had run out.[114] An Imperial Decree of 25 March 1813 offered 'full grace and pardon' to anyone who took the Oath by 1 May 1813. No one did so, leading Public Worship to propose that they all be treated as felons, that no special concessions be made to anyone who now took the Oath and that, as the Oath was a political not a spiritual act, they all be declared rebels.[115] The regime had been driven to distraction, changing its policy over and over again but to no avail. The military commission of Turin, which had brought the first great bandit chiefs to heel in Napoleonic Italy, did not have the same effect on the fifty priests still held in Pinerolo, who all refused.[116]

The policy of enforcing the Oath had failed, utterly. Yet it is indicative of the regime that there were calls from within its ranks to extend the Oath still further. D'Auzers declared, after several years of dealing with Spina, that the Ligurian clergy ought to be subject to it:

> By forcing them to take it, all the troublemakers will be unmasked.
> Either way, they will be placed in an embarrassing position, either
> to lose their influence in their faction, or to come into the open.[117]

D'Auzers, it should be noted, was among the most moderate of the senior French officials in Italy. There was even a ministerial project in 1812 to extend a new Oath, based on the Concordat of Fontainebleau, to the auxiliary clergy and vicars-general of the Roman departments.[118] Events overtook it, however.

The failure of the Concordat of Fontainebleau

The hopes that Pius VII would accept the new Concordat concocted by the *Concile Nationale*, and their subsequent disappointment, offer a poignant window on the relationship between the Napoleonic state and Italian spirituality. In its death throes, the regime lashed out at its chosen scapegoats – the Roman clergy – but between February and March 1813 the French administrators and their Italian charges ran the whole gamut of hopes and fears when it appeared that Pius had accepted the Concordat of Fontainebleau. At the false dawn on 2 February, Norvins declared the news of the Papal surrender would even have a good influence on brigandage. He thought the educated classes welcomed the news, as it would heal the rifts driven between families by the issue of collaboration, a revealing insight into his own belief that so much hinged on simple loyalty to the former sovereign. Lagarde, in Florence, also reported the initial joy at the news from

Paris, and noted that the Tuscans were especially pleased at the prospect of the Pope's return, a reform of the Gallican articles and a more traditional reorganization of the Italian dioceses. For once, he said, the clergy sang a *Te Deum* with genuine enthusiasm.[119]

However, Norvins reported the stirrings of a 'White Terror' among the lower classes, and a thirst for revenge against the collaborators.[120] The juring clergy feared the refractories would now feel able to take a new Oath, and that they would be sacrificed to appease them, losing their cures to the returning heroes.[121] Within a week it was clear that the news from Paris had stiffened opposition to the French, not lessened it. Conscription was collapsing and local government paralyzed as the false rumours spread that the new Concordat included a complete restoration of Papal authority. From Civitavecchia came news that the imprisoned refractories were 'triumphant', that they felt they could not lose – either supporting the new Concordat, if its terms suited them, or declaring it a forgery, if they did not.[122] The Tuscan clergy were now looking hard at the terms of the new Concordat, realizing that the number of parishes would be greatly reduced; 'the brilliant conjectures have been retracted' – conjectures that hoped for a wholesale restoration of the old order.[123]

For a moment, however, Norvins believed that Pius had lost his standing among his subjects, his seemingly impenetrable resistance at last broken, that 'the old idol had been dethroned'.[124] Lagarde agreed, thinking the Tuscan clergy had lost faith in him for signing the new Concordat.[125] By early March it was clear that Rome would not be returned to Pius and that he had refused the new Concordat. Meanwhile the fuss had only served to alienate the most useful episcopal collaborator in the area, the Bishop of Anagni. He had served as the French-appointed Vicar-General of Rome, but learned that – when a solution looked possible – he would not continue under the new Concordat. Thus, when the government pushed ahead with the new Concordat regardless, he refused to attend the obligatory *Te Deum*.[126] Every hope had been raised and dashed in these few weeks; all that was left was confrontation. Norvins now believed firmly in Roman counter-revolution, the power of the refractory Church and the need to take institutional steps to reduce its presence in society. The terms of the new Concordat would achieve this: one parish per 5,000 souls, making a total of 204 parish clergy for the two Roman departments 'will reduce my police work by half, and reduce the relationship between the clergy and the people'. Finally, he lashed out even at Tournon's tepid form of appeasement:

> The other churches [than the 204 parish churches] should be closed. They should be converted to administrative uses, or kept as historic monuments by custodians. The chapels and oratories, where the malcontents gather together under the pretext of piety – to pray to God to strike France and bad mouth the emperor – should be

demolished. Then the nobility and the monks will no longer have their workshops of discontent, and would be forced to worship publicly, and be unable to profane religion with sedition and hatred.[127]

The local reactions to the high politics at Fontainebleau exposed the fissures between the religion of the rulers and that of the ruled all the more starkly. Norvins – once an emigré himself – emerged from the process something close to an Hébertiste in his tirades about nobles and monks, after entertaining the fleeting hope that only the diplomatic technicality of a civic oath stood between the Roman elite and collaboration. The Church was hated and feared, and to be pruned to its bare bones under the new Concordat. If Norvins had come to be wary of the forces ranged against him, Lagarde was more disdainful:

> Italy regards the Pope and his court as its property, to be kept on its territory. To put him in Avignon is akin to looting relics. There is less the influence of religious feeling here, than of a national sentiment which has shown itself in different parts of Italy for many years. It sees itself as a body stripped of its former grandeur, but destined to regain it at some time or other.[128]

Lagarde may have been a prescient prophet, but he persisted in the original French failure to accept the power of religion in Italian life. Norvins, by contrast, had learned to fear it. In 1813, at the end, French sensibility ranged between contemptuous complacency and almost paranoid hatred. When Napoleon and Pius finally tore up the Concordat they had forged together, they both pleased hosts of enthusiastic lieutenants. It did not speak well for the essence of the imperial relationship in Napoleonic Italy.

The priests, the police and the people

The war waged against God in Napoleonic Italy encompassed more than the increasingly blatant confrontation between the Church and the Napoleonic regime. These years also witnessed another, equally vital struggle within the Church, a battle with itself that it had to win before it could hope to confront the power of the Napoleonic state. Pius VII – himself from a neo-Jansenist background[129] – and many of his clergy had to move further from their roots than did Napoleon, from his original role as 'the saviour of the Church' to the gaoler of the Pope. The ex-Jansenist theology professor came to embrace Marian devotion at its most populist; Napoleon was, after all, a protégé of Robespierre's brother. It was less of a wrench for one gaoled at Thermidor to send Catholic clergy before military commissions, than for an Italian Jansenist to oppose the abolition of missions, or accept the mendicant orders as the witnesses of his own persecution, but this was the case, even if it took the sustained shock of Napoleonic imperialism to bring it about.

The struggle within the Church was partially prefigured by the anti-Jansenist, anti-revolutionary campaigns of 1785–98, but they turned principally on inter-clerical politics; their goal was precise and immediate – the buttressing of Curial authority – however imbued with the anti-Jansenist animus.[130] The Napoleonic Concordats forced the Italian Church to confront older, more profound tensions between itself and the laity; it now had to face the unfinished business of Trent. The post-Tridentine Church was reasonably adept at living with paradox but, when combined with the intellectual currents of the eighteenth century, the older aversion to missions and miracles, and an increasing ambivalence to the Madonna, infused the whole Church. Jansenism might be contained, but this of itself did not prevent the drift towards those rocks best discerned by Gramsci as a split between an 'intellectual Catholicism' and a Church 'for simple souls'. Gramsci points directly to the almost eternal struggle of the Catholic Church to prevent this.[131] At few points in its history, at least in Italy, had the Church come closer to letting this occur than in the second half of the eighteenth century. The threat of the Napoleonic Concordats forced the Church to confront this problem with renewed intensity.

Pius VII probably spoke more truth than he knew when he castigated the French for confusing superstition with Catholicism. The Church had gradually recognized this distinction over time, whereas for the French legitimate belief was almost – if not wholly – confined to the sphere of the fixed patterns of the liturgy. The boundaries between acceptable and unacceptable piety had agonized eighteenth-century Italian clerics but now, increasingly, they dissolved. This did not take the shape of the great battles of the eighteenth century about the relative importance of external devotion and internalized faith, which pitted cleric against cleric, and so the French officials usually missed the point altogether. The change took place in their full view – and they hastened to scotch it – but few among the new rulers seemed to grasp its import.

Although a willingness to embrace many aspects of the faith 'of the simple souls' was common both to Pius VII in his exile and to the humblest friar or *parocco*, this was not the result of a well-coordinated project, unlike the Curialist movement of the 1790s. Rather it was atomized, finding expression in a myriad of minor local realignments that would have been unlikely – if not always unthinkable – before the intrusion of the Concordats. This war was won by a multitude of individual deeds rather than formal polemics. Parish clergy supported, rather than curbed, the exuberant devotions of the confraternities; bishops came to commend the extra-parochial devotions of oratories and field chapels, where once they had disliked them. Everywhere

the poverty of the Church won it support among all classes, as the traditional poverty of the friars blended with the new-found, 'Oath-made'
hardships of the Roman clergy: in this way, many within the secular Church
found common cause with those elements of the regular orders, such as the
Capuchins, who had been regarded with some ambivalence by an earlier
generation. In these ways, the Church put itself in closer contact with the
laity, as the tensions implicit in Trent were set aside during the war against
the Concordats. The millenarian climate prevalent in the last decades of the
eighteenth century in Italy saw the flowering of miracles, of 'an eschatolog-
ical tension' created by the impact of traumatic events on collective
mentalities, beginning with the dissolution of the Jesuits and heightened by
the events of the *triennio*,[132] fitting into a pattern common in the history of
modern Europe. 'Modern European apparitions have occurred in clusters,
usually at periods of particular stress', as David Blackbourn has accurately
observed.[133] It did not end there, however; the nature of Napoleonic rule
meant the crisis was sustained. The Napoleonic reforms made the Church
enter into this crisis and master it. At the level of cultural experience, the
events of the *epoca francese* represent a powerful demonstration of the
dictum that popular religion was not the preserve of the lower classes.[134]
Nor was it confined to the most geographically isolated parts of the
periphery. Mario Rosa has pointed to 'a clear distinction between the bourgeois culture of the towns and the rural popular culture of the countryside'
that he feels had developed at the heart of Italian Catholicism in the course
of the eighteenth century.[135] The events that took place under Napoleonic
rule examined here must, at the very least, heavily qualify this. Above all, the
conflict between the Napoleonic reforms and Italian Catholicism resulted in
the advance of popular piety, in stark contrast to the general trend perceived
by modernization theory.

The confrontation between the Napoleonic regime and Italian popular
piety showed how vibrant and deep-rooted was the latter, and how determined it remained to resist the Concordat and its associated reforms. This
was as true at the centre as on the periphery, and it touched the elites as well
as the masses. The widespread, generally uniform character of this popular,
passive resistance by the laity bears both comparison and contrast with the
observation made of passive resistance during the *Kulturkampf* that '[h]erein
lay the power of popular Catholic culture: it patterned proximate events as
universal struggle'.[136] The universality of Catholic imagery and belief were
the only real common factors in Italian life in the early nineteenth century,
and this made for the similarity of passive resistance everywhere. Beside this,
however, are the differences between the traditional popular religion of the
period and the later, more clerical-inspired popular piety of the Catholic
revival. In the very different environment of mid-century, passive resistance
became a national affair, as in Bismarckian Germany. The new popular
piety was now engendered and sustained by well-constructed support

networks. In Napoleonic Italy this similarity of character and purpose from one locality to another remained just that, similarity; there were as yet no structures to transform localized opposition into anything more widespread.

There is strong evidence that the experience of Napoleonic rule left Italian popular religion badly bruised, certainly in terms of its material resources in the case of the confraternities and as regards places and objects of worship outwith parish structures. Nevertheless, the essence of popular piety, the mentalities that drove it and the forms through which it found expression, emerged enhanced from the years of repression and official discouragement. Gramsci, writing as late as 1919, could rhapsodize about the benefits the revolution would gain when 'Catholicism ... became the crowd itself, emanated from the masses, embodied itself in a hierarchy that asked the consent of the masses', a telling tribute to the enduring power of the Church.[137] Many currents of change would erode popular piety in settenorial Italy by the end of the nineteenth century, and the Church would soon master and tame many of them, although it never again attempted to turn away from popular religiosity to the extent it had in the eighteenth century. Its retreat was not effected by the Napoleonic state, however.

The regime harried and harassed Italian popular religion, but it never caught it. A comparison with the military role of the *partidas* in Spain is not inappropriate, all the more so because the Italian hierarchy, like the Cortez, found it had to accommodate these disorderly elements at first, but then came to praise them, and finally to imitate their defiance when the French, at last, came for them, ostensibly over the Oath. For their part, the Tridentine clergy showed a coolness under fire worthy of Wellington's troops at Torres Verdes; their response to French harassment was a vindication of the Borromean ideal in times of crisis, however compromised it might be in normal circumstances. This is not to argue that other, more structural currents of modernity would not, sooner rather than later, bring an end to the world of the *casacce* or the hill chapels, but it seems hard to count the Napoleonic state among them in terms of effectiveness, however strong its resolve to take a lead in their destruction. This world would succumb to economic and social change, but only temporarily to French pressure. Indeed, where communities remained vibrant, so did popular piety – which the clergy attacked only in the last quarter of the century.[138] Although religious observance declined at the centre in northern and central Italy, it remained both strong and highly politicized on the peripheries at the end of the nineteenth century, where, in the place of socialist, secular radicalization, 'a resentful "clerico-populism"' settled over the static and traditional countryside'.[139]

The Church, for its part, learned anew to confront the secular state with the traditional symbols and rituals most deeply rooted in the collective tradition common to all social strata. These were the ways in which the Church rebuilt its authority with the laity, its mind concentrated less by the prolonged influence of the Enlightenment than by the short, sharp shock of the Concordats. Turchi, the last pre-Napoleonic Bishop of Parma, was regarded as among the greatest predicators of the eighteenth century, and he used these gifts to castigate the Enlightenment and the works of the French Revolution, the Jansenists included, from 1790 onwards.[140] His skilful, highly politicized predications, notably his oft reprinted 'Important Advice for the People' of 1790, did much to undermine the new republican regime in Milan during the *triennio*, even if it was less spectacular than the *sanfedismo* of Ruffo in the south.[141] This 'hard-line' stood in contrast to the more restrained tone of the official Papal press before 1793, it should be noted.[142] The perceived need for resistance to the French reforms – and to the Revolution itself – came from the dioceses and the parishes from the outset, not from the top down.

When Pius VII at last turned to face Napoleon and attack the Concordat directly, he had this to draw on, as well as to foster. The Church came to terms with itself and its faithful in these years, and so faced the secular challenge of the new regime with renewed confidence and widespread support. The French failed to understand the ability of the Tridentine Church to compromise with the archaism of the faithful and add old weapons to its arsenal.

It is all the more remarkable that this alliance with popular, often archaic, religiosity was achieved without compromising the corporate discipline of the Tridentine Church. The example of the Roman clergy is the most striking evidence of this, but the capacity of the Church to sustain itself in the Roman departments through ordained chains of command in the face of continued mass arrests is, perhaps, an even greater tribute to the power of hierarchy and corporate discipline in the face of an unprecedented crisis. It was heralded by events in the Archdiocese of Florence, and engendered the rallying of the local clergy to the Roman clergy, wherever they were sent. These were the great *causes célèbres* nonetheless. The true test of clerical solidarity came in the routine running of the dioceses and parishes in the face of the reforms of the Concordat, and it was not found wanting. Ultimately this exasperated and infuriated the French. It was an example of self-discipline and resolve later imitated during the *Kulturkampf*.[143]

With the exception of Lagarde in Florence – who confronted a Church already battered by some aspects of the Leopoldine reforms – most French officials learned to fear the Church to some degree, even if they felt a deep cultural distaste for its values. Their appreciation – if that is the right term – for its ability to exercise social control both at the centre and the periphery stands in stark contrast to the contempt the French reserved for the weakness of the secular states they succeeded. The new rulers soon learned that the Church was the most potent indigenous influence they had to deal with in Italy, even if they never discovered its secrets or appreciated its methods. The recognition of this power – negligible in the face of military conquest but very influential in that of routine administration – is always present in the intemperate outbursts of the French in Italy. It probably amounts to the highest form of praise, in the circumstances. In his anger Norvins said of the Roman clergy that

> The priests control everything, they dominate the great and the small, holding the former in childish ignorance, the latter in need .... They do the confessing, and so dispense all the hopes and fears of everyone.[144]

Roederer admitted to his superiors that

> When I first arrived, I soon discerned the bad will of the bishops [of Umbria] but that was nothing. The important thing was to understand their power, and to take in the consequences of their opposition.[145]

D'Auzers called the Ligurian clergy nothing less than 'this powerful corps, which from time immemorial has been able to rouse the people of town and country at its will'. Deprived by the Concordat of its predicators, it now turned to the 'even more dangerous confessional, against which the police are powerless'. They had a long experience of 'using the conscience to manipulate the human passions ... of fostering an anathema for evidence, by recourse to superstition' and so were able to unsettle a government.[146] This is more than a recognition of influence, however; it is an admission of defeat. The confessional was a weapon forged by Trent, and its effectiveness was a tribute to its success among the laity.

Finally, the pacific character of the Italian clergy stands out in an age of brutal mass warfare, all the more striking because their passive resistance came at the height of Napoleonic power. Pius and the Roman clergy – and those of Florence before them – made their stands, and their way to prison, not in the death throes of the empire, but when there was no continental coalition in the field. They defied the regime in the aftermath of Wagram, not in the flushes of optimism that marked the start of the new wars and renewed coalitions. Until 1813 there was no realistic hope of liberation from Napoleonic rule. In these circumstances the actions of the Roman clergy, of Spina, of the humblest Capuchin or Franciscan who refused the Oath, deserve to stand out as a beacon of opposition to Napoleon, alongside the Spanish *partidas*. Violence attracts the gaze of history more readily than dignified suffering, just as the martyrdom of Pius VII and the Roman clergy attracted the compassion of contemporaries more than the subtlety of a Spina. They all deserve a place in the clouds around the sun of Austerlitz, however. Through their example, a different vision of the world survived a time of rampant militarism and secularization. It found mass support. Pius had willed non-violence from the start. In 1808 he referred to 'the experience of the vicissitudes of deadly revolutions' as reason enough to adopt pacific resistance and avoid all violence.[147] His call would have meant nothing had not the conflict between Church and state touched a profound popular nerve. As the French police came to see, violent revolt is not the sole – or perhaps even the best – indicator of opposition to a regime, even if its well-springs remained a mystery to them.

7

THE WAR AGAINST GOD

It remains to place the conflict between the Napoleonic regime and the Italian Church in the wider pattern of the history of Church and state both before and after the *epoca francese*.

The French reforms sat in a long line of attempts to 'civilize' the Italian peripheries and to educate the urban masses. Almost all of these initiatives were the work of the post-Tridentine Church, itself the object of French persecution by the end of the occupation. Yet, at the end, that cannot allow the significant – if highly paradoxical – identity of interest between that Church and the Napoleonic state to go unremarked. Here it is essential to make distinctions within the forces of the Catholic Reformation, the better to evaluate the aspirations of the 'Napoleonic project' for the regeneration of the Italian masses. There can be no other viable conclusion than that a project for the moral regeneration of the Italians – coherent and sustained, if ultimately futile – existed among the French. Beyond the conflict that engulfed Church and state in the *epoca francese* was the *longue durée* of the civilizing mission, in which the Napoleonic reforms have their place. Looking forward, it must also be asked to what extent the conflict between Church and state was a watershed for the future, in the formation of the turbulent history of Church–state relations in the succeeding century.

Borromeo and Bonaparte

Although the Jesuits – and later the Capuchins – came to work closely with the secular hierarchy in the course of the late sixteenth and seventeenth centuries – the former priding themselves on their subordinate role to the latter[1] – the way of the Jesuits and their successor orders was not synonymous with that of the episcopal reformers, who are epitomized by Carlo Borromeo. The French often failed to grasp these differences, and it was their loss, in a very real sense. In a myriad of local elites, clientage networks and alien political structures at the centre and on the periphery, the French found Italian society difficult enough to penetrate without the loss of the crucial sources of influence and information which only the episcopate, in particular, could supply. They failed signally even to perceive that there were real differences within the Catholic Reformation that might have made their relationship with the episcopacy and sections of the secular clergy much easier.

Although the Napoleonic reformers shared many attitudes and concerns even with the Jesuits, there was a fundamental rift between the ultimate vision of the Gallican Church of the Concordat and the ideal of society held by the most potent missionaries of Trent. Their shared contempt for what they perceived as popular culture – for archaism – is a misleading point of contact, as is their shared interest in the externals of public worship. Both strove to conquer the public sphere of celebration and ritual from popular piety by instituting demonstrative, but highly orchestrated, rituals of their own. Jesuits fought to win back Easter from *carnevale*, as did the empire; both sought to replace collective, traditional spontaneity with regimented, prescribed acts of public allegiance. It is tempting to reduce the differences between the Napoleonic quest for legitimacy in the public sphere and the Jesuit missionaries' drive to establish orthodoxy at the heart of the great Church festivals to simply a matter of taste, of interpreting 'Baroque enthusiasm' and 'Enlightened sensibilities' as being only skin-deep, and to see the revulsion of the French for Jesuit-inspired practices as those of aesthetic predilection alone. This would be mistaken. There was an unbridgeable difference between the passive, submissive and – above all – pacific society of the Jesuit mission and the world of controlled, channelled individualism – and aggression – desired by the French. The Napoleonic state did not wish the *Pax* to be universal; it worked incessantly to bring peace to divided communities by secular and – where it could – clerical means, but this was in the interests of the narrowly defined national community. The *Grande Nation* – however widely flung – was not the universal Church. Ferocity, initiative – *machismo* – were still to be cultivated, if only for export. The civilized Napoleonic polity was still a very masculine world. Its imperial officials were right to sense the utter incompatibility of this version of the civilizing mission with that of the Jesuits. If there was a Jesuit watchword, it was patience. Gradual assimilation, achieved through acceptance, was their preferred route to social control. Nothing could have been further from Napoleonic *dirigisme*. It was indicative of the gentle – or, conversely, 'sissified' – nature of their vision that the Jesuits often targeted women and children as their way into the rude, peripheral community or the rudderless urban poor. In the education of the elites, their Noble Colleges held out against teaching fencing and riding. The most damaging competitors to the Noble Colleges by the eighteenth century were, significantly, the new military academies.[2] The Jesuit ideal of 'perfecting the knight' corresponded with the premium the French put on clever conversation, worldly knowledge and polished manners, but the French knight was also a working knight as it were. The Jesuits missed out half of the crucial Napoleonic equation, *gai et guerrier* if, indeed, it was an equation at all.

The secular hierarchy was not quite the same. Its leaders expected to serve the state, with most – if not all – its faults. The Italian episcopate was nothing if not realistic and for the French to fail to work effectively through the bishops was truly picking a needless fight. It displays a gravely misconceived rigidity in their commitment to the terms of the Concordat, but given the nature of the Italian episcopate – in contrast to the legacy of the Jesuits among the lower clergy, the regular orders and, indeed, the laity – it need not obscure completely the real identity of interest between the Napoleonic state and this most orthodox sector of the Italian Church. Most bishops preached obedience to conscription and sought to calm the unrest it provoked, but even here the French were dissatisfied, as often as not, because the episcopate worked through mediation not intimidation. Their attitude to the 'unpoliced' periphery was not alien to that of the French, and stretched beyond the policing of the laity to that of their own clergy as well. It was less the day-to-day management of the dioceses that drove them apart, than the realization when faced by local crises that the new secular order was too significantly different from the old.

The response of the episcopate and the parish clergy was to draw closer to the laity, to meet it on its own ground and, finally, to stand up to the French through passive opposition, like the regulars before them. It is, perhaps, too readily assumed that the power of popular religion was waning by the end of the eighteenth century simply because a growing section of the clergy were combating it. That would be to confound activity with achievement too readily. There is too much evidence to the contrary to accept Owen Chadwick's verdict that neo-Jansenist changes were making steady, if slow progress among the laity by the end of the eighteenth century, that 'they made a turning point in the later history of the Church'.[3] Indeed, even at the height of the Catholic revival, clerical control over Marian apparitions and their links to local folk superstitions could be tenuous, as David Blackbourn has shown in the case of Marpingen in the Rhineland.[4] In this period and place, there are strong grounds for describing the conflict as between modernity, as embodied by aggressive reform, and tradition. Faced with so stark a choice, the waverers in the Church finally opted for tradition in the face of the Napoleonic onslaught, so placing Church–state conflict in a very different context to that drawn by Blackbourn for the *Kulturkampf* later in the century, when there were other sources of modernity in society beyond those espoused by the state.[5] A useful comparison might be with Mexico during the *Juarista* reforms of the 1860s, during which the clergy sided with their communities against many modernizing state reforms. This gave the Church lay support in its own confrontation with the state over its anti-clerical reforms and also strengthened its bonds to those same communities, with which they had been in conflict over the nature of popular religion.[6]

The forces of tradition were still strong. In Napoleonic Italy, unlike in much of later nineteenth-century Europe, the confraternities, Marian devotion and the new-found influence of the mendicant orders were all too powerful for the Church to ignore. However damaged they were by the French reforms, it would be wrong to conclude they counted for nothing in these years. They became foci of popular resistance, and the laity resisted fiercely when rallied around these forces, so fiercely that many Italian clerics saw sense in making common cause with them. That confraternities and local *feste* were at the centre of passive resistance to Napoleonic rule gave it shape and focus, if only at local level. It contradicts the picture painted for France and the Rhineland of a declining popular religion, only unleashed when the Revolution dismantled clerical control,[7] or of a situation in flux, 'as previously existing forms of clerical authority were dissolving without anything definite emerging to take their place'.[8] The French and Rhenish clergy did not make common cause with popular religion as unreservedly as their Italian counterparts, yet Spina and other Italian prelates ensured a continuity in their hold over the laity, however compromised by the standards of eighteenth-century reformers. Whereas in other parts of western Europe, historians detect a dangerous gap in relations between the Church and the laity, in the decades between the Revolution and the ultramontane, clerical-controlled revival of the mid-nineteenth century, this was not the case in French Italy. In the Rhineland, popular religion was increasingly – if not universally – regarded as a threat by the hierarchy in the changed circumstances of 1790–1820;[9] in France, the continuity between the attitudes of the *ancien régime* clergy and those of the restoration period produced 'the inverse correlation ... between formal religious practice and the practice of popular religion'. The renewal of close ties between the French laity and its clergy had to await the emergence of a new generation of priests, drawn from the people, from mid-century onwards.[10] Under the pressure of the reforms of the Concordat, the Italian Church threw itself back on the people and compromised with popular piety. In so disparate a country as Italy, the Church responded to the Napoleonic challenge with considerable uniformity and with startling difference from its counterparts elsewhere. In the immediate context of Church–state relations in the *epoca francese*, this willingness to turn its back on the eighteenth century and embrace popular religion as a form of resistance spelt the complete collapse of any real understanding between the secular church and the French.

In the final analysis, the French were incapable of establishing good working relations with any part of the Italian Church. The regulars were simply swept away, more often than not with overt ruthlessness, while ultimately it proved impossible to bind the episcopate to the regime on any but the most utilitarian grounds. In general, the parish clergy certainly became more suspect to the regime, and probably more hostile to it, over the course of Napoleonic rule. *De facto*, if never *de jure*, as had been the case in the 1790s, the Napoleonic regime was anti-clerical, at least in its Italian possessions. Napoleon died an excommunicate, after having torn up the Concordat he had staked so much on. This set of circumstances heralded many bitter clashes between Church and state all over western Europe and in Latin America in the century ahead.

Church and state in the nineteenth century

The weight of evidence compiled by the French themselves reveals beyond doubt the continued strength of popular piety in Italy. The emphatic judgement must be that the Napoleonic reforms failed in their attempts to take up the burden of Trent to 'civilize' and 'enlighten' the masses. As in Sperber's evaluation of the history of such reforms in the Rhineland, so in French Italy the continuum of Enlightened, Revolutionary and Napoleonic reforms had failed.[11] The French battered the material resources of the regulars and the confraternities, but the popular culture that sustained the latter and the more orthodox reverence which upheld the former emerged, if anything, strengthened by Napoleonic persecution. Chadwick's judgements that, at the turn of the century, 'monks and nuns were too many to be respected because they were monks or nuns' and that 'social ideas moved against the beggar and the mendicant friars' are utterly disproved by the Italian response to the Napoleonic assault on the Church.[12] The laity – rich and poor, urban and rural – showed no signs of growing 'more sensitive, or more austere, or more bourgeois', of moving 'away from an older freedom of popular devotion'.[13] Quite the reverse.

Restored regimes in an older reforming tradition, such as the Prussians in the Rhineland, saw efforts patterned on those of the French and earlier enlightened regimes continue to fail into the mid-nineteenth century.[14] The House of Savoy too was still fighting *ancien régime* battles in Liguria into the 1830s against the alliance that Spina had forged. The report of the new Piedmontese police chief, made to his underling in Genoa in 1816, has a familiar ring to it:

> the inhabitants of Piazza Santa Maria Angeloruno, of this city, celebrated the festival of the Holy Name of Mary with a zeal unbecoming religion, by erecting an altar with a sacred image of the Virgin at night, after the festival had been held officially that day, which was expressly prohibited … . His Majesty [the King of Sardinia] is decided in his will to prevent any so-called solemnities that, under the cloak of Religion, are practised by the crowd, which are in the main motivated only by irreverence, scandal and civil disorder.[15]

The will to fight popular piety was a rare strand of continuity between the French and the restored House of Savoy, but perhaps the most important point is the survival of that piety over the course of Napoleonic rule, at the centre as well as on the periphery. The *casacce* were finally done away with by Charles-Albert, not the French, because they had the strength to revive in 1814.[16]

In the Rhineland, a reforming, Enlightened episcopate had continued to attack the confraternities and other forms of popular piety over the revolutionary period and into the restoration, only to see them continue in wholly secularized form, while watching those populist practices of which it approved, notably pilgrimage, wither on the vine.[17] This was not the case in Italy. The Church did not have to await the mid-nineteenth century revival here, because it compromised with the vestiges of popular religion earlier. Popular piety, however unreconstructed, henceforth ceased to have the proportions of the threat of 'inherent laicization' that Sperber has discerned in the context of the Rhineland.[18] In this way the bond was unbroken and, when popular religion did begin to be curbed, it came from the shifting priorities of the Church itself and from the restored regimes it supported. This was the case in Piedmont and in the Papal states themselves, although it was hard-fought even then.[19] When and where Italian popular piety was brought under tighter clerical control and 'civilized', it was not the work of the Napoleonic regime but of a later generation of reformers working within the framework of the Church or essentially loyal to it. Firmer episcopal and Curial control over the parish clergy and the religious education of the laity was achieved under the restoration, not the French, if often in the face of passive resistance in the parishes.[20] The regimes of the restoration were remarkably well attuned to partnership with the Church as it emerged from the Napoleonic period and, aware of their own inherent weaknesses, they drew on the Church for support.[21] The drive to transform popular piety along more orthodox lines would await a new generation of clergy, forged in the struggle against the post-unitary state at the end of the century. That this particular battle still had to be fought had at least some of its roots – in the north and centre, if not in the Mezzogiorno – in the compromise made between the clergy and popular religion against Napoleon.[22]

The influence of the Church in Italian society was undoubted, however compromised, and unlike elsewhere it was unbroken by Napoleon. Gramsci recognized this all too clearly, seeing the inability of the liberal, post-unitary state to forge a partnership with the hierarchy as one of its fundamental weaknesses. Hindsight confirms that this was a cardinal legacy of the Napoleonic regime to the united Italy. Gramsci had an acute insight not only when he pointed to the essential incompatibility of the liberal state and the Church, but also when he located the root of that incompatibility in the impossibility for the Church as a whole – and not just the Papacy – to subordinate itself to the state in any way.[23] This was a fundamental shift of attitude within the Church: Whereas the eighteenth-century episcopate had been prepared to work with the lay power in a subordinate role, the experience of Napoleonic rule had destroyed this tradition: *vis-à-vis* the conservative states of the restoration, the Church now had the upper hand as a vital source of social control.[24] In relation to the new, all-embracing post-unitary liberal state, the hierarchy now found its enhanced, post-Napoleonic position impossible to renounce without an unthinkable 'act of humiliation of pontifical authority, a renunciation of its own life, from part of the ecclesiastical hierarchy'.[25] What had been possible before Napoleon was unimaginable after him. Having survived the revolutionary tide better than the secular powers of the *ancien régime*, the Church entered the restoration 'above all ... free from any dangerous solidarity with legitimism'.[26] The experience of the Napoleonic period had created a tradition and set an example for the later policy of intransigence that dogged the post-unitary state, not just at the level of the hierarchy but at the grassroots where the *Opera dei Congressi* strove to create a Catholic 'counter-culture' to that of the liberal regime. Gramsci here located the real importance of that power which the new state was so desperate to harness to its own purposes, although his attitude towards it is overlaid with Marxian inflexibility:

> The new Italian state lacked the cooperation of the ecclesiastical hierarchy and the religious spirit [it could provide], which alone might have appeased the innumerable individual consciences of a backward, opaque people, driven by irrational and capricious impulses.[27]

The alliance forged by the Church with popular piety against Napoleon was still the mainspring of its power and so of its potential usefulness – almost indispensability – to the post-unitary state. That state soon found itself in the same dilemma as the polity that was, in so many ways, its mentor.

When new challenges confronted the Church throughout Catholic Europe from mid-century onwards, it could draw on the renewed prestige and popular support it had won in the face of Napoleonic persecution. The reforms of the Concordat, in the tradition of the Port Royal, sought to return to the primitive Church; the Napoleonic persecutions achieved exactly that, if hardly in a way the regime wished. This, in turn, created a tradition of resistance that the Church drew upon in the great clashes with the state at the end of the century. These conflicts took place in a very different world, spiritual and material, to that of the struggle in Napoleonic Italy. They took place behind the backdrop of economic change and urbanization, and in societies where the Church had a much firmer grip on lay piety than at the turn of the century. The Catholic revival of the mid-nineteenth century was clerically inspired and controlled, at least in Germany and France. When the French clergy began to welcome popular religion back into the fold from about the 1830s, it was on their own terms and they were quickly able to 'sanitize' it.[28] It was, at least in part, this very ability to control a large, disciplined faithful that made the new emergent states in Germany, France and Italy so fearful of the Church. Perhaps the closest parallel with the experience of Napoleonic Italy is Mexico in its late colonial period. The Hildago revolt of 1810–15 drew only 9 per cent of parish clergy to its ranks, but it was central to the rebels' concept of the revolt. According to its major historian,

> The church in its full sense of the body of communicants – priests and laity – remained an especially powerful set of relationships in the late colonial period.[29]

This was equally true in Napoleonic Italy, where violent resistance was rare among the clergy, but, together with the laity, they proved a formidable presence in the face of French reform.

When the history of clashes between Church and state in the nineteenth century is traced, it emerges clearly that the Catholic Church was more capable of reinventing itself than its liberal opponents. Just as Spina threw in his lot with traditional popular piety and the Roman clergy rediscovered 'the desert' and the primitive Church, so the Church developed a whole new range of devotional practices, organizational structures and proselytizing techniques, all deployed in the mid-century revival. Liberalism – for all its diversity in other ways – remained predictable and moribund in its response to resurgences of clericalism. German liberals during the *Kulturkampf* saw themselves as being in the vanguard of progress, a vanguard Catholics seemed determined to halt through their perceived return to obscurantism. As David Blackbourn has said,

> for liberals generally this 'struggle of civilizations' was concerned with far more than church–state relations in the narrow and formal sense: it was a clash between their own 'modern' outlook embodied in a liberal nationalism, and the backwardness and stubborn parochialism imputed to German Catholics.[30]

There is obviously no direct political line of descent from Napoleonic authoritarianism to Protestant German liberalism, but their respective views about popular Catholicism bear as close a resemblance as possible, over historical time and space. The lineal connection between the 1902 Combes government of the Third Republic and the First Empire is clearer, even if it would have horrified the anti-Bonapartists in its ranks to admit as much. Its aggressively anti-clerical policies culminated in a very Gallican dispute over the appointment of bishops and ended in the destruction of Napoleon III's Concordat, the suspension of diplomatic relations between Paris and Rome, and the separation of Church and state. In this sphere, at least, the Third Republic might be said to be a truer heir of the First Empire than was the Second Empire. Indeed, when Napoleonic policies in Italy are set beside those of Combes, the latter emerge as the more moderate. Despite 'a spectacular exodus of monks' when restrictions on clerical teaching were rigidly enforced, even the arch-republican historian Maurice Agulhon concluded that 'many congregations submitted to the rules, and the network of private schools was in the end little harmed'.[31] The regular orders in Napoleonic Italy were left no rules to hide behind.

When the tensions at local level tipped over into confrontation, the response of later liberal regimes differed not at all from that of the French in Italy: Prussian troops swarmed into areas where Virgins appeared; seven German bishops were gaoled and four were exiled during the *Kulturkampf* – a smaller total than Napoleon managed in Italy – along with uncountable numbers of priests who were briefly gaoled, harassed or forced to go 'on the run' from pulpit to pulpit in order to avoid arrest for violation of the May Laws.[32] Again the only significant difference between these reactions and those of the French in Italy is the relative leniency of the Prussians. Napoleon ordered the Roman clergy – and others who supported them – into far harsher exile than did Bismarck. Gendarmes made their appearance when church buildings were barricaded against the anti-clerical laws in 1905–6 in France and 'in rural territory ... peasants armed with pitchforks and cudgels rediscovered ... the traditional weapons and actions of a resistance uprising'.[33] Nor had the attitude of the reformers changed. Combes' ministers sought combat, 'for they wanted to be a fighting government'.[34] During the *Kulturkampf* there were German liberals 'who viewed the state as a social and cultural steamroller, and clearly enjoyed the vicarious experience of watching its power being applied'.[35] Roederer had heirs, both lineal, within the hexagon, and spiritual, beyond it. Confrontation with the Church drew out the authoritarian, often brutal, element in liberalism throughout the century. In this respect, the Napoleonic experience in Italy is a harbinger of the future, and important in that it is the first incidence of how liberals would react to Catholic resistance to reform when in control of a strong, effective state, especially when that state proved less powerful than they had assumed. They became bullies, but frustrated ones. David Blackbourn could have been writing on Napoleonic Italy when he remarked of the *Kulturkampf* 'just as the actions of the Prussian state denoted weakness as much as strength, so the violent bombast of liberal rhetoric denoted impotence'.[36]

The result for the state was ultimately the same too: failure. The 'heavy-handed response was not necessarily a sign of strength'.[37] In the Second

Reich and the Third Republic, as in Napoleonic Italy, the Church turned to passive resistance in the struggles of the late nineteenth century. The changed circumstances of the period sharpened the edge through the new phenomena of mass demonstrations and the emergence of Catholic political parties – the Centre in Germany, *Action Française* in the Third Republic – which were unthinkable in the first decade of the century. The tactics used by the Mexican hierarchy during the *Juarista* persecutions of the 1860s bear the closest comparison, in spirit and detail, with those first deployed in Napoleonic Italy.[38] The principles and the binding force of passive resistance remained the same, however. Helmut Smith's assessment of the Catholic experience of the *Kulturkampf* can also serve as a universal model:

> The experience of persecution and resistance created the conditions for the formation of a Catholic community that transcended, at least in part, differences of class and status, a community that shared a common emotive rhetoric ... . Herein lay the popular Catholic culture: it patterned proximate events as universal struggle.[39]

Neither the Napoleonic empire nor its successor liberal states could match this. They had no comparable iconography and no deeply ingrained popular traditions to sustain them. In Germany, 'the reach of the Prussian state was not always the same as its grasp';[40] in the Third Republic, 'French society and culture in general remained impregnated with religion. Neither Jules Ferry nor even Émile Combes had changed anything in that respect'.[41] In so many countries the state – over the course of a century of unheralded change – had achieved nothing in this regard, and learned less.

> The image of an embattled Church – wounded and bleeding – constituted a powerful symbol, one that placed a claim on the devout, demanding sacrifice and abnegation.[42]

This was the Church's deepest, most powerful tradition. Governments stirred it at their peril, but they went on doing so, partly because anti-clericalism was a powerful unifying force within governments throughout the nineteenth century. It defined the broad republican left for much of the Third Republic, when it was otherwise riven by personal rivalries and the deepening divisions between the socialist and non-socialist left. It provided a unifying 'republican spirituality', expressing a philosophy of science and progress against the clerical resurgence of the early years of the Republic, even if challenged later by Guesde.[43] Bismarck's whole *raison d'être* in provoking the *Kulturkampf*, in many interpretations, was to bind the liberals to the government and, more profoundly, to shape a sense of national unity and identity around the anti-Catholic struggle.[44] It certainly bound the

German liberals together, however much it divided the German polity as a whole or Protestants from Catholics.[45] French republicans and German liberals first buried other differences to fight the common foe in the nine-teenth-century spirit of confidence in 'progress', and then drew together in the face of their increasing vulnerability and isolation. This pattern was set in Napoleonic Italy: Roederer and Tournon were juxtaposed to each other in the new Roman departments precisely because of their diverse political and cultural backgrounds, but the differences between them over religious resis-tance were questions of nuance not substance. The *ancien régime* roué Norvins and the ex-Terrorists Lagarde and Nardon had even less to separate their views. D'Auzers, the moderate patrician, and Degerando, the repub-lican intellectual, shared a common distaste for the Church, the faithful and their ways. The powerful capacity of anti-clericalism to unite a very consciously elitist elite, and then to cut it off from the society it was supposed to guide, is already present here.

A theology for reaction and liberation?

The most important difference between the earlier experience of Church–state conflict under the First Empire and the later confrontations is obviously that of conventional political organization and consciousness. Nevertheless the Napoleonic regime, like Bismarck and the German liberals later in the century, conceived of political culture only in terms of the state, extended from the national to the imperial but legitimized only by public institutions and committed to 'progress'. They saw the Church as an active agent of opposition to this concept of public life, both in terms of the universalist values it stood for and the cultural influence it exercised to the detriment of public service. To Napoleonic imperialists, the Papal states themselves were the antithesis of a polity. Norvins lashed out in 1813:

> Rome has never acted as a sovereign state in its dealings with Europe. Its government was neither commercial nor warlike in char-acter. It depended on the credulity of Catholics, on the spiritual influence of the great Saint, and so it could not make common cause with other governments, who all had age-old interests based on family ties, fleets, armies, and on tangible territorial power ... . [T]here was nothing this singular people could have accepted, or understood [of such common interests], for it does not possess the most basic makings of a nation; it is under the yoke of its priests and its lawyers, who have replaced the victors of the Capitol as its rulers.[46]

Clericalism was the negation of *civisme*. The French believed Italians had too narrow a vision of the world, rooted in a *campanilismo* encouraged by their priests. The comparison with the German liberals' view of the Church during the *Kulturkampf* is too obvious to avoid. German liberals saw the Church as a barrier to national unity, as well as to progress:

> From the liberals' point of view, material and cultural 'backwardness' went together: both were the product of a tightly disciplined, clerically controlled and 'medieval' Catholicism.[47]

Although within itself the Church was constantly evolving in the face of the changes of the nineteenth century and responding to its challenges, liberalism – whether Napoleonic or German – saw it as an immovable foe.

Taken together, this is damning proof of the narrowness of the liberal vision of political culture and powerful evidence as to how much 'liberalism', so defined, was the ethos of the Napoleonic regime. The French Revolution invented the framework of 'conventional politics' and, even if the Napoleonic state neutered its representative aspects, its fundamental preconceptions were based on that framework. If public life did not revolve around public institutions at a national or imperial level, if it did not mean service to the state, if it did not involve organized elections – even the rubber stamping of electoral colleges or the sham of the plebiscites – then it was not politics. The conventions of politics were set.

It is the term 'conventional' that matters, however. There is a growing sense among historians of the counter-revolution, perhaps more in a French context than elsewhere, that an earlier literature has set the criteria for political consciousness too high, certainly in terms of the early nineteenth century, possibly even at a more general level. Historians of the French Second Republic, if not without their critics, have opened a powerful debate on popular, especially rural, radicalization.[48] Donald Sutherland and Réné Dupuy, working on Chouannerie, have done much to reposition the 'threshold' of politicization in the context of reaction. For Dupuy, Chouannerie was the culmination of a political process begun in 1788, and the point of the insurrection for the majority of peasants was to 'recover power that had been confiscated by fraud'.[49] The clergy, and their own opposition to the Oath which crystallised in the nocturnal processions of 1791, had been a part of that process. As Dupuy notes, the refractory clergy were not wrong to say that the new regime sought to impose a new religion on the people.[50] This, too, was part of the process of the 'confiscation of power'. Sutherland, although less convinced of the sophistication of his subjects, is still clear that 'inarticulate and unconscious as it was, the countrypeople's notion of community was a critical factor in the ideological make-up of Chouannerie' and that Chouannerie was 'one of the great moral struggles of the revolutionary era', in which the clergy and popular religion · had their parts to play.[51] Politicization can come from the right as well as the left, depending on the source of repression, and there is much in the ethos of its religious policies to link the First Empire more to the Revolution than to the old order.

If Napoleon's regime was indeed 'the first modern dictatorship', it was a dictatorship of the modern left. As such, the religious resistance to it might, almost perversely, be a forerunner – but not, it must be stressed, a direct ancestor – of liberation theology, at least in the hands of the laity and at grassroots level. The experience of Napoleonic Italy is, most certainly, an important and early instance of how the Church and the faithful would react and resist an authoritarian regime. For contemporaries – not least the French themselves – the problems posed by the widespread passive resistance provoked by their religious policies were far more pressing than the conspiracies of the *Carbonari* and other conventionally 'political' sources of opposition.[52] The majority of examples of religious resistance in Napoleonic Italy – lay as well as clerical, on the periphery as well as at the centre – were not spontaneous or quietist, even if they were peaceful. Those involved on both sides, at the grassroots, knew – and often said – that these confrontations were about a way of life that the French were determined to end and local communities were determined to preserve. The political awareness of the regular clergy and the Roman priests was remarkably astute, nor should this be wondered at. But it did not end there. Lay brothers, local clergy and Marian visionaries were all combating French policies; they were defying the new laws deliberately. Such defiance was one part of the assertion of an indigenous political culture against the model of the state forcibly imported by the French. The resistance was not, for the most part, spasmodic or erratic. Even the apparitions and miracles continued beyond the frequently quoted examples of the *triennio*. Fear of impending change and upheaval are usually cited as the circumstances in which politics and apparitions and other forms of popular religiosity connect.[53] In Napoleonic Italy they persisted throughout the period of occupation which indicates not only the enduring nature of the trauma, but also that these forms of disobedience became embedded in local communities. Their longevity indicates not just the tenacity of tradition, but the power of organization and the persistent awareness of these communities in the face of Napoleonic rule. There was a dynamic element in much of this resistance, notably in the 'mobilization' of 'wronged madonnas' in the defence of hill chapels and oratories. Nor, as has been seen, were the authorities themselves unaware of this. If anything, the French police may often have attributed too high a degree of politicization to some of these events in linking them directly to Papal intrigue. That is, they endowed them with the highly precise politics of counter-revolution, rather than seeing in them the more diffuse, but still politicized, qualities Colin Lucas and Roger Dupuy have called 'anti-revolution'.[54] Persistent manifestations of collective anti-revolutionary protest – and those of the confraternities are among the most tenacious – might reasonably be described as politicized acts. They opposed one form of social and political associative life, based on clientage, kinship, corporatism and shared ritual, to the model of the secular, imperial state regarded by the French as the only definition of political organization. As has been seen, the collective resistance of the *epoca francese* took place in an atomized world that did not have the wider organizational networks possessed by the mid-nineteenth century revival, nor did it have any secular political framework above local level. This did more than condition its character. In the context of politicization, this atomized character was the essence of its political culture. The resistance to French rule was meant to preserve exactly this and popular religion – with its roots in local madonnas, local saints, confraternities and sacred spaces – was the touchstone of that political culture, the conduit through which it expressed itself and, in more practical ways, the means through which it worked. *Campinalismo*, sacred and secular, was Italian political culture. To refuse to recognize the politicized nature of religious resistance is to miss the point in the same way as the French did.

The exception to this was the Papal states. Here the nature of sovereign power allowed an entire nation – one of the oldest states in Europe, whatever the French thought – to mobilize, peacefully, against the Napoleonic reforms and foreign occupation. It produced something close to a national campaign of disobedience, centred on the Oath and led by the clergy, but that went far beyond these issues and came close to paralysing local government and the administration of justice. The tactics developed by the Roman episcopate to cope with the mass arrests and deportations were replicated in Germany during the *Kulturkampf* and later in Mexico, when the whole country was placed under a Papal interdict in the 1920s.[55] The Church first learnt how resist, tentatively, in the Archdiocese of Florence, and then in its own heartland. It was a lesson it never forgot. The remarkable phenomenon discerned by Helmut Smith during the *Kulturkampf* when 'dutiful and law-abiding Catholic men and women now held the authorities in contempt'[56] appeared most emphatically in the Papal states between 1809 and 1814. The response to the French occupation and the French reforms in the Papal states set a pattern for the future on far more than a local scale, for in such circumstances the Church proved it was truly a universal body, able to oppose the universalist creed of liberalism wherever they clashed. It is more than apt that, in its table of contents, a leading general study of modern Italy groups the Church alongside the anarchists, socialists and the republicans as 'the subversives'.[57]

The conflict described in this study was more than a clash between Church and state. It was between the concept of society that emerged from the French Revolution, as nurtured by the Napoleonic regime, and the Catholic religion, as it was practised in northern and central Italy. Its example stretched far beyond the Alps, if not by direct imitation in every case, then whenever and wherever a set of historical circumstances presented themselves. Its normative power is perhaps an even stronger indication of its wider significance than any evidence of direct imitation, although the tactics developed by the clergy obviously influenced the conduct of later conflicts. Eventually every facet of that spiritual culture felt the ire of the new regime, and every component of that culture fought back as best it could. It drew on the discipline of the Tridentine clergy and the vibrant, human *sociabilità* that was so much part and parcel of popular religion, and which gave the lie to Stendhal's quip that 'these people had been bored for a hundred years'.[58] In the end the imperial reformers were repulsed. Perhaps traditional piety or, indeed, a sense of life that was spiritual – archaic or otherwise – was doomed to disappear or be subsumed into the religious evolutions of the next generation. But it did not submit to Napoleonic hectoring. That the last Emperor of the West failed to win this battle deserves to be recorded.

NOTES

Preface: The eagle of empire and the lamb of God

1 T. Tackett, *Religion, Revolution, & Regional Culture in Eighteenth Century France. The Ecclesiastical Oath of 1791* (Princeton, 1986). T.J.A. Le Goff and D.M.G. Sutherland, 'Religion and rural revolt in the French Revolution', in J.M. Bak and G. Benecke (eds), *Religion and Rural Revolt* (Manchester, 1984), pp. 123–45. T.C.W. Blanning, 'The Role of Religion in European Counter-Revolution, 1789–1815', in D.E.A. Beales and T.C.W. Blanning (eds), *History, Society and the Churches: Essays in Honour of Owen Chadwick* (Cambridge, 1985). Idem, *The French Revolution in Germany. Occupation and resistance in the Rhineland, 1792–1802* (Oxford, 1983).
2 R. Gibson, *A Social History of French Catholicism, 1789–1914* (London, 1989). J. Sperber, *Popular Catholicism in Nineteenth Century Germany* (Princeton, 1984). R.J. Ross, 'Enforcing the Kulturkampf in the Bismarckian State and the Limits of Coercion in Imperial Germany', *Journal of Modern History*, 56 (1984), pp. 456–82. D. Blackbourn, *Marpingen. Apparitions of the Virgin Mary in Nineteenth Century Germany* (New York and Oxford, 1993). Idem, 'Progress and Piety: Liberals, Catholics and the State in Bismarck's Germany', in D. Blackbourn (ed.), *Populists and Patricians. Essays in Modern German History* (London, 1987), pp. 143–67. J. Devlin, *The Superstitious Mind. French Peasants and the Supernatural in the Nineteenth Century* (London and New Haven, 1987) approaches the subject from a different angle. Latterly: R. Harris, *Lourdes. Body and Soul in the Secular Age* (London, 1999).
3 E. Said, *Orientalism. Western Concepts of the Orient* (London, 1978). Idem, *Culture and Imperialism* (London, 1993).
4 L. Colley, *Britons. Forging the Nation, 1707–1837* (London and New Haven, 1992). E. Weber, *From Peasants into Frenchmen. The Modernization of Rural France, 1871–1914* (Stanford, 1975).
5 J. Schneider (ed.), *Italy's 'Southern Question'. Orientalism in One Country* (Oxford and New York, 1998).
6 A. Bloom, *The Closing of the American Mind* (New York, 1987), p. 202.

Chapter 1: The last barbarian invasion?

1 M.P. Carroll, *Veiled Threats. The Logic of Popular Catholicism in Italy* (Baltimore and London, 1996), pp. 200–8.
2 M. Rosa, 'The Italian Churches', in W.J. Callahan and D. Higgs (eds), *Church and Society in Catholic Europe of the Eighteenth Century* (London, 1979), pp. 66–76, 74. Rosa believes the major historian of popular religiosity in this

190

period, De Rosa, has overdrawn the depth of the split between orthodox and neo-pagan practices, and generalizes too much. They are agreed, however, that the levels of sheer ignorance in the Mezzogiorno were so much greater than in the north as to constitute a fundamentally different problem.

3 A. Valente, *Gioacchino Murat e l'Italia meridionale* (Turin, 1965).
4 M. Broers, *Europe under Napoleon, 1799–1815* (London, 1996), pp. 70–7.
5 Cited in local context in C. Bullo, 'Dei movimenti insurrezionali del Veneto sotto il dominio napoleonico e specialmente del brigantaggio politico del 1809', *Nuovo archivio Veneto*, 17 (1899), pp. 61–110, 77.
6 S. Pollard, *The Integration of the European Economy since 1815* (London, 1981), p. 24.
7 C. Botta, *Histoire des peuples d'Italie* (4 vols; Brussels, 1825). Idem, *Storia d'Italia dal 1789 al 1814* (Paris, 1824; Milan, 1854).
8 The classic overview on which much else is predicated: G. Candeloro, *Storia d'Italia moderna* (Milan, 1965), vols 1 and 2.
9 A. Grab, 'State Power, Brigandage and Rural Resistance in Napoleonic Italy', *European History Quarterly*, 25 (1995), pp. 39–70. J. Davis, *Conflict and Control. Law and order in nineteenth century Italy* (London, 1988). M. Broers, 'Policing Piedmont: "The Well Ordered Police State" in the age of revolution, 1794–1821', *Criminal Justice History*, 15 (1994), pp. 39–57.
10 W. Roberts, 'Napoleon, the Concordat of 1801, and its consequences', in F.J. Coppa (ed.), *Controversial Concordats. The Vatican's Relations with Napoleon, Mussolini and Hitler* (Washington, 1999), pp. 34–80, 35. See also O. Hufton, 'The Reconstruction of a Church, 1796–1801', in G. Lewis and C. Lucas (eds), *Beyond the Terror* (Cambridge, 1983), pp. 21–52.
11 D.K. Van Kley, *The Religious Origins of the French Revolution* (New Haven, 1996). M. Cottret, *Jansénismes et Lumières. Pour un autre XVIIIᵉ siècle* (Paris, 1998), pp. 227–40 for a stimulating correlation between the paramount place accorded the primitive Church for Jansenists and Enlightened notions of nature.
12 O. Hufton, 'The French Church', in Callahan and Higgs (eds), *Church and Society*, p. 19.
13 Ibid., p. 19.
14 R. Chartier, *The Cultural Origins of the French Revolution*, trans. L.G. Cochrane (Durham and London, 1991), pp. 104–5.
15 A. Cabanis, 'Un idéologue bonapartiste: Roederer', *Revue de l'Institut Napoléon*, 133 (1977), pp. 3–19.
16 Chartier, *Cultural Origins*, p. 109.
17 Ibid., p. 109.
18 For the former view: Chartier, *Cultural Origins*. M. Vovelle, *Piété baroque et déchristianisation. Attitudes provençales devant la mort au siècle des Lumières d'après les clauses des testaments* (Paris, 1973). Idem, *Religion et Révolution: la déchristianisation de l'an II* (Paris, 1977). Tackett, *Religion*.
19 Sperber, *Popular Catholicism*, p. 278.
20 G. Pignatelli, *Aspetti della propaganda cattolica a Roma da Pio VI a Leone XII* (Rome, 1974). For the classic overview: F. Venturi, *Settecento riformatori*, vol. 1, *Da Muratori a Beccaria* (Turin, 1969).
21 O. Chadwick, *The Popes and the European Revolution* (Oxford, 1981), pp. 612–3.
22 For an overview: R. Rusconi, 'Gli ordini religiosi maschili dalla Controriforma alle soppressioni settecentesche. Cultura, predicazione, missioni', in M. Rosa (ed.), *Clero e Società nell'Italia moderna* (Rome and Bari, 1992), pp. 207–74.

Chapter 2: Centre and periphery

1 Among the most important recent studies for this period: O. Raggio, *Faide e Parentele. Lo stato Genovese visto dalla Fontanabuona* (Turin, 1990). G. Tocci (ed.), *Le Comunità negli stati Italiani d'Antico Regime* (Bologna, 1989). C. Casanova, *Le Mediazioni del Privilegio. Economie e poteri nelle Legazioni Pontifice del'700* (Bologna, 1984). B. Sordi, *L'Amministrazione Illuminata. Riforme delle Comunità e progetti di Costituzione nella Toscana Leopoldina* (Milan, 1991). M. Bellabarba, *La giustizia ai confini. Il principato vescovile di Trento agli inizi dell'età moderna* (Bologna, 1996). C. Wickham, *The Mountain and the City. The Tuscan Apennines in the Early Middle Ages* (Oxford, 1988) has shown its centrality to Italian history, in the longest of *longues durées*.
2 Cited in L. Riall, *The Italian Risorgimento. State, society and national unification* (London, 1994), p. 58.
3 Wickham, *Mountain*, p. 365.
4 Raggio, *Faide*, pp. ix–x.
5 Wickham, *Mountain*, p. 365.
6 Tocci, 'Introduzione', in *Le Comunità*, pp. 10–11.
7 For an overview: G. Hanson, *Early Modern Italy, 1550–1800* (Basingstoke, 2000), pp. 165–70.
8 Raggio, *Faide*, *passim*.
9 For an overview: Hanson, *Italy*, pp. 91–104, 238–9.
10 For an overview: M. Broers, 'The parochial revolution: 1799 and the counter-revolution in Italy', *Renaissance and Modern Studies*, 33 (1989), pp. 159–73.
11 On Bologna and central Italy: L. Antonielli, *I Preffetti dell'Italia Napoleonica* (Bologna, 1983). Grab, 'State Power'. On the cities of the Veneto: Bullo, 'Dei movimenti'.
12 On the Veneto: P. Ginsborg, 'Peasants and revolutionaries in Venice and the Veneto, 1848', *Historical Journal*, 27 (1974), pp. 503–50.
13 Tocci, *Le Comunità*, pp. 10–11.
14 On the success of the Counter Reformation in Siena: O. Di Simplicio, *Peccato, Penitenza, Perdono. Siena, 1575–1800. La formazione della coscienza nell'Italia moderna* (Milan, 1994). G. Hanlon, 'The decline of a provincial military aristocracy: Siena 1560–1740', *Past & Present*, 155 (1997), pp. 64–108.
15 R. Zangheri, *La proprietà terriera e le origini del Risorgimento nel Bolognese* (Bologna, 1961). P. Villani, *La vendità dei beni dello stato nel Regno di Napoli (1806–1815)* (Milan, 1963). C. Zaghi, *Napoleone e l'Italia* (Naples, 1966).
16 A. Prosperi, '"Otras Indías": Missionari della Contro-riforma tra contadini e selvaggi', in Atti del Convegno Internazionale di Studi, Florence, 1980, *Scienze, credenze occulte, livelli di cultura*, (Florence, 1982), pp. 205–34. Idem, *Tribunali della coscienza. Inquisitori, confessori, missionari* (Turin, 1996), pp. 551–601.
17 A. Gramsci, 'Quaderni del Carcere', 27 (2) in T. La Rocca (ed.), *La religione come senso comune* (Milan, 1997), pp. 233–4.
18 The distinction is drawn upon usefully in Gibson, *Social History*, esp. p. 134. Gibson draws on G. Cholvy, *Géographie réligieuse de l'Hérault contemporain* (Paris, 1968), p. 136.
19 For an overview: L. Chatellier, *The Religion of the Poor: rural missions in Europe and the formation of modern Catholicism, 16th–19th centuries*, trans. B. Pearce, (Cambridge, 1997).
20 C. Russo, 'La religiosità popolare nell'età moderna. Problemi e prospettivi', in idem, *Problemi di Storia della Chiesa nei secoli XVII–XVIII* (Naples, 1982), pp. 137–90, 142. Carlo Ginzburg's rejection of the term 'popular religion' is well known. In the context – and from the vantage point – of the social structures of the Italian periphery, his preference for 'culture' or 'folklore' carries much force.

It was not, however, the framework in which contemporary ecclesiastical authorities worked. It also seriously undervalues the inroads made by Trent in introducing new forms of orthodox piety, the Rosary and the Forty Hours chief among them. For the debate, see Russo, 'Religiosità'. For Ginzburg's views see the preface to the Italian edition of *The Cheese and the Worms. The Cosmos of a Sixteenth-Century Miller*, trans. J. Tedeschi and A. Tedeschi (London, 1980). See also idem, *The Night Battles: witchcraft and agrarian cults in the sixteenth and seventeenth centuries* (London, 1983).

21 Wickham, *Mountain*, p. 359.

22 Gramsci, 'Quaderni del Carcere', 27 (2) in *Religione*, pp. 234–5.

23 For an overview in English: Broers, 'Parochial revolution', *passim*.

24 On the longevity of Tuscan violence and the distorting effect its image could have on wider perceptions: T. Dean, 'Marriage and mutilation: Vendetta in Late Medieval Italy', *Past & Present,* 157 (1997), pp. 3–36.

25 Archives Nationales de Paris (ANP) F7 8867 (Ombronne) Prefect to Min. 3e arrond., Police-Générale, 15 July 1810.

26 ANP F7 6531 (Rome) D. Gen. Police, Rome, to Min. 3e arrond., Police-Générale, 25 September 1812.

27 ANP F7 8820 (Gênes) 'Rapport sur François Assereto' to Min. 3e arrond., Police-Générale, 3 April 1812.

28 ANP F7 6531 (Rome) D. Gen. Police, Rome, to Min. 3e arrond., Police-Générale, 3 November 1812.

29 ANP F7 8805 (Arne) D. Gen. Police, Florence, to Min. 3e arrond., 29 December 1811.

30 ANP F7 8818 (Gênes) Prefect to Min. 3e arrond., Police-Générale, 14 April 1808. The work of Raggio on the valley of the Fontanabuona in the early modern period lends a fair degree of accuracy to the opinion of the Prefect.

31 V. Paltrinieri, *I moti contro Napoleone negli stati di Parma e Piacenza (1805–1806)* (Bologna, 1927).

32 ANP F1E 85 'Rapport au Gouverneur-Générale de la situtation des États', 17 June 1806.

33 ANP F7 8794 (Apennines) Prefect to Min. 3e arrond., Police-Générale, 24 November 1809.

34 ANP F7 8794 (Apennines) D. Gen. Police, Turin, to Min. 3e arrond., Police-Générale, 16 December 1809.

35 ANP F7 8794 (Apennines) D. Gen. Police, Turin, to Min. 3e arrond., Police-Générale, 9 July 1811.

36 ANP F7 6531 (Rome) D. Gen. Police, Rome, to Min. 3e arrond., Police-Générale, 10 October 1812.

37 See particularly the correspondence in ANP F7 8791–2–3 (Apennines).

38 Archives de la Guerre (Vincennes) (AG) XF150 Organisation, Gendarmerie, Piémont, 1800–1801 'Coup d'oeil sur le Piémont, year ix/1801'. Cited in M. Broers, *Napoleonic Imperialism and the Savoyard Monarchy, 1773–1821. State Building in Piedmont* (Lampeter, 1997), p. 285.

39 See the corpus of work by Mona Ozouf, most notably *L'homme régénéré* (Paris, 1989).

40 ANP F7 8867 (Ombronne) Prefect to Min. 3e arrond., Police-Générale, 15 July 1810.

41 ANP AP29 16 (Fonds Roederer) A. Roederer to P.-L. Roederer, 3 December 1811.

42 ANP F7 8795 (Apennines) Prefect to D'Auzers, 12 October 1812.

43 J.-C. Waquet, *Corruption. Ethics and Power in Florence, 1600–1770*, trans. L. McCall (University Park, 1992), pp. 17–18, 92–3.

44 ANP F1E 87–88 'Rapport sur la situtation de l'Administration de Parme', Subdélégué, Parma, to the Administrative Prefect, Parma, 15 June 1806.
45 ANP F1E 85 Directeur, Lycéé de Parme, to Min. Int., 25 August 1806.
46 ANP F1E 85 Nardon to Min. Int., 1 September 1806.
47 ANP F1E 85 Nardon to Min. Int., 8 September 1806.
48 ANP AP29 15 (Fonds Roederer) A. Roederer to P.-L. Roederer, 28 April 1813.
49 ANP AP29 15 (Fonds Roederer) A. Roederer to P.-L. Roederer, 11 June 1813.
50 M. Patrizi, *The Patrizi Memoirs: a Roman family under Napoleon, 1796–1815*, trans. Mrs Hugh Fraser (London, 1915).
51 On the policy of *ralliement*: F. Bluche, *Le Bonapartisme. Aux origines de la droite autoritaire, 1800–1850* (Paris, 1980). On the Piedmontese: M. D'Azeglio, *Things I Remember*, trans. E.R. Vincent (Oxford, 1966). C. Bona, *Le Amicizie: Società Segrete e Rinascita Religiosa (1770–1830)* (Turin, 1962). On French militarism and the Italian elites: M. Broers, 'Noble Romans and Regenerated Citizens: The morality of conscription in Napoleonic Italy, 1800–1814', *War in History*, 8 (2001), pp. 249–70.
52 M.P. Carroll, *The Cult of the Virgin Mary. Psychological Origins* (Princeton, 1986).
53 L. Hunt, *The Family Romance of the French Revolution* (Berkeley, 1992).
54 M. Duchet, *Anthropologie et histoire au siècle des Lumières* (Paris, 1971).
55 Waquet, *Corruption*, p. 89.
56 Prosperi, *Tribunali*, *passim*. Di Simplicio, *Peccato*, *passim* for an urban context.
57 ANP F20 102 'Rapport sur Rome et les états romains', 1810.
58 Tournon to his mother, 23 September 1810, in J. Moulard (ed.), *Lettres inédites du comte Camille de Tournon, préfet de Rome, 1809–1814: 1re Partie: la politique et l'esprit public* (Paris, 1914).
59 M. Broers, 'Cultural Imperialism in a European Context? Political culture and cultural politics in Napoleonic Italy', *Past & Present*, 160 (2001), pp. 152–80. Idem, 'Noble Romans'.
60 Said, *Orientalism*, *passim*.
61 For an analysis of this, in a generally secular context: Broers, 'Cultural Imperialism'.
62 Van Kley, *Religious Origins*, *passim*.
63 Roberts, 'Napoleon', pp. 47–52.
64 Ibid., p. 37.

Chapter 3: The religion of the rulers

1 Tournon to his mother, 3 November 1810, *Lettres inédites*.
2 ANP F19 1925 'Proposition d'un Concile Général', 22 November 1809. On the Concordat of the Italian Republic of Italy: C. Zaghi, *Potere, Chiesa e Società. Studi e ricerche sull'Italia Giacobina e Napoleonica* (Naples, 1984), pp. 501–627.
3 ANP AFIV 1045 Min. Cultes to Napoleon, 14 thermidor an xii/2 August 1804.
4 ANP AFIV 909 'Rapport: Organisations des dix séminaires metropolitaines. Projet du Décret', 13 August 1806.
5 ANP F7 8796 (Apennines) S. Préfet, Sarazzana, to Prefect, 14 July 1811.
6 C. Fatnappiè, *Riforme Ecclesiastiche e Resistenze Sociali. La sperimentazione istituzionale nella diocesi di Prato alle fine dell'antico regime* (Bologna, 1986).
7 The findings of the 1811 'Inchiesta' are analysed in C. Bernardi, *La Drammaturgia della Settimana Santa in Italia* (Milan, 1991), pp. 342–9.
8 ANP F7 8794 (Apennines) D'Auzers to Min. 3e arrond., Police-Générale, 14 May 1810.
9 ANP F7 8794 (Apennines) Min. Cultes to D'Auzers, 29 June 1810.

10 Voltaire, 'Superstition', *Philosophical Dictionary*, cited at http://history.hanover.edu/texts/voltaire/volsuper.htm.

11 ANP F7 8823 (Gênes) Prefect to Min. 3e arrond., Police-Générale, 5 August 1810.

12 Tournon to his mother, 3 November 1810, *Lettres inédites*.

13 J. Moulard, *Le Comte Camille de Tournon* (3 vols; Paris, 1927), vol. 2, *La Préfecture de Rome*, II, pp. 112–3.

14 ANP F20 102 'Rapport sur Rome et les États Romains', 1810.

15 Rusconi, 'Ordini', p. 223.

16 ANP F1E 87–88 Nardon to Min. Int., 14 October 1806.

17 ANP F1E 87–88 'Arrêté de l'Administration Générale', 8 October 1806.

18 Rusconi, 'Ordini', pp. 222–3.

19 R. Muchenbled, *Culture populaire et Culture des élites* (Paris, 1977), pp. 369–70.

20 ANP F1E 87–88 Min. Int. to Nardon, 30 October 1806.

21 ANP F7 7018 (Rome) Norvins to Min. Police-Générale, 21 May 1812.

22 ANP F7 7018 (Rome) Norvins to Min. Police-Générale, 11 April 1812.

23 E. Brigidi, *Giacobini e realisti, o Il Viva Maria: Storia del 1799 in Toscana* (Siena, 1882) makes the pogrom in Siena its centrepiece.

24 Archivio di Stato di Firenze (ASF) Buon Governo 461 (1808) Archbishop of Pisa to President of the Buon Governo, 1 April 1808.

25 ASF Buon Governo 464 (1808) Archbishop of Pisa to President of the Buon Governo, 14 March 1808.

26 ASF Buon Governo 464 (1808) Prefect, Ombronne, to President of the Buon Governo, 26 June 1808.

27 ASF Buon Governo 464 (1808) Prefect, Ombronne, to President of the Buon Governo, 3 June 1808.

28 ASF Buon Governo 464 (1808) Prefect, Ombronne, to President of the Buon Governo, 8 June 1808.

29 Moulard, *Comte Camille*, pp. 515–6.

30 ANP F7 6530 1st Instruction, 22 May 1808.

31 A reference to the missions of the Lazzarites and Jesuits, ordered by the bishops in the 1790s.

32 ANP F1E 87–88 'Rapport sur la situation de l'Administration de l'arrondissement de Parme', 15 June 1806.

33 Said, *Orientalism, passim*.

34 Voltaire, 'Bishop', *Philosophical Dictionary*, cited at http://history.hanover.edu/texts/voltaire/volbisho.htm.

35 ANP F7 6523A Notes to the margin of S. Prefect, Pisa, to Lagarde, 30 March 1813.

36 ANP F20 102 'Rapport sur Rome et les États Romains', 1810.

37 ANP F20 102 'Rapport sur Rome et les États Romains', 1810.

38 ANP F7 6523A Min. 3e arrond., Police-Générale, to Lagarde, August 1810.

39 R. Darnton, *The Forbidden Best-Sellers of Pre-Revolutionary France* (London, 1996). Particularly his analysis of *Thérèse Philosophe*, pp. 89–114.

40 Russo, 'Religosità', pp. 150–1, stresses the 'top-down' policies behind this.

41 Rusconi, 'Ordini', pp. 208–23.

42 Ibid., p. 228.

43 J. McManners, *Church and Society in Eighteenth Century France* (2 vols; Oxford, 1998), vol. 1, *The Clerical Establishment and its Social Ramifications*, pp. 571–614.

44 For a detailed exposition of its workings, based on local examples: Prosperi, *Tribunali*, pp. 290–315. For its successful application in an extremely inaccessible region, which draws the contrast between the absence of the state and the

ability of the Church to 'police' the populace in this respect: C. Giorgini, *La Maremma Toscana nel Settecento. Aspetti sociali e religiosi* (Teramo, 1968), pp. 186–7.

45 Prosperi, *Tribunali*, pp. 312–5. Giorgini, *Maremma*, pp. 34–5.
46 ANP F19 1082 Bishop of Casale to Min. Cultes, 9 March 1806.
47 ANP F19 1082 'Circulaire de M. l'Évêque de Casal', 6 March 1806.
48 ANP F19 1072B Petition of Canon Bergancini to Min. Cultes, 8 March 1809.
49 ANP F19 1072B Bishop of Vercelli to Min. Cultes, 15 April 1809.
50 On the extent and results of secularization in Piedmont, making some reference to the Vercellese: M. Broers, 'Sexual Politics and Political Ideology under the Savoyard Monarchy, 1814–21', *The English Historical Review*, 457 (1999), pp. 607–35.
51 ANP AFIV 1048 Min. Cultes to Napoleon, 26 February 1812. The Minister also noted that the practice of posting the names of non-communicants on church doors had been banned under the Leopoldine legislation, but the issue of *biglietti* had not, thus perpetuating the system.
52 J. Bossy, 'The Counter-Reformation and the Peoples of Catholic Europe', *Past & Present*, 47 (1970), pp. 51–70, 63–4.
53 Rusconi, 'Ordini', p. 272.
54 G. Tocci, 'Il Ducato di Parma e Piacenza', in L. Marini, G. Tocci, C. Mozzarelli (eds), *I Ducati Padani, Trento, Trieste*, vol. 17, G. Galasso (ed.), *Storia d'Italia* (Turin, 1979), pp. 306–7.
55 Fatnappiè, *Riforme Ecclesiastiche*, p. 43.
56 Rusconi, 'Ordini', p. 264.
57 Ibid., pp. 266–7, for one such polemic by a Jansenist friar in Florence in 1782.
58 McManners, *Church and Society*, vol. 2, *The Religion of the People and the Politics of Religion*, pp. 89–90. In contrast, missions conducted by curés themselves confined to their own parishes were still very numerous into the 1780s: p. 87.
59 T. Rey-Mermet, *Le Saint du Siècle des Lumières. Alfonso de Liguori (1696–1787)* (Paris, 1992), pp. 323–37.
60 Rey-Mermet, *Saint*, p. 324.
61 Prosperi, *Tribunali*, pp. 564–6.
62 Rusconi, 'Ordini', pp. 258–9.
63 Giorgini, *Maremma*, pp. 129–30.
64 S. Da Campaganola, *Adeolato Turchi uomo-oratore-vescovo (1724–1803)* (Rome, 1961), pp. 304–7.
65 Giorgini, *Maremma*, pp. 127–35.
66 Rusconi, 'Ordini', p. 265.
67 Prosperi, *Tribunali*, pp. 560–1.
68 J.-C. Martin, *La Vendée et la France* (Paris, 1987), pp. 58–9.
69 ANP AFIV 1046 'Circulaire du Min. Police-Générale aux Préfets et Commissaires-Généraux de l'Empire', 1 October 1809.
70 ANP AFIV 909 'Rapport: Organisations des dix séminaires metropolitaines. Projet du Décret', 13 August 1806.
71 ANP AFIV 909 'Dictées de l'Empereur pour le Ministre des Cultes', 26 August 1806.
72 ANP AFIV 1046 Cardinal Fesch to Napoleon, 30 September 1809.
73 ANP F19 1076 Bishop of Piacenza to Min. Cultes, 12 October 1809.
74 R. Fantini, 'Due Cardinali "Napoleonisti": Caselli, Vescovo di Parma, e Oppizzoni, Arcivescovo di Bologna', *Aurea Parma*, 53 (1969), pp. 153–64, 154.
75 ANP F19 1076 Bishop of Parma to Min. Cultes, 14 October 1809.
76 T. Chiuso, *La Chiesa in Piemonte* (2 vols; Turin, 1887), vol. 2, pp. 101–2. Tocci, 'Il Ducato di Parma', pp. 318–9.

77 ANP F7 8791–2–3 (Apennines) Commissaire-Général Police, Genoa, to Min. 3e arrond., Police-Générale, 12 September 1808.

78 ANP F7 8791–2–3 (Apennines) Prefect to Min. 3e arrond., Police-Générale, 24 September 1808.

79 ANP F7 8791–2–3 (Apennines) Commissaire-Général Police, Genoa, to Min. 3e arrond., Police-Générale, 12 September 1808.

80 Prosperi, *Tribunali*, pp. 551–3.

81 ANP F7 8791–2–3 (Apennines) Commissaire-Général Police, Genoa, to Min. 3e arrond., Police-Générale, 12 September 1808.

82 Prosperi, *Tribunali*, pp. 565–6.

83 ANP F7 8791–2–3 (Apennines) Prefect to Min. 3e arrond., Police-Générale, 24 September 1808.

84 Archivio di Stato di Genova (ASG) Prefettura Francese, Pacco 170, fasciolo 230 (Police-Générale, 1808–13) D'Auzers to Prefect, 8 September 1808.

85 ASG Prefettura Francese, Pacco 170, fasciolo 230 (Police-Générale, 1808–13) Lt. Gend., brigade, Nervi, to Gend. Comdt, Genoa, 1 October 1808.

86 ANP F7 8791–2–3 (Apennines) Min. Police Générale to Min. Cultes, 24 September 1808.

87 Giorgini, *Maremma*, p. 171.

88 Russo, 'Religosità', p. 173.

89 Chadwick, *Popes*, pp. 513–5.

90 G.S. Pene Vidari, 'Famiglia e diritto di fronte al "Codice Civile"', in Archivio di Stato di Torino (ed.), *Ville de Turin* (2 vols; Turin, 1990), vol. 2, pp. 63–91, 76–82.

91 M.G. Lulli, 'Il problema del divorzio in Italia dal secolo XVIII al codice del 1865', *Il Diritto di Famiglia e delle Persone*, 3 (1974), pp. 1,230–47.

92 G.S. Pene Vidari, 'Famiglia e diritto', pp. 63–91, 75.

93 ANP F7 8926 (Taro) Min. 3e arrond., Police-Générale, to Min. Police-Générale, 20 February 1806.

94 Di Simplicio, *Peccato*, p. 381.

95 Ibid., p. 378.

96 M.T. Silvestrini, *La Politica della Religione. Il Governo Ecclesiastico nello Stato Sabaudo del XVIII Secolo* (Florence, 1997), pp. 325–6.

97 G. Ricuperati, 'Il Settecento', in P. Merlin, C. Rosso, G. Symcox, G. Ricuperati (eds) *Il Piemonte Sabaudo*, pp. 441–833, 449–50, *Storia d'Italia*, G. Galasso (ed.), vol. VIII (Turin, 1994).

98 ANP F7 8791–2–3 (Apennines) Commissaire-Général Police, Genoa, to Min. 3e arrond., Police-Générale, 12 September 1808.

99 Bossy, 'Counter-Reformation', pp. 56–7.

100 I. Fazio, 'Valori economici e valori simbolici: il declino della dote nell'Italia dell'ottocento', *Quaderni Storici*, 79 (1992), pp. 291–316.

101 ANP F7 8794 (Apennines) D'Auzers to Min. 3e arrond., Police-Générale, 20 April 1810.

102 ANP F7 8794 (Apennines) Proc.-Gen.-Imp. Cour Crim., Apennines, to Min. 3e arrond., Police-Générale, 16 March 1810.

103 ANP F7 8794 (Apennines) Prefect to Min. 3e arrond., Police-Générale, 9 May 1806.

104 ASF Buon Governo 464 (1808) Capo-Squadro, Pitigliano, to President, Buon Governo, 31 May 1808.

105 ANP F19 397 Tournon to Miollis, December 1810.

106 ANP AFIV 909 'Dictées de l'Empereur pour le Ministre des Cultes', 26 August 1806.

107 Cited in Muchenbled, *Culture populaire*, pp. 359–60.

Chapter 4: The religion of the ruled

1 M. Agulhon, *Pénitents et Francs-Maçons de l'ancienne Provence* (Paris, 1968), pp. 155–6.
2 MacManners, *Church and Society*, vol. 2, pp. 172, 188.
3 Devlin, *Superstitious Mind*. Harris, *Lourdes*.
4 Muchenbled, *Culture populaire*, pp. 383–8.
5 Harris, *Lourdes*, esp. the map on pp. 34–5.
6 Agulhon, *Pénitents*, p. 366.
7 A theme throughout A. Forrest, *Conscripts and Deserters: the French army and society during the Revolution and Empire* (Oxford, 1989).
8 ANP AFIV 1303 Napoleon to Min. Cultes, 12 February 1806.
9 ANP AFIV 1303 Min. Cultes to Napoleon, 21 January 1807.
10 ASG Prefettura Francese, Pacco 78, fasciolo 106 (Culto, pratiche diverse) S. Prefect, Novi, to Prefect, 22 March 1812.
11 ANP F19 1077 Bishop of Piacenza to Min. Cultes, 31 December 1808.
12 ASF Buon Governo 810 (1808) President, Buon Governo, to Menou, 9 January 1808.
13 A comparative reading of Devlin, *Superstitious Mind*, pp. 6–18 and M.P. Carroll, *Madonnas that Maim. Popular Catholicism in Italy since the Fifteenth Century* (Baltimore, 1992), pp. 59–61 reveals the identical nature of these beliefs in France and northern and central Italy. Such a comparative reading contradicts the assertion of the latter author that 'a multiplicity of madonnas distinguishes Italian Catholicism from other variants': p. 66. In a French regional context: Harris, *Lourdes*, pp. 15–18 on the nineteenth century; pp. 36–44 on the traditional power of Marian devotion in the Pyrenees.
14 Carroll, *Madonnas*, pp. 52–4, 94, 104–5.
15 Ibid., pp. 64–5.
16 R. Leveroni, *Cicagna. Appunti di storia religiosa e civile* (Chiavari, 1912), pp. 99–107.
17 ASG Prefettura Francese, Pacco 11, fasciolo 18 (Chiese e parrocchi) Vicar-Gen., Archdiocese of Genoa, to Prefect, 19 February 1808.
18 For an overview: Broers, 'Parochial revolution'. Among the local studies for the states that would form the *départements réunis*: G. Assereto, *La Repubblica Ligure: lotte politiche e problemi finanziari, 1797–1799* (Turin, 1975), p. 179. A. Cretoni, *Roma Giacobina* (Rome, 1971), pp. 87–98. Brigidi, *Giacobini*. More widely: G. Lumbroso, *I moti popolari contro i francesi, 1796–1800* (Florence, 1932).
19 The classic regional study remains G. Turi, *'Viva Maria!': La reazione alle riforme Leopoldine, 1790–1799* (Florence, 1969) which stresses the social and economic forces driving the revolts.
20 Carroll, *Veiled Threats*, pp. 23–4.
21 ANP F7 8829 (Taro) S. Prefect, Piacenza, to Prefect, 8 May 1810.
22 ANP F7 8823 (Gênes) Comm-Gen. Police, Genoa, to Min. 3e arrond., Police-Générale, 4 August 1811.
23 Carroll, *Cult*, p. 224.
24 H. Gross, *Rome in the Age of Enlightenment. The post-Tridentine syndrome and the ancien regime* (Cambridge, 1990), p. 270.
25 M. Rosa, 'Politica ecclesiastica e riformismo religioso in Italia alla fine dell'antico regime', in D. Menozzi (ed.), *Chiesa Italiana e Rivoluzione francese*, (Bologna, 1990), pp. 17–45, 28, 34.
26 A.D. Wright, *The Counter-Reformation* (London, 1982), p. 207.
27 G.P. Brizzi, *La formazzione della classe ditigente nel sei-settecento* (Bologna, 1976), p. 224.

28 Carroll, *Madonnas*, pp. 104–5.
29 Rusconi, 'Ordini', pp. 268–9.
30 Fantappiè, *Riforme Ecclesiastiche*, pp. 141–2.
31 Carroll, *Veiled Threats*, pp. 20–2.
32 K. Eisenbichler, 'The Suppression of Confraternities in Enlightenment Florence', in N. Terpstra (ed.), *The Politics of Ritual Kinship. Confraternities and Social Order in Early Modern Italy* (Cambridge, 2000), pp. 262–78, 277.
33 Russo, 'Religiosità', p. 159.
34 Giorgini, *Maremma*, p. 55.
35 Carroll, *Cult*, pp. 113–4. G. Christian, *Local Religion in Sixteenth Century Spain* (Princeton, 1981), p. 136.
36 Carroll, *Cult*, p. 14.
37 Archivio di Stato di Bologna (ASB) Legazione e Prefettura di Bologna, Fondi Dipt Reno, Titolo XXIV (1811) Rubrico 16 Petition of the ex-Sabbatini of the Blessed Virgin of S. Lucca to Prefect, November 1811.
38 Gross, *Rome*, p. 271.
39 M. Ruggiero, *La Rivolta dei Contadini Piemontesi* (Turin, 1974), p. 61.
40 W.B. Taylor, *Magistrates of the Sacred: Parish Priests and Indian Parishioners in Eighteenth Century New Spain* (Stanford, 1996).
41 For an overview: B. Hamnett, *A Concise History of Mexico* (Cambridge, 1999), pp. 127–41. For the classic monograph in English: H. Hamill, *The Hildago Revolt* (Gainesville, 1966). The case for the central role of popular religion is made in E. Van Young, *Hacienda and Market in Eighteenth Century Mexico. The Rural Economy of the Guadalajara Region, 1675–1820* (Berkeley, 1981).
42 S. Gruzinski, *La colonization de l'imaginaire. Sociétés indigènes et occidentalisation dans la Mexique espagnole, xvie–xviiie siècles* (Paris, 1988), pp. 123–4.
43 McManners, *Church and Society*, vol. 2, pp. 106–7, 110. Van Kley, *Religious Origins*, pp. 108, 162–3.
44 For a summation of the Marxist critique: M. Vovelle, *The Revolution against the Church*, trans. A. José (Oxford, 1991).
45 A. Gérard, *Pourquoi la Vendée?* (Paris, 1990), pp. 155, 223.
46 Martin, *Vendée*, p. 73.
47 Harris, *Lourdes*, p. 13.
48 Devlin, *Superstitious Mind*, pp. 2–7. Marian devotion could be strong in urban areas, too. In Lyon in mid-century, the Jesuits fostered several Marian congregations among the artisans: McManners, *Church and Society*, vol. 2, p. 185.
49 P. Burke, 'The Virgin of the Carmine and the Revolt of Masaniello', *Past & Present*, 99 (1983), pp. 3–21.
50 Leveroni, *Cicagna*, pp. 121–4, 141–61.
51 John Davis astutely notes that the local revolts of 1799 in Naples centred on the relics of local patron saints, 'all symbols of local identity, and as a result … more likely to lead to conflict with neighbouring or rival communities than to give royalist movements a broader solidarity. In contrast … the emblems of the *Santafede* remained highly abstract.' See J.A. Davis, '1799: The "Santafede" and the crisis of the ancien régime in southern Italy', in J.A. Davis and P. Ginsborg (eds), *Society and Politics in the Age of the Risorgimento* (Cambridge, 1991), pp. 1–25, 16. The clergy and elites of the Tyrol organized resistance to the French in 1796, specifically by vowing the province to the Sacred Heart: L. Cole, 'Nation, Anti-Enlightenment and Religious Revival in Austria: the Tyrol in the 1790s', *Historical Journal*, 43 (2000), pp. 475–97. The Sacred Heart became the emblem of the Royal and Catholic Army, whose leadership always struggled to break the hold of localism on its troops.

52 J.A. Meyer, 'The *Cristada* peasant war and religious war in revolutionary Mexico, 1926–29', in J.M. Bak and G. Benecke (eds), *Religion and rural revolt* (Manchester, 1984), pp. 441–52.

53 Taylor, *Magistrates*, p. 462. Taylor's general analysis of relations between priests and rural communities, and his general observation that tensions between priests and people over popular religion 'usually expressed a spirit of local independence from outside authority' in Indian highland regions, all bear close comparison with the Italian peripheries in the same period.

54 Carroll, *Cult*, p. 224.

55 Blackbourn, *Marpingen*, p. 363.

56 ANP F7 7018 Bulletin de Police, 21 May 1812.

57 For a wider discussion of this, as related to Marian devotion and pilgrimages: Russo, 'Religosità', pp. 151–2.

58 Burke, 'Virgin', p. 20.

59 Carroll, *Cult, passim*, for a general discussion.

60 ANP F7 8929 (Taro) Prefect to Min. 3ère arrond., Police-Générale, 28 June 1810.

61 ANP F7 8862 (Montenotte) Police-Comm.-Gen., Livorno, to Min. 3ère arrond., Police-Générale, 12 February 1811.

62 ANP F7 8804 (Arne) Lagarde to Min. 3ère arrond., Police-Générale, 25 January 1811.

63 ANP F7 8804 (Arne) Lagarde to Min. 3ère arrond., Police-Générale, 11 September 1811.

64 Rusconi, 'Ordini', pp. 266–7.

65 Carroll, *Veiled Threats*, p. 45.

66 ANP F7 8796 (Apennines) D'Auzers to Min. Police-Générale, 22 August 1811.

67 Bernadette saw a small girl in white, which bore an uncomfortable resemblance to several genres of neo-pagan, truly 'folkloric' spirits common to the Pyrenees: Harris, *Lourdes*, pp. 72–9.

68 ANP F7 8796 (Apennines) D'Auzers to Min. Police-Générale, 22 August 1811.

69 ASG Prefettura Francese, Pacca 163, fasciolo 219 (Pratiche relative al Culto) Cardinal Spina to Lebrun, 22 October 1805.

70 Carroll, *Veiled Threats*, pp. 20–3.

71 ANP F7 8819 (Gênes) Police-Comm., Genoa, to Min. 3ère arrond., Police-Générale, 31 July 1809.

72 ANP F7 8819 (Gênes) Police-Comm., Genoa, to Min. 3ère arrond., Police-Générale, 30 September 1809.

73 Bloom, *Closing*, p. 202.

74 ANP F7 8819 (Gênes) Police-Comm., Genoa, to Min. 3ère arrond., Police-Générale, 3 August 1810.

75 ANP F7 8823 (Gênes) Police-Comm., Genoa, to Min. 3ère arrond., Police-Générale, 4 August 1810.

76 ANP F7 8826 (Gênes) D. Gen., Turin, to Min. Police-Générale, January 1811.

77 ANP F7 8805 (Arne) Lagarde to Min. 3ère arrond., Police-Générale, 10 December 1811.

78 ANP AFIV 1048 Min. Cultes to Napoleon, 29 April 1812.

79 ANP F7 6530 Bulletin de Savone, 8 September 1810.

80 Archivio di Stato di Torino (AST) Esteri, Vescovi e Archivescovi. Correspondenza, Mazzo 1 (1814–21) Bishop of Mondovì to For. Min., 20 July 1816.

81 N. Terpstra, 'The Politics of Ritual Kinship', in idem, *Politics of Ritual*, pp. 1–8, 1.

82 Eisenbichler, 'Suppression', pp. 271–4.

83 Agulhon, *Pénitents*, p. 366.
84 McManners, *Church and Society*, vol. 2, p. 188.
85 Bossy, 'Counter-Reformation', p. 68.
86 Chartier, *Cultural Origins*, p. 104.
87 'Confréries', *Dictionnaire de Spiritualité Ascétique et Mystique* (Paris, 1979), vol. 102, ii, pp. 1,469–77, 1,471.
88 Eisenbichler, 'Suppression', pp. 274–8.
89 On the Revolutionary regimes and the guilds: W.H. Sewell, *Work and Revolution in France: The Language of Labour from the Old Regime to 1848* (Cambridge, 1980). M.D. Sibalis, 'Corporatism after corporations: the debate on the restoration of the guilds under Napoleon I and the Restoration', *French Historical Studies*, 15 (1988), pp. 718–30. For the assimilation of the confraternities into the new order, on the social level, and the limits of their counter-revolutionary potential: Agulhon, *Pénitents*, pp. 254–84.
90 Vovelle, *Revolution*, p. 6.
91 Bernardi, *Drammaturgia*, p. 506, which draws on the established literature in these specific contexts.
92 Bossy, 'Counter-Reformation', pp. 59–60.
93 Ibid., p. 60 believes the confraternities to have been weak, already, and so to have posed no problem to the advance of Trent. The evidence for this much later period shows this was not the case, at least in northern and central Italy.
94 Bernardi, *Drammaturgia*, pp. 330–2.
95 ASB Legazione e Prefettura di Bologna, Fondi Dipt Reno, Titolo XX Polizia (1805) Rubrico 8 Min. Int., Milan, to Prefect, 16 January 1805.
96 Cited in Bernardi, *Drammaturgia*, pp. 348–9.
97 Eisenbichler, 'Suppression', pp. 277–8.
98 ANP F7 8867 (Ombronne) Prefect to Min. 3e arrond., Police-Générale, 15 July 1810.
99 The name seems to be derived from 'casa', to describe the decorated houses the brothers first met in, before they acquired their oratories: Bernardi, *Drammaturgia*, p. 332.
100 Bernardi, *Drammaturgia*, pp. 332–40. See also E. Grendi, 'Morfologia e dinamica della vita associativa urbana. Le confraternite a Genova fra i secoli xvi e xviii', *Atti della Società Ligure di Storia Patria*, 79 (1965), pp. 284–98.
101 Cited in L. Levati, *I Dogi di Genova e vita genovese degli stessi anni. Feste e costumi genovesinel secolo xviii* (4 vols; Genoa, 1912–16), vol. 4, p. 415.
102 ANP F7 8822 (Gênes) Comm. Gen. Police, Genoa, to Min. 2e arrond., Police-Générale, 4 May 1807.
103 Gross, *Rome*, pp. 96–7.
104 Fantappiè, *Riforme Ecclesiastiche*, pp. 71–88, 198–9, 379–87.
105 Ibid., pp. 73, 86. Bernardi, *Drammaturgia*, pp. 334, 339–40.
106 Fantappiè, *Riforme Ecclesiastiche*, pp. 146–7.
107 ANP F19 703 Prefect, Po, to Min. Cultes, 3 October 1808. For these conflicts during the *ancien régime*: A. Torre, 'Confraternite e conflitti sociali nelle campagne piemontesi di Ancien Régime', *Quaderni Storici*, 15 (1980), pp. 1,046–61.
108 Bernardi, *Drammaturgia*, p. 353.
109 Ibid., p. 253. Giorgini, *Maremma*, pp. 165–71.
110 ASB Legazione e Prefettura di Bologna, Fondi Dipt Reno, Titolo XXIV (1811) Rubrico 15 Podestà of Budrio to Prefect, 28 April 1811.
111 Russo, 'Religoisità', p. 168.
112 ANP F19 703 Maire of Cuneo to Min. Cultes (undated, *c.* 1810).

113 ANP F7 8932 (Taro) Min. 3e arrond., Police-Générale, to Min. Police-Générale, 27 September 1812.
114 Bossy, 'Counter-Reformation', pp. 67–8.
115 Terpstra, *Politics of Ritual*, p. 7.
116 Eisenbichler, 'Suppression', pp. 264–7.
117 Terpstra, *Politics of Ritual*, pp. 7–8.
118 G. Mori, 'Clero e istituzioni religiose nel distretto napoleonico delle Alpi Apuane', *Studi Parmensi*, 24 (1979), pp. 179–223, 203.
119 Russo, 'Religosità', pp. 161–2.
120 Archivio Comunale di Genova (ACG) Impero Francese Filza 328 (Commissarii di Polizia) Police Comm., Molo, to Maire of Genoa, 23 December 1805.
121 ANP F7 8819 (Gênes) Police Comm., Genoa, to Min. 3e arrond., Police-Générale, 31 July 1809.
122 ANP F7 8819 (Gênes) Police Comm., Genoa, to Min. 3e arrond., Police-Générale, 2 August 1811.
123 ANP F7 7017 Police Comm., Genoa, to Prince Borghese, Turin, 12 July 1808.
124 Bernardi, *Drammaturgia*, p. 340.
125 See the mass of correspondence in AST Segretaria di Stato per Affari Interni, Serie V (Miscellanea) Buon Governo e Polizia (1814–20).
126 ASG Prefettura Francese, Pacco 12, fasciolo 19 (Oratorii) S. Prefect, Novi, to Prefect, 8 fruct. an xiii/26 August 1805.
127 ASG Prefettura Francese, Pacco 12, fasciolo 19 (Oratorii) S. Prefect, Novi, to Prefect, 2 December 1809.
128 ASG Prefettura Francese, Pacco 12, fasciolo 19 (Oratorii) S. Prefect, Novi, to Prefect, 29 December 1809.
129 ASG Prefettura Francese, Pacco 78, fasciolo 106 (Culto. Pratiche diverse) Maire of Pasturana to S. Prefect, Novi, 1 July 1810.
130 ASG Prefettura Francese, Pacco 78, fasciolo 106 (Culto. Pratiche diverse) Vicar-Gen. Casale to S. Prefect, Novi, 12 July 1810.
131 ASG Prefettura Francese, Pacco 78, fasciolo 106 (Culto. Pratiche diverse) Min. 3e arrond., Police-Générale, to Prefect, 28 August 1810.
132 ASG Prefettura Francese, Pacco 78, fasciolo 106 (Culto. Pratiche diverse) S. Prefect, Novi, to Prefect, 4 July 1810.
133 ASG Prefettura Francese, Pacco 78, fasciolo 106 (Culto. Pratiche diverse) S. Prefect, Novi, to Prefect, 6 August 1811.
134 ASG Prefettura Francese, Pacco 78, fasciolo 106 (Culto. Pratiche diverse) S. Prefect, Novi, to Prefect, 22 March 1812.
135 ANP F7 8818 (Gênes) Prefect to Min. 3e arrond., Police-Générale, 20 May 1809.
136 ASG Prefettura Francese, Pacco 78, fasciolo 106 (Culto. Pratiche diverse) Vicar-Gen. Casale to Prefect, 4 June 1812.
137 ASG Prefettura Francese, Pacco 492, Maire of San Quirico to Prefect, 12 October 1813.
138 On Mayno and counter-insurgency: Broers, *Napoleonic Imperialism*, pp. 340–9.
139 A striking example of how wealthy confraternities could be, even in provincial centres, came in Voghera in 1811. After the government seized the property of the confraternities, leaving their oratories bare, the brothers simply bought new church furnishings and tried to reoccupy their oratories. They went on holding their services, as before: ASG Prefettura Francese, Pacco 12, fasciolo 19 (Oratorii) S. Prefect, Voghera, to Prefect, 5 July 1811.
140 ANP F7 8826 (Gênes) Prefect, Apennines, to Min. 3e arrond., Police-Générale, 3 February 1811.

141 ANP F7 8906 (Rome) Norvins to Min. 3e arrond., Police-Générale, 18 April 1811.
142 J. Bossy, 'The Mass as a Social Institution, 1200–1700', *Past & Present*, 100 (1983), pp. 29–61, 58–60.
143 Cited in Bossy, 'Counter-Reformation', p. 59.
144 ASF Buon Governo 464 (1808) Archpriest of the Metropolitan of Florence to President, Buon Governo, 26 May 1808.
145 ANP F19 1080 Min. 3e arrond., Police-Générale, to Min. Cultes, 13 July 1809.
146 ANP F7 8906 (Rome) Norvins to Min. 3e arrond., Police-Générale, 2 July 1812.
147 ASF Buon Governo 463 (1808) 'Testimone dei fedeli della parocchia del S. Niccosia, Pisa', to President, Buon Governo (undated, *c.* March 1808).
148 ASF Buon Governo 463 (1808) President, Buon Governo, to the Giuntà (undated, *c.* May 1808).
149 ANP F19 1072B Insp. Gend. Imp. to Min. Cultes, 27 June 1808.
150 ANP F19 1079 Prefect, Trasimène, to Min. Cultes, 29 October 1812.
151 ANP F19 1076 Min. 3e arrond., Police-Générale, to Min. Cultes, 9 May 1811.
152 Chadwick, *Popes*, pp. 513–5.
153 Cited in Moulard, *Comte Camille*, vol. 2, pp. 162–3.
154 ANP F19 1079 Miollis to Min. Cultes, 6 June 1811.
155 ANP F19 1079 Min. 3e arrond., Police-Générale, to Min. Cultes, 28 December 1809.
156 ANP F19 1082 Tournon to Min. Cultes, 14 March 1810.
157 ANP F19 1079 Miollis to Min. Cultes, 14 June 1811.
158 ANP F19 1079 'Rapport adressé au Tribunal de Première Instance de Viterbe', 21 January 1811.
159 ANP F19 1079 Min. 3e arrond., Police-Générale, to Min. Cultes, 26 January 1813.
160 ANP F7 8906 (Rome) Prefect, Trasimène, to Min. Cultes, 2 August 1812.
161 ANP F7 8927 (Taro) Prefect to Min. 3e arrond., Police-Générale, 2 June 1809.
162 ANP F7 8819 (Gênes) Police Comm., Genoa, to Min. 3e arrond., Police-Générale, 31 July 1809.
163 I. Prociani, *La festa della nazione. Rappresentazione dello Stato e spazi sociali nell'Italia unita* (Bologna, 1997), pp. 174–7, 208.
164 A. Latreille, *L'Église Catholique et la Révolution française* (2 vols; Paris, 1946), vol. 2, p. 129.
165 ANP F19 355–6–7 Prefect, Sesie, to Min. Cultes, 19 August 1806.
166 ANP F19 355–6–7 Bishop of Vercelli to Min. Cultes, 19 August 1809.
167 ANP F19 355–6–7 Cardinal Spina to Min. Cultes, 9 November 1811.
168 ANP F7 8936 (Rome) Min. 3e arrond., Police-Générale, to Napoleon, 12 February 1812.
169 ANP F7 8895 (Rome) Norvins to Min. 3e arrond., Police-Générale, 20 August 1811.
170 ANP F7 8895 (Rome) Min. 3e arrond., Police-Générale, to Norvins, 27 September 1811.
171 ANP F7 8899 (Rome) Norvins to Min. 3e arrond., Police-Générale, 16 August 1812.
172 ASG Prefettura Francese, Pacca 78, fasciolo 106 (Culto. Pratiche diverse) S. Prefect, Bobbio, to Prefect, 13 November 1811.
173 Prociani, *Festa*, pp. 203–4.
174 Corpus Christi had been successfully 'subverted' in eighteenth-century France, as well as in Italy, from the most solemn of the great festivals to pure *carnevale*: McManners, *Church and Society*, vol. 2, pp. 123–4. Russo, 'Religosità', pp.

151–60, on the greater popularity of local saints and the Virgin over Christocentric devotions, and continued reassertion of this in various forms.
175 Muchenbled, *Culture populaire*, pp. 341–8.
176 Russo, 'Religosità', pp. 137–42.

Chapter 5: The Concordat and the Italian clergy

1 ANP AFIV 1046 Elisa to Min. Cultes, 27 May 1809.
2 ANP AP29 15 (Fonds Roederer) A.-L. Roederer to his father, 11 January 1812.
3 ANP F19 894 Prefect, Taro, to Min. Cultes, 20 February 1807.
4 ANP AFIV 1046 Min. Cultes to Napoleon, 28 February 1807.
5 ANP AFIV 1046 Min. Cultes to Napoleon, 7 March 1807.
6 ANP AFIV 1046 Min. Cultes to Napoleon, 7 July 1807.
7 ANP F19 900 Prefect, Arne, to Min. Cultes, 21 February 1809.
8 M. Rosa, 'Politica ecclesiastica e riformismo religioso in Italia alla fine dell'antico régime', in D. Menozzi (ed.), *Chiesa Italiana e Rivoluzione Francese* (Bologna, 1990), pp. 17–45, 28–33.
9 Brizzi, *Formazzione, passim*.
10 ANP AFIV 1046 Min. Cultes to Napoleon, 28 February 1807.
11 ANP F1E 87–88 'Rapport sur la situation de l'Administration de l'arrondissement de Parme', 15 June 1806.
12 Zaghi, *Potere*, p. 100.
13 ANP F19 355–6–7 Cardinal Spina to Min. Cultes, 9 August 1812.
14 ANP F19 703 Bishop of Biella to Charbonnière, 28 vend. an. xi/20 Oct. 1802.
15 ANP F19 355–6–7 Bishop of Vercelli to Min. Cultes, 19 August 1809.
16 ANP F1E 78 'Mémoire sur le Piémont', an xi/1802.
17 ANP F19 355–6–7 Bishop of Vercelli to Min. Cultes, 19 August 1809.
18 ANP F7 8489 (Sesie) D'Auzers to Min. 3e arrond., Police-Générale, 4 September 1809.
19 AST Governo Francese, Serie 1, Cart. 19 (Dossier Prov. Alba) Commissario d'Alba to Min. of Int., Turin, 15 fruct. an viii/2 September 1800.
20 Chiuso, *Chiesa*, vol. 2, p. 100.
21 ANP F19 703 Bishop of Biella to Charbonnière, 28 vénd. an xi/20 October 1802.
22 Broers, *Napoleonic Imperialism*, pp. 304–9.
23 ANP F1E 85 Vicar-Gen., Piacenza, to Min. Cultes, 1 July 1806.
24 Chadwick, *Popes*, p. 551.
25 Tocci, 'Il Ducato di Parma', p. 316.
26 ANP AFIV 1317 'Rapport sur la situtation ecclésiastique des ci-devant États de Parme, Plaisance et Guastelle', 5 February 1806.
27 J. Lefon, *Pie VII* (Paris, 1958), p. 104.
28 ANP F19 355–6–7 Bishop of Piacenza to Min. Cultes, 17 March 1808.
29 ANP F19 1077 Min. of War to Min. Cultes, 8 December 1808.
30 ANP F19 1077 Bishop of Piacenza to Min. Cultes, 31 December 1808.
31 ANP F7 8927 (Taro) Prefect to Min. Police-Générale, 2 June 1809.
32 ANP F7 8927 (Taro) Prefect to Min. Police-Générale, 15 June 1809.
33 ANP F7 8927 (Taro) Min. 3e arrond., Police-Générale, to D'Auzers, 2 February 1811.
34 ANP AFIV 1046 Min. Cultes to Napoleon, 7 March 1807.
35 ANP F19 703 Bishop of Amiens to Min. Cultes, 10 floréal an xii/21 April 1804; Menou to Min. Cultes, 19 prairial an xi/8 June 1803.
36 For the full administrative consequences of the introduction of the Concordat in Piedmont: ANP F19 703 'Rapport, Min. Cultes à l'Empereur', 5 therm. an

xiii/14 July 1805. Pius VII fought Napoleon hard over the reduction of the dioceses, according to the French Minister in Rome: ANP F19 703 Cacault to Min. Cultes, 18 ventôse an xi/9 March 1802.

37 Cited in G. Tuninetti, 'Gli arcivescovi di Torino e la politica ecclesiastica di Napoleone', in Archivio di Stato di Torino (ed.), *All Ombra dell'Aquila Imperiale. Trasformazioni e continutià istituzionali nei territori sabaudi in età napoleonica (1802–1814)* (2 vols; Rome, 1994), vol. 1, pp. 413–28, 420.

38 Tuninetti, 'Gli arcivescovi di Torino', pp. 415–6.

39 ANP AFIV 1045 Min. Cultes to Napoleon, 19 floréal an xiii/9 May 1805.

40 G.P. Romagnani, *Prospero Balbo. Intellettuale e Uomo di Stato (1762–1837)* (2 vols; Turin, 1987, 1990), vol. 2, *Da Napoleone a Carlo Alberto (1800–1837)*, pp. 80–1, 116–7.

41 Tuninetti, 'Gli arcivescovi di Torino', pp. 421–8.

42 Fantini, 'Due Cardinali "Napoleonisti"', pp. 154–61.

43 ANP F19 355–6–7 Min. Cultes to Bishop of Piacenza, 9 April 1808.

44 C. Grandi, *La Repubblica di Asti nel 1797* (Asti, 1851), pp. 137–41.

45 ANP AFIV 1046 Min. Cultes to Napoleon, 19 January 1809.

46 ANP AFIV 1046 Min. Cultes to Napoleon, March 1809.

47 McManners, *Church and Society*, vol. 1, pp. 240–1.

48 Ibid., vol. 2, pp. 683, 695.

49 ANP AFIV 1048 Min. Cultes to Napoleon, 14 January 1811.

50 AST Esteri, Lettere Ministri. Roma, Mazzo 312 (1814) D'Azeglio to the King, 26 June 1814.

51 AST Esteri, Lettere Ministri. Roma, Mazzo 312 (1814) D'Azeglio to the King, 16 June 1814.

52 ANP AFIV 1048 Min. Cultes to Napoleon, 12 January 1811.

53 ANP AFIV 1048 Min. Cultes to Napoleon, 12 January 1811.

54 It is interesting that the government had considerable trouble in getting the Chapter of Ghent – which D'Osmond had done much to pacify during his administration – to accept a successor without a bull: ANP AFIV 1048 Prefect, Escault, to Min. Cultes, 6 December 1811.

55 ANP AFIV 1048 Elisa to Min. Cultes, 15 January 1811.

56 ANP F7 8820 (Gênes) Lagarde to Elisa, 24 December 1810.

57 ANP F7 8820 (Gênes) Lagarde to Min. 3e arrond., Police-Générale, 24 December 1810.

58 ANP F7 8820 (Gênes) Lagarde to Min. 3e arrond., Police-Générale, 2 January 1811.

59 ANP F7 8820 (Gênes) Prefect, Arne, to Min. 3e arrond., Police-Générale, 22 December 1810.

60 ANP F7 8820 (Gênes) Prefect, Arne, to Min. 3e arrond., Police-Générale, 22 December 1810.

61 ANP F7 8820 (Gênes) Prefect, Arne, to Min. 3e arrond., Police-Générale, 16 January 1811.

62 ANP F7 8820 (Gênes) Min. 3e arrond., Police-Générale, to Prefect, Arne, 21 December 1810.

63 ANP F7 8805 (Arne) Lagarde to Min. 3e arrond., Police-Générale, 10 December 1811.

64 ANP F7 8805 (Arne) Lagarde to Min. 3e arrond., Police-Générale, 1 February 1812.

65 ANP F7 8803 (Arne) Lagarde to Min. 3e arrond., Police-Générale, 16 March 1811.

66 ANP F7 8805 (Arne) Archbishop of Florence to Elisa, 30 November 1811.

67 ANP F7 8805 (Arne) Lagarde to Min. 3e arrond., Police-Générale, 1 February 1812.
68 ANP F7 8805 (Arne) Lagarde to Min. 3e arrond., Police-Générale, 6 July 1812.
69 ANP F7 8805 (Arne) Lagarde to Min. 3e arrond., Police-Générale, 28 October 1812.
70 ANP F7 8805 (Arne) Lagarde to Min. 3e arrond., Police-Générale, 30 April 1813.
71 ANP F7 8805 (Arne) Lagarde to Elisa, 20 December 1813.
72 ANP F7 8805 (Arne) Lagarde to Min. 3e arrond., Police-Générale, 26 October 1812.
73 ANP F19 1072A Archbishop of Florence to Min. Cultes, 11 March 1811.
74 ANP F19 1072A Min. 3e arrond., Police-Générale, to Min. Cultes, 9 May 1811.
75 ANP F7 8804 (Arne) Min. 3e arrond., Police-Générale, to Prefect, 2 September 1811.
76 ANP F7 8804 (Arne) Prefect to Elisa, 17 July 1811.
77 ANP F7 8804 (Arne) Lagarde to Min. 3e arrond., Police-Générale, 2 May 1812.
78 ANP F7 8804 (Arne) Lagarde to Elisa, 3 April 1812.
79 ANP F19 1072A Archbishop of Florence to Min. Cultes, 15 December 1812.
80 ANP F19 1072A Min. 3e arrond., Police-Générale, to Min. Cultes, 21 November 1812.
81 ANP F7 8805 (Arne) Lagarde to Min. 3e arrond., Police-Générale, 13 April 1813.
82 ANP F7 6523A Bulletin de Police: la Toscane, 1 August 1812.
83 ANP F7 8805 (Arne) Lagarde to Min. 3e arrond., Police-Générale, 16 July 1813.
84 ANP F7 8805 (Arne) Lagarde to Min. 3e arrond., Police-Générale, 26 October 1812.
85 AST Materie Politiche. Lettere Ministri, Roma, Mazzo 405 (1817) Registro II, Barbaroux, Rome, to For. Sec., Turin, 28 August 1817.
86 ANP AFIV 909 'Organisation des Dix Séminaires métropolitaines. Projet de Décret', 13 August 1806.
87 ANP F19 704 Min. Cultes to Napoleon, 27 August 1806.
88 ANP F19 355–6–7 Min. 3e arrond., Police-Générale, to Min. Cultes, 12 September 1811.
89 ANP F19 1081 Vicar-Gen. Casale, to Prefect, Genoa, 1 October 1810.
90 ANP F19 704 Bishop of Piacenza to Min. Cultes, 12 February 1810.
91 Zaghi, *Potere*, pp. 96–9.
92 Mori, 'Clero e istituzioni', p. 223.
93 ANP F19 355–6–7 Prefect, Méditerranée, to Min. Cultes, 6 May 1811.
94 ANP F19 355–6–7 Archbishop of Pisa to Min. Cultes, 6 May 1811.
95 Fatnappiè, *Riforme Ecclesiastiche*, pp. 399, 443.
96 L. Allegra, 'Il parocco: un mediatore fra alta e bassa cultura', *Storia d'Italia. Annali*, vol. 4, *Intellettuali e Potere* (Turin, 1981), pp. 895–950.
97 ANP F7 4308 Jourdan to Min. Police-Générale, 15 germinal an x/27 March 1802.
98 ANP F1E 85 Moreau de St-Méry to Eugène de Beauharnais, 29 December 1805.
99 Bullo, 'Dei movimenti', p. 77.
100 ANP F7 8791–2–3 (Apennines) Lagarde to Min. 3e arrond., Police-Générale, 16 June 1809.
101 Zaghi, *Potere*, pp. 71–4, 96–7.
102 ANP F7 8791–2–3 (Apennines) D'Auzers to Min. 3e arrond., Police-Générale, 28 June 1808.

103 ANP F7 8795 (Apennines) D'Auzers to Min. 3e arrond., Police-Générale, 2 April 1811.
104 ANP F7 8795 (Apennines) D'Auzers to Min. 3e arrond., Police-Générale, 20 May 1813.
105 ANP F7 8795 (Apennines) D'Auzers to Min. 3e arrond., Police-Générale, 3 August 1810.
106 ANP F7 8933 (Taro) Prefect to Min. 3e arrond., Police-Générale, 21 September 1810.
107 ANP F7 4308 Jourdan to Min. Police-Générale, 15 germinal an x/27 March 1802.
108 ANP F7 8934 (Trasimène) Prefect to Min. 3e arrond., Police-Générale, 8 March 1811.
109 ANP F7 8791–2–3 (Apennines) Prefect to Min. 3e arrond., Police-Générale, 16 August 1809.
110 Archivio di Stato di Cuneo (ASC) Epoca Francese, Mazzo 48 (Preti e Parrochi) S. Prefect, Saluzzo, to Prefect, Sture, 8 ventôse an xi/30 April 1803.
111 ASF Buon Governo 460 (1808) Petition of Nenci, Parocco of Bettolle, to President, Buon Governo, 21 March 1808.
112 ASF Buon Governo 460 (1808) Govenor of Siena to President, Buon Governo, 18 March, 1808.
113 ANP F19 703 Bishop of Casale to Bishop of Vercelli, 22 October 1805.
114 ANP F7 8867 (Ombronne) Prefect to Min. 3e arrond., Police-Générale, 21 May 1808.
115 Di Simplicio, *Peccato*, *passim*.
116 ANP F7 8867 (Ombronne) Lagarde to Min. 3e arrond., Police-Générale, 13 June 1810.
117 ANP F7 8867 (Ombronne) Prefect to Min. 3e arrond., Police-Générale, 7 May 1810.
118 ANP F7 8867 (Ombronne) Min. 3e arrond., Police-Générale, to Lagarde, 9 July 1810.
119 ANP F19 355–6–7 Cardinal Spina to Min. Cultes, 9 August 1812.
120 ANP BB18 700 Proc.-Gen., Cour Imp. Rome, to Min. Justice, 1 April 1812.
121 ANP BB18 700 Min. Justice to Min. Police-Générale, 18 April 1812.
122 ANP BB18 702 Proc.-Gen., Cour Imp. Rome, to Min. Justice, 24 December 1812.
123 ANP F19 1076 Bishop of Piacenza to Min. Cultes, 4 January 1807.
124 ANP F7 8805 (Arne) Lagarde to Min. 3e arrond., Police-Générale, 10 December 1811.
125 ANP F7 8935 (Trasimène) Norvins to Min. 3e arrond., Police-Générale, 20 July 1811.
126 ANP F1E 87–88 'Rapport sur la situation de l'Administration de l'arrondissement de Parme', 15 June 1806.
127 ANP AFIV 1046 'Circulaire du Ministre de Police-Générale aux Préfets et Commissaires-Généraux de l'Empire', 1 October 1809.
128 ANP F19 703 Bishop of Biella to Charbonnière, 28 vend. an. xi/20 October 1802.
129 ANP F19 703 'Plans rélatifs au circonscription des cures, Piémont', March 1810.
130 ANP F1E 87–88 Pierre Caragnari to Min. Interior, 26 August 1805.
131 Cited in Moulard, *Comte Camille*, vol. 2, p. 64.
132 ASG Prefettura Francese, Pacco 11, fasciolo 18 (Culto) 'Obsérvations sur le plan d'organisation des paroisses du Diocèse de Casal', 1810.
133 ANP F19 1076 Bishop of Montalcino to Min. Cultes, 2 September 1810.

134 ASF Prefettura dell'Arno 485 Sacerdote Lorenzo dei Pazzi of San Lorenzo, commune Marradi, to Menou, 4 August 1808.
135 ASG Prefettura Francese, Pacco 78, fasciolo 106 (Culto, pratiche diverse) S. Prefect, Novi, to Prefect, 2 December 1812.
136 ANP F7 8797 (Apennines) Norvins to Min. 3e arrond., Police-Générale, 24 August 1812.
137 ANP F7 8797 (Apennines) Norvins to Min. 3e arrond., Police-Générale, 11 August 1812.
138 ASG Prefettura Francese, Pacco 11, fasciolo 18 (Chiese e parrocchi) 'Réparations d'églises et presbytères', November 1811.
139 Joseph II also found a Church far poorer than he had imagined, and the constraints this placed on him were largely what prevented the full implementation of reforms that would have made the Church in the Austrian provinces very like that of 1791 in France. A compromise emerged, which left more dioceses and parishes in place than he wished, with revenues still administered by the Church, if under tighter state supervision: P.G.M. Dickson, 'Joseph II's reshaping of the Austrian Church', *Historical Journal*, 36 (1993), pp. 89–114.
140 ASF Prefettura dell'Arno 476, 'Obsérvations sur la translation de cures ou érections succusiales demandées par les Évêques des Diocèses du ci-devant État de la Toscane', Préfet de l'Arne, January 1811.
141 ANP F19 703 'Rapport sur la circonspection et limites des diocèses', 1810.
142 ANP F19 703 Bishop of Vercelli to Bishop of Casale, 1 March 1806.
143 ANP F19 703 Petitions of the People of Giara, 30 June 1808 and 4 January 1810.
144 ASG Prefettura Francese, Pacco 11, fasciolo 18 (Culto) Petition of the People of Sturla-Marina to Prefect (undated, *c.* autumn 1810).
145 ASG Prefettura Francese, Pacco 11, fasciolo 18 (Culto) Petition of the People of the parish of Santa Maria di Grenacolo (Genova-Extramuros) to Prefect, 23 October 1810.
146 ASG Prefettura Francese, Pacco 11, fasciolo 18 (Culto) Cardinal Spina to Prefect, 14 December 1812.
147 ASG Prefettura Francese, Pacco 11, fasciolo 18 (Culto) Maire, commune S. Fructuoso, to Prefect, 26 September 1810.
148 ASF Segretaria di Stato I, 820 (Lettere e Rapporti, 1808–9) Regio Diritto to Menou, 4 January 1808.
149 ASF Buon Governo 466 (1808) Sacerdote Clemente Querxi, commune Tizzana, to President, Buon Governo, 23 June 1808.
150 See ASG Prefettura Francese, Pacco 11, fasciolo 18 (Culto).
151 ANP F19 703 Prefect, Po, to Archbishop of Turin, 29 August 1809.
152 For an example of this, in the Fontanabuona, in the Ligurian hinterland: Raggio, *Faida*, pp. 233–8. Levroni, *Cicagna*, pp. 133–4. For its wider history: Bossy, 'Counter-Reformation', pp. 54–7.
153 ANP F7 8818 (Gênes) Prefect to Min. 3e arrond., Police-Générale, 20 May 1809.
154 ASG Prefettura Francese, Pacco 231, fasciolo 8 (Correspondenza, Prefetto, Culto) D'Auzers to Prefect, 24 May 1811.
155 ANP F7 8802 (Arne) Min. 3e arrond., Police-Générale, to Prefect, 12 January 1811.
156 ANP F7 8893 (Rome) Norvins to Min. 3e arrond., Police-Générale, 10 June 1810.
157 ASG Prefettura Francese, Pacco 163, fasciolo 219 (Pratiche relative al Culto) Maire of Voghera to Prefect, 12 October 1810.

158 ASG Prefettura Francese, Pacco 11, fasciolo 18 (Culto) Sen. Fabra to Prefect, 20 October 1812.

159 Fatnappiè, *Riforme Ecclesiastiche*, pp. 46–7.

160 ASF Prefettura dell'Arno 476, 'Obsérvations sur la translation de cures ou érections succusiales demandées par les Évêques des Diocèses du ci-devant État de la Toscane', January 1811.

161 ANP AFIV 1317 'Rapport sur la situation ecclésiastiques des ci-devant États de Parme, Plaisance et Guastelle', 5 February 1806.

162 J. Fava, '*La Historique* di Moreau de St-Méry', *Aurea Parma*, 69 (1985), pp. 74–83, 79.

163 Fatnappiè, *Riforme Ecclesiastiche*, pp. 47–50.

164 ANP F19 397 'Projet pour les diocèses romains', 21 May 1810.

165 ANP F19 397 'Rapport au Ministre', 6 October 1810.

166 Cited in Moulard, *Comte Camille*, vol. 2, pp. 63–4.

167 ANP F19 703 Prefect, Marengo, to Min. Justice, 2 ventôse an xi/20 February 1803.

168 ANP F20 102 'Rapport sur le budget de 1811. Obsérvations du Préfet', 5 December 1810.

169 ANP F19 1077 'Note pour le Ministre des Cultes, dictée par S.M. dans le Conseil des Ministres', 13 June 1810.

170 ASB Legazione e Prefettura di Bologna, Fondi Dipt Reno, Titolo XXIV Religione, 1810 (Rubrico 17: Chiese ed Oratori) Director of Domain to Prefect, 10 July 1810.

171 ANP F19 596 Prefect, Genoa, to Min. Cultes (undated, *c.* January 1811).

172 ASG Prefettura Francese, Pacco 11, fasciolo 18 (Culto) Petiton of the Curé and the People of San Vincenzo, Genoa, to Prefect (undated, *c.* autumn 1810).

173 ASG Prefettura Francese, Pacco 11, fasciolo 18 (Culto) Vicar-Gen., Archdiocese of Genoa, to S. Prefect, Genoa, 10 August 1811.

174 ASF Buon Governo 465 (1808) S. Prefect, Siena, to President, Buon Governo, 27 June 1808. Prefect, Mediterranée, to President, Buon Governo, 27 June 1808. Bishop of Pistoia to President, Buon Governo, 29 June 1808. S. Prefect, Arezzo, to President, Buon Governo, 30 June 1808.

175 ANP F19 1080 Archbishop of Florence to Min. Cultes, 7 May 1810.

176 ANP F19 1080 Min. Interior to Min. Cultes, 12 September 1811.

177 ASG Prefettura Francese, Pacco 12, fasciolo 19 (Chiese, confraterniti, missioni, conventi) Maire of Voghera to S. Prefect, Voghera, 27 April 1811.

178 ASG Prefettura Francese, Pacco 12, fasciolo 19 (Chiese, confraterniti, missioni, conventi) Vicar-Gen. Casale to Prefect, 4 June 1811.

179 Moulard, *Comte Camille*, vol. 2, p. 70.

180 ANP F19 1079 Min. Cultes to Miollis, 13 April 1811.

181 ANP F7 8906 (Rome) Roederer to Min. 3e arrond., Police-Générale, 30 January 1811.

182 ASG Prefettura Francese, Pacco 163, fasciolo 219 (Pratiche relative al Culto) S. Prefect, Genoa, to Prefect, 20 fruct. an xiii/7 September 1805.

183 Hanson, *Early Modern Italy*, pp. 122–32.

184 ANP F19 894 Tardy to Min. Cultes, 10 March 1809.

185 ANP F19 355–6–7 Bishop of Chiusi and Pienza to Min. Cultes, 8 July 1811.

186 ANP F19 355–6–7 Min. Cultes to Bishop of Chiusi and Pienza, 27 September 1811.

187 ANP F19 397 'Rapport fait par M. le Baron Dalpozzo à la Consulte, Séance du 31 décembre 1810'.

188 ANP F19 397 Min. Cultes to Tournon, 5 November 1813.

189 ANP AFIV 1317 'Rapport sur la situation ecclésiastiques des ci-devant États de Parme, Plaisance et Guastelle', 5 February 1806.
190 Tocci, 'I Ducati Padani', p. 319.
191 ANP F19 1072A Min. Police-Générale to Min. Cultes, 18 January 1810.
192 ASF Buon Governo 461 (1808) Archbishop of Pisa to President, Buon Governo, 14 April 1808.
193 ANP AFIV 1317 Cardinal Fesch to Napoleon, 23 floréal an xii/13 May 1804.
194 ANP F7 8906 (Rome) Police Comm., Genoa, to Min. 3e arrond., Police-Générale, 15 September 1810.
195 ANP AFIV 1303 'Vues sur l'organisation du Culte Catholique', 1812.
196 Moulard, *Comte Camille*, vol. 2 , p. 70.
197 AG Serie C4–41 (Correspondance du Maréchal Junot, Gouverneur-Général des États de Parme, Plaisance et Guastelle, janvier–juillet, 1806) Junot to Bishop of San Donnino, 18 March 1806.
198 ANP F19 703 Min. Cultes to Napoleon, 5 therm. an xiii/25 July 1805.
199 ANP F1E 85 'Rapport au Ministre de l'Interieur', 8 prairial an xiii/19 May 1805.
200 ANP F1E 87–88 'Rapport sur la situation de l'Administration de Parme', 15 June 1806.
201 N. Watchel, 'Acculturation', in J. Le Goff and P. Nora (eds), *Faire de l'histoire* (Paris, 1974), pp. 130–1.
202 ANP F7 6523A S. Prefect, Pisa, to Lagarde, 30 March 1813.
203 ANP F7 8805 (Arne) Lagarde to Min. 3e arrond., Police-Générale, 6 July 1812.
204 Moulard, *Comte Camille*, vol. 2, pp. 119–20.
205 Latreille, *L'Église*, vol. 2, p. 117.
206 C. Maylole de Lupé, *La captivité de Pie VII* (2 vols; Paris, 1916), vol. 2, p. 22.
207 E.E.Y. Hales, *Napoleon and the Pope* (London, 1962), pp. 146–7.
208 Harris, *Lourdes*, p. 14.
209 Ibid., esp. pp. 219–20 on the role of the Assumptionists in late nineteenth-century France in this process.
210 Ibid., *passim* on this process.
211 ANP AFIV 1046 Min. Cultes to Napoleon, 7 July 1807.
212 Cited in Zaghi, *Potere*, p. 515.
213 McManners, *Church and Society*, vol. 1, pp. 571–614.
214 He did not even succeed in this in the Austrian provinces: Dickson, 'Joseph II'.
215 For a recent overview: C. Capra, 'Stato e Chiesa in Italia negli anni di Giuseppe II', in H. Reinalter (ed.), *Der Jodephinismus. Bedeutung, Einflüsse und Wirkungen*, (Frankfurt, 1999), pp. 103–19.
216 Tocci, 'I Ducati Padani', pp. 299, 306.
217 Zaghi, *Potere*, pp. 509–12.
218 Assereto, *Repubblica Ligure*, pp. 86–7.
219 ANP AFIV 1046 Min. Cultes to Napoleon, 11 September 1811.
220 F. Carabellese (ed.), *In Terra di Bari dal 1799 al 1806* (Trani, 1900), p. xxxviii.
221 J. Borel, *Gênes sous Naopoléon 1er* (Paris, 1929), pp. 46–7.
222 Chiuso, *Chiesa*, vol. 2, pp. 168–78.
223 ANP F19 355–6–7 Jourdan to Min. Cultes, 2 prairial an x/22 May 1802.
224 ANP F19 355–6–7 Jourdan to Min. Cultes, 2 prairial an x/22 May 1802.
225 ANP F19 355–6–7 Jourdan to Min. Cultes, 2 prairial an x/22 May 1802.
226 Moulard, *Comte Camille*, vol. 2, pp. 54–5.
227 ANP AFIV 1303 Min. Cultes to Napoleon, 13 October 1810.
228 ANP AFIV 1317 'Rapport sur la situation ecclésiastique des ci-devant États de Parme, Plaisance et Guastelle', 5 February 1806.
229 ANP AFIV 1045 Min. Cultes to Napoleon, 20 floréal an xiii/9 June 1805.

230 ANP F19 596 Imperial Decree, St Cloud, 13 September 1810.
231 ASG Prefettura Francese, Pacco 163, fasciolo 219 (Pratiche relative al Culto) Min. Cultes to Prefect, 18 December 1811. Cardinal Spina to Prefect, 11 December 1807.
232 ASF Buon Governo 466 (1808) President, Buon Governo, to Giunta di Governo, 2 July 1808.
233 ANP AFIV 909 Napoleon to Min. Cultes, 14 April 1806.
234 ANP AFIV 1045 Min. Cultes to Napoleon, 16 fructidor an xiii/3 September 1805.
235 ASF Buon Governo 467 (1808) President, Buon Governo, to the Vicari, February 1808.
236 ANP F7 6523A Bulletin de Police: la Toscane, 2 October 1810.
237 ANP F19 1077 'Note pour le Ministre des Cultes dictée par S.M. dans le Conseil des Ministres', 13 June 1810.
238 Moulard, *Comte Camille*, vol. 2, p. 56.
239 ANP F19 1077 'Note pour le Ministre des Cultes dictée par S.M. dans le Conseil des Ministres', 13 June 1810.
240 C.A. Naselli, *La soppressione napoleonica delle corporazione religiose. Contributo alla storia religiosa del primo ottocento italiano* (Rome, 1986), p. 12. ANP AFIV 1047 Min. Cultes to Napoleon, 31 May 1810 puts the figure at 5,145.
241 Tournon to Janet, 5 June 1810, *Lettres inédites*.
242 Tournon to Janet, 12 June 1810, ibid.
243 Moulard, *Comte Camille*, vol. 2, esp. pp. 57–8.
244 ANP F19 1077 'Rapport fait par M. Dal Pozzo sur les évenéments qui ont lieu la nuit du 14–15 juin, 1810'.
245 ASB Legazione e Prefettura di Bologna, Fondi Dipt Reno, Titolo XXIV (Religione) 1810, Rubriche 13–17, Mother Superior, Convent of Santa Maria Maddalena, Cento, to Prefect, 15 May 1810.
246 ANP F7 8906 (Rome) Prefect to Min. 3e arrond., Police-Générale, 10 October 1810.
247 ANP F7 8935 (Trasimène) Prefect to Min. 3e arrond. Police-Générale, 30 August 1813.
248 G.F. Sconamiglio, 'L'Alta Valdarda all'inizio del 1800', *Archivio Storico per le Provincie Parmensi*, Serie IV, 28 (1976), pp. 155–60.
249 ASF Prefettura dell'Arno 476, Prefect to Min. 3e arrond., Police-Générale, 28 August 1810.
250 ASF Prefettura dell'Arno 476, Prefect to Min. 3e arrond., Police-Générale, 28 August 1810.
251 Tournon to Dal Pozzo, 18 May 1810, *Lettres inédites*.
252 ASF Buon Governo 467 (1808) Procuratore of the Camaldi Hermits to President, Buon Governo (undated, c. February 1808).
253 For the zeal with which the regime prosecuted *délits forestiers*: I. Woloch, *The New Regime. Transformations of the French Civic Order, 1789–1820s* (New York, 1994), p. 358. On the origins of the problem and the Code: O. Festy, *Les Délits ruraux et leurs répression sous la Révolution, le Directoire et le Consulat* (Paris, 1956).
254 ACG Impero Francese, Correspondenza, Registro 222 (1810–11) Maire of Genoa to Prefect, 22 October 1811.
255 Cited in L. Ginetti, 'Sull'insurrezzione dell'alto piacentino nel 1805–1806', *Aurea Parma*, 2 (1913), pp. 205–10, 205.
256 ANP F7 8906 (Rome) Roederer to Min. 3e arrond., Police-Générale, 30 January 1811.

257 ANP F19 1082 S. Prefect, Perugia, to Prefect, Trasimène, 15 October 1810.

258 ANP F7 8935 (Trasimène) Prefect to Min. 3e arrond., Police-Générale, 22 May 1812.

259 The nuances detected by Plongeron among the Parisian regulars in 1791 seem absent here. The division between the propertied and mendicant orders in the Papal states was clearer: B. Plongeron, *Les Réguliers de Paris devant le Serment Constitutionelle* (Paris, 1964), p. 429.

260 ANP F7 8906 (Rome) Roederer to Min. 3e arrond., Police-Générale, 30 January 1811.

261 ANP F19 1082 Roederer to Min. Cultes, 16 April 1813.

262 ASB Legazione e Prefettura di Bologna, Fondi Dipt Reno, Titolo XXIV Religione, 1810. (Rubico 19: Soppressione di Conventi) Vicar-General, Archdiocese of Bologna, to Prefect, 13 August 1810.

263 M. Dall'Aglio Maramotti, *L'Assistenza ai poveri nella Parma del Settecento* (Reggio Emilia, 1985), p. 91.

264 ANP AFIV 1317 'Rapport sur la situation ecclésiastique des ci-devant États de Parme, Plaisance et Guastelle', 5 February 1806.

265 ASB Legazione e Prefettura di Bologna, Fondi Dipt Reno, Titolo XXIV Religione, 1810. (Rubico 17: Chiese ed Oratori) Vicar-General, Archdiocese of Bologna, to Prefect, 3 July 1810.

266 ASG Prefettura Francese, Pacco 145, fasciolo 188 (Culto e Polizia) Maire of Voghera to Prefect, 12 May 1809.

267 ASG Prefettura Francese, Pacco 145, fasciolo 188 (Culto e Polizia) Min. Cultes to Prefect, 13 June 1809.

268 ANP F19 1082 Tournon to Min. Cultes, 26 July 1810.

269 ASB Legazione e Prefettura di Bologna, Fondi Dipt Reno, Titolo XXIV Religione (1810) (Rubrico 17: Chiese ed Oratori) 'Istruzione per l'esecuzione del Reale Decreto di 25 aprile', 1810.

270 ANP F7 6523A Bulletin de Police: la Toscane, 12 October 1810.

271 ANP AFIV 909 Napoleon to Min. Cultes, 14 April 1810.

272 ASF Buon Governo 467 (1808) Petition of Frà Francesco Antonio Carme to President, Buon Governo, 20 February 1808.

273 ANP AFIV 945 Min. Cultes to Napoleon, 18 June 1806.

274 ACG Impero Francese, Correspondenza, Registro 222 (1810–11) Maire of Genoa to Maire of Todi, 14 November 1810.

275 ANP F19 1079 Miollis to Min. Cultes, 15 June 1812.

276 ANP F19 1072A Inspector-Gen. Comdt Gend. 29th Military Division to Min. Cultes, 27 February 1811.

277 ASF Segretario di Stato I. Protocolli 1140 (1808) for these invitations.

278 ANP F19 1076 Min. Cultes to Bishop of Sarazana, 2 January 1810.

279 ANP F19 1076 Bishop of Sarazana to Min. Cultes, 16 January 1810.

280 See ANP F19 1078 for these responses.

281 ANP F19 1078 Bishop of Civita Castellana to Min. Cultes, 26 August 1813.

282 ANP F19 1076 Min. Cultes to Bishop of Savona, 3 February 1810.

283 ANP F19 1079 Min. 3e arrond., Police-Générale, to Min. Cultes, 30 May 1814.

284 ANP F19 894 Tardy to Min. Cultes, 10 March 1809.

285 ASF Buon Governo 409 (1808) for these petitions.

286 ASB Legazione e Prefettura di Bologna, Fondi Dipt Reno, 1811. Titolo XX, Polizia (Rubrico 4: Oziozi e Mendicanti) Gend. Capt. to Prefect, 8 November 1811.

287 ANP F19 1072A Vicar-General, diocese of Montefiascone, to Min. Cultes, 18 April 1812.

288 ANP F19 1079 Bishop of Montefiascone to Min. Cultes, 20 July 1811.

289 ANP F19 1082 Tournon to Min. Cultes, 26 July 1810.
290 ANP F19 1081 Min. Cultes to Napoleon, 23 March 1810.
291 ACG Impero Francese, Correspondenza, Filiza 220 (1808) Maire to Min. Cultes, 15 September 1808.
292 ACG Impero Francese, Correspondenza, Filiza 220 (1808) Prefect to Maire, 24 October 1808.
293 ANP F19 1072B Miollis to Min. Cultes, 17 March 1812.
294 ANP F7 8893 (Rome) Miollis to Min. Cultes, 20 June 1811.
295 AST, AC Segretaria di Stato per Affari Interni, Serie V, Miscellanea, Registro Lettere, Buon Governo e Polizia (1814–1820), President, Buon Governo, to Preffeto of Tortona, 11 March 1817. Cited in Broers, 'Sexual Politics', p. 619.
296 AST Materie Politiche. Lettere Ministri. Roma. Mazzo 405 (1818) Registro II, Barbaroux, Rome, to For. Sec., Turin, 12 March 1818.
297 Moulard, *Comte Camille*, vol. 2, p. 67.
298 ANP F19 1072A Min. Police-Générale to Min. Cultes, 18 January 1810.
299 ANP F19 1082 S. Prefect, Perugia, to Roederer, 15 October 1810.
300 ACG Municipio Francese, Filiza 317 (Stabilimenti religiosi, 1806–1814) Prefect to Maire, 18 June 1813.
301 ANP F19 1079 Min. 3e arrond., Police-Générale, to Min. Cultes, 29 April 1813.
302 ANP F19 1072B Maire of Moncrivello to Bishop of Vercelli, 8 June 1809. Bishop of Vercelli to Min. Cultes, 11 September 1809.
303 ANP F7 8935 (Trasimène) Norvins to Min. 3e arrond., Police-Générale, 22 May 1811.
304 ANP F7 8935 (Trasimène) Norvins to Min. 3e arrond., Police-Générale, 11 June 1811.
305 ANP AFIV 1046 Min. Cultes to Napoleon, 15 July 1807.
306 ANP F7 8802 (Arne) Lagarde to Min. 3e arrond., Police-Générale, 3 November 1811.
307 ASB Legazione e Prefettura di Bologna, Fondi Dipt Reno, Titolo XXIV Religione (1810) (Rubrico 19: Soppressione di Conventi) D. Gen. Police, Milan, to Prefect, 28 June 1810.
308 ASB Legazione e Prefettura di Bologna, Fondi Dipt Reno, Titolo XXIV Religione. (1810) (Rubrico 19: Soppressione di Conventi) Prefect to D. Gen. Police, Milan, 6 July 1810.
309 Watchel, 'Acculturation', pp. 130–1.
310 ANP AFIV 1045 Min. Cultes to Napoleon, 16 fructidor an xiii/3 September 1805.
311 ANP F7 8795 (Apennines) D'Auzers to Min. 3e arrond., Police-Générale, 20 July 1810.
312 Fantappiè, *Riforme Ecclesiastiche*, pp. 65–7.
313 ANP F19 596 Prefect, Arne, to Min. Cultes, 1810.
314 ASB Legazione e Prefettura di Bologna, Fondi Dipt Reno, Titolo XXIV Religione (1810) (Rubrico 17: Chiese ed Oratori) 'Istruzione per l'esecuzione del Reale Decreto di 25 aprile', 1810.
315 ASB Legazione e Prefettura di Bologna, Fondi Dipt Reno, Titolo XXIV Religione. (1810) (Rubrico 19: Soppressione di Conventi) Prefect to Podestà, comune Burdio, 16 August 1810.
316 ASB Legazione e Prefettura di Bologna, Fondi Dipt Reno, Titolo XXIV Religione. (1810) (Rubrico 19: Soppressione di Conventi) Prefect to Vice-Prefetto, Imola, 9 October 1811.
317 ANP F19 1079 Prefect, Po, to Min. Cultes, 6 July 1810.

318 AST Intendenza di Pinerolo, Sezione IV (Correspondenza) Cat. 2 (Epoca Francese), Articolo 50 (1811) D'Auzers to S. Prefect, Pinerolo, 29 December 1812.
319 A. Spina (ed.), *Diario della deportazione in Corsica del canonico di Albano G.B. Loberti (1810–1814)* (Albano, 1985), p. 8. Also cited in Nardi, *Napoleone e Roma*, p. 148.
320 E. Duffy, *The Stripping of the Altars. Traditional Religion in England 1400–1580* (London and New Haven, 1992), pp. 587, 593.
321 ASB Legazione e Prefettura di Bologna, Fondi Dipt Reno, Titolo XXIV (1810) Rubrico 18 (Confraternite e Consorzi Secolari) D. Gen. Police, Milan, to Prefect, 2 June 1810.
322 ANP F19 1082 Tournon to Min. Cultes, 26 July 1810.
323 ANP F19 1075 'Dichiarazione del Clero di Siena sul giuramento di religiosi soppressi', 15 October 1810.

Chapter 6: The Roman clergy and the crisis of the Oath

1 Latreille, *L'Église*, pp. 117–8.
2 Roberts, 'Napoleon', p. 45.
3 For the fullest account of the Italian Concordat: Zaghi, *Potere*, pp. 501–627.
4 Cited in Latreille, *L'Église*, pp. 111–2.
5 Cited in ibid., p. 116.
6 Ibid.
7 ANP F7 6530 1st Instruction, 22 May 1808.
8 ANP F19 1925 'À la perpetuelle mémoire de la chose', 10 June 1809.
9 ANP F19 703 Cacault to Min. Cultes, 18 ventôse an xi/29 April 1803.
10 ANP AFIV 1045 Min. Cultes to Napoleon, 14 thermidor an xii/2 August 1804.
11 ANP AFIV 1045 Min. Cultes to Napoleon, 16 fructidor an xiii/3 September 1805.
12 Latreille, *L'Église*, pp. 119–20. On Lucca: pp. 112–3.
13 Ibid., pp. 114–6.
14 Ibid., p. 117.
15 ANP F7 8936 (Trasimène) Prefect to Min. 3e arrond., Police-Générale, 10 February 1812.
16 ANP F19 1077 'Note pour M. le Ministre des Cultes, dictée par S.M. dans le Conseil des Ministres', 13 June 1810.
17 For a statistical approach, but lacking Parisian sources: A. Mercati, 'Elenchi di ecclesiastici dello Stato Romano deportati per rifiuto del giuramento imposta da Napoleone', *Rivista di Storia della Chiesa in Italia*, 7 (1953), pp. 51–98.
18 Tackett, *Religion*, p. 288 notes that non-juring increased with distance from Paris and the central belt in France, the revolutionary power centre. The initial but short-lived behaviour as regards Rome displays a similar pattern of conformity related to proximity to the political centre.
19 ANP F7 8906 (Rome) Norvins to Min. 3e arrond., Police-Générale, 23 July 1811.
20 ANP F19 1077 Miollis to Min. Cultes, 31 July 1810.
21 ANP F7 8887 (Rome) Norvins to Min. 3e arrond., Police-Générale, 19 August 1810.
22 ANP F7 8936 (Trasimène) S. Prefect, Perugia, to Min. Police-Générale, 13 April 1811.
23 ANP F7 8934 (Trasimène) Min. 3e arrond., Police-Générale to Prefect, June 1811.

24 C. Langlois, 'La rupture entre l'Église Catholique et la Révolution', in F. Furet and M. Ozouf (eds), *The French Revolution and the Creation of Modern Political Culutre* (3 vols; Oxford, 1989), vol. 3, *The Transformation of Political Culture 1789–1848*, pp. 375–90, 382.

25 Roberts, 'Napoleon', p. 40.

26 Tackett, *Religion*, pp. 287–99.

27 On France: Tackett, *Religion, passim*. On the Cisapline Republic: A. Valenti, 'Il dibattito sul giuramento civico nella Repubblica Cisalpina', in Menozzi, *Chiesa Italiana*, pp. 181–232.

28 Zaghi, *Potere*, p. 589.

29 Plongeron, *Réguliers*, p. 427.

30 Tackett, *Religion*, pp. 41–4. Most of the oaths so denounced were invalid, having been restrictive oaths in the first place, but this was not clear to contemporary observers.

31 Roberts, 'Napoleon', p. 49.

32 ANP F7 6530 Bulletin de Savone, 16 July 1810.

33 Lupé, *Captivité*, vol. 1, p. 15.

34 ANP F7 6530 Bulletin de Savone, 16 July 1810.

35 ANP F7 8906 (Rome) Norvins to Min. 3e arrond., Police-Générale, 11 December 1811.

36 ANP F7 8903 (Rome) Tournon to Min. 3e arrond., Police-Générale, 27 April 1813.

37 Bossy, 'Mass', pp. 52–3.

38 H.W. Smith, *German Nationalism and Religious Conflict. Culture, ideology, politics, 1870–1914* (Princeton, 1995), p. 46.

39 ANP F7 8906 (Rome) Prefect, Trasimène, to Min. 3e arrond., Police-Générale, 13 October 1810.

40 ANP F7 8906 (Rome) Prefect, Trasimène, to Min. 3e arrond., Police-Générale, 18 August 1810.

41 ANP F7 8906 (Rome) Norvins to Min. 3e arrond., Police-Générale, 13 October 1810.

42 ANP F7 8906 (Rome) Roederer to Min. 3e arrond., Police-Générale, 3 August 1810.

43 Tackett, *Religion*, pp. 290–1.

44 ANP F7 8906 (Rome) Tournon to Min. 3e arrond., Police-Générale, 3 August 1810.

45 ANP F7 8906 (Rome) Norvins to Min. 3e arrond., Police-Générale, 22 July 1812.

46 ANP F7 8906 (Rome) Tournon to Min. 3e arrond., Police-Générale, 3 August 1810.

47 P. Prodi, *The Papal Prince. One body and two souls: the papal monarchy in early modern Europe*, trans. Susan Haskins (Cambridge, 1987), pp. 154–6.

48 ANP F7 8889 (Rome) Police Comm., Civitavecchia, to Min. 3e arrond., Police-Générale, 19 November 1810.

49 ANP F7 8889 (Rome) Police Comm., Civitavecchia, to Min. 3e arrond., Police-Générale, 8 October 1810.

50 ANP F7 8888 (Rome) Norvins to Min. 3e arrond., Police-Générale, 1 April 1811.

51 Hufton, 'The Reconstruction', pp. 21–52.

52 ANP F19 1079 Norvins to Miollis, 27 June 1813.

53 ANP F7 8934 (Trasimène) Roederer to Min. 3e arrond., Police-Générale, 15 May 1811.

54 ANP F7 8936 (Trasimène) Roederer to Min. 3e arrond., Police-Générale, 24 May 1812.

55 ANP F7 8894 (Rome) Norvins to Min. 3e arrond., Police-Générale, 10 August 1810.

56 ANP F7 6530 Roederer to Min. 3e arrond., Police-Générale, 26 April 1810.

57 ANP F7 6530 Roederer to Min. 3e arrond., Police-Générale, 26 April 1810.

58 ANP F7 8936 (Trasimène) S. Prefect, Foligno, to Min. 3e arrond., Police-Générale, 21 January 1811.

59 ANP F19 1079 Norvins to Miollis, 27 June 1813.

60 ANP F7 8935 (Trasimène) Min. 3e arrond., Police-Générale, to Min. 2e arrond., Police-Générale, 15 April 1811.

61 ANP F7 8935 (Trasimène) Norvins to Min. 3e arrond., Police-Générale, 17 September 1811.

62 ANP F7 8935 (Trasimène) Roederer to Min. Cultes, 12 April 1811.

63 ANP F7 8935 (Trasimène) Norvins to Min. 3e arrond., Police-Générale, 10 January 1812.

64 ANP F7 8935 (Trasimène) Roederer to Min. 3e arrond., Police-Générale, 29 December 1810.

65 ANP F7 8935 (Trasimène) Norvins to Min. 3e arrond., Police-Générale, 3 January 1810.

66 On Umbria: ANP F7 8934 (Trasimène) Roederer to Min. 3e arrond., Police-Générale, 12 December 1810. On the Papal states as a whole: ANP AFIV 1047 Miollis to Min. Cultes, 1 August 1810. Miollis to Min. 3e arrond., Police-Générale, 6 September 1811.

67 ANP F7 8936 (Trasimène) Miollis to Min. 3e arrond., Police-Générale, 6 September 1811.

68 ANP F7 8906 (Rome) Norvins to Min. 3e arrond., Police-Générale, 2 February 1813.

69 ANP F7 7018 (Rome) Norvins to Min. 3e arrond., Police-Générale, 2 August 1811.

70 ANP F7 8893 (Rome) Norvins to Min. 3e arrond., Police-Générale, 29 July 1811.

71 ANP BB18 700 Min. Justice to Napoleon, 31 October 1811.

72 ANP BB18 700 Proc.-Gen.-Imp. Cour Imp. Rome, to Min. Justice, 16 July 1811.

73 ANP BB18 700 1st President, Cour Imp. Rome, to Min. Justice, 20 April 1812.

74 These figures are taken from two consolidated lists: ANP F19 1077 'État nominatif des prêtres romains déportés', 3 September 1812, and F19 1082 Min. Cultes to Napoleon, 5 June 1812. These figures correspond to those in Mercati, 'Elenchi', passim. Those given in Chadwick, Popes, are misleadingly small because they are only for department Rome and do not include that of Trasimène, thus rendering his verdict false that 'a majority was not persuaded of the sacredness of the temporal power.' Chadwick puts the figures at 15 juring bishops and 900 juring priests to 9 non-juring bishops and 500 non-juring priests: p. 513. Nor was the temporal power the real point of the protest.

75 ANP F7 8906 (Rome) Police Comm., Civitavecchia, to Min. 3e arrond., Police-Générale, 22 June 1810.

76 ANP F19 1077 Prefect, Taro, to Min. Cultes, 22 January 1811.

77 ANP F19 1077 Prefect, Taro, to Min. Cultes, 4 April 1811.

78 ANP F7 8905 (Rome) Police Comm., La Spezia, to Min. 3e arrond., Police-Générale, 12 April 1811.

79 ASB Legazione e Prefettura di Bologna, Fondi Dipt Reno, Titolo XXIV (1813) Rubrico 6 (Religione) Prefect to Police Comm., district of Levante, 22 February 1813.

80 F7 8905 (Rome) D'Auzers to Min. 3e arrond., Police-Générale, 2 May 1813.

81 Tackett, *Religion*, p. 289.

82 Archivio di Stato di Parma (ASP) Fondo Dipartimento del Taro. Sezione II. Buste 69. Fasciolo 104 (Preti Romani, 1810) S. Prefect, Piacenza, to Prefect, 1 July 1810.

83 ASP Fondo Dipartimento del Taro. Sezione II. Buste 69. Fasciolo 104 (Preti Romani, 1810) Min. Cultes to Prefect, 6 August 1810.

84 ASP Fondo Dipartimento del Taro. Sezione II. Buste 69. Fasciolo 104 (Preti Romani, 1810) S. Prefect, Parma, to Prefect, 10 August 1810.

85 ASP Fondo Dipartimento del Taro. Sezione II. Buste 69. Fasciolo 104 (Preti Romani, 1810) Bishop of Parma to Prefect, 12 August 1810.

86 ASP Fondo Dipartimento del Taro. Sezione II. Buste 69. Fasciolo 104 (Preti Romani, 1810) Min. Cultes to Prefect, 17 September 1810.

87 ASP Fondo Dipartimento del Taro. Sezione II. Buste 69. Fasciolo 104 (Preti Romani, 1810) Min. Cultes to Prefect, 27 June 1810.

88 ASP Fondo Dipartimento del Taro. Sezione II. Buste 69. Fasciolo 104 (Preti Romani, 1810) S. Prefect, Piacenza, to Prefect, 6 August 1810.

89 ASB Legazione e Prefettura di Bologna, Fondi Dipt Reno, Titolo XXIV (1810) Rubrico 6 (Ecclesiastici in genere) Podestà, Bologna, to Prefect, 8 December 1810.

90 ANP F19 1021 For. Min., Kingdom of Italy, to Min. Cultes, 5 March 1811.

91 ASB Legazione e Prefettura di Bologna, Fondi Dipt Reno, Titolo XXIV (1813) Rubrico 6 (Ecclesiastici in genere) Prefect to Chief of Police, Bologna, 26 July 1813.

92 ANP F7 8907 (Rome) Commander-in-Chief, Corsica, to Min. 3e arrond., Police-Générale, 13 August 1812.

93 ANP F19 1021 Vicar-Gen., Parma, to Min. Cultes, 24 December 1810.

94 ANP F19 1019 Vicar-Gen., Parma, to Min. Cultes, 22 January 1811.

95 ANP F19 1019 Roederer to Min. Cultes, 14 August 1811.

96 ANP F19 1019 Prefect, Taro, to Min. Cultes, 2 September 1811.

97 ANP F19 1019 Maire of Poggio to Min. Cultes, 29 March 1811.

98 ANP F19 1019 Maire of Rieti to Min. Cultes, 29 June 1810. Maire of Bastia to Min. Cultes, 14 January 1811.

99 ANP F19 1020 Maire of Valentano to S. Prefect, Viterbo, 2 December 1811.

100 ASB Legazione e Prefettura di Bologna, Fondi Dipt Reno, Titolo XXIV (1813) Rubrico 6 (Ecclesiastici in genere) Prefect to Chief of Police, Bologna, 26 July 1813.

101 ANP F7 8932 (Taro) Min. 3e arrond., Police-Générale, to Min. Police-Générale, 27 September 1812.

102 ANP F19 1019 Vicar-Gen., Parma, to Min. Cultes, 3 September 1810.

103 ANP F7 8931 (Taro) Prefect to Min. 3e arrond., Police-Générale, 22 January 1811.

104 ANP F7 7017 (Gênes) Comm. Gen. Police, Genoa, to Min. Police-Générale, 20 February 1811.

105 ANP F19 1022 Prefect, Taro, to Min. Cultes, 12 June 1812.

106 ANP F19 1021 Prefect, Taro, to Min. Cultes, 24 June 1812.

107 ANP F19 1021 For. Min., Kingdom of Italy, to Min. Cultes, 10 February 1813.

108 ANP F19 1021 Min. Cultes to Napoleon, 7 April 1813.

109 ANP F19 1077 Prefect, Taro, to Min. Cultes, 31 March 1813.

110 ANP F19 1021 Prefect, Taro, to Min. Cultes, 24 June 1812.

111 ANP F19 1079 Norvins to Miollis, 27 June 1813.

112 ANP F19 1077 Prefect, Taro, to Min. Cultes, 23 July 1812.

113 ANP F19 1077 'État nominatif des prêtres déportés dans l'Île de Corse, du 14 séptembre 1812 au 1re janvier, 1813'.

114 ANP F19 1077 Prefect, Po, to Min. Cultes, 8 October 1812.

115 ANP F19 1077 Min. Cultes to Napoleon, 2 July 1813.

116 ANP F19 1077 Min. Cultes to Napoleon, 12 July 1813.

117 ANP F7 8826 (Gênes) 'Rapport administratif et politique de la ville de Gênes', January 1811.

118 ANP F19 1077 Tournon to Min. Cultes, 7 August 1812.

119 ANP F7 7016 (Florence) Bulletin, 3 February 1813.

120 ANP F7 7018 (Rome) Bulletin, 2 February 1813.

121 ANP F7 7018 (Rome) Bulletin, 6 February 1813.

122 ANP F7 7018 (Rome) Bulletin, 11 February 1813.

123 ANP F7 7016 (Florence) Bulletin, 3 March 1813.

124 ANP F7 7018 (Rome) Bulletin, 24 February 1813.

125 ANP F7 7016 (Florence) Bulletin, 3 March 1813.

126 ANP F7 7018 (Rome) Bulletin, 8 March 1813.

127 ANP F7 7018 (Rome) Bulletin, 18 March 1813.

128 ANP F7 7016 (Florence) Bulletin, 3 March 1813.

129 Lefon, *Pie VII*, pp. 66–87.

130 Pignatelli, *Aspetti*. On Jansenism: M. Rosa, 'Jansénisme et Révolution en Italie', in C. Maire (ed.), *Jansénisme et Révolution* (Paris, 1990), pp. 229–40.

131 Gramsci, 'Senso Comune, Religione e Filosofia', in *Religione*, pp. 160–1.

132 M. Caffiero, 'Rivoluzione e millenio. Le correnti millenaristiche in Italia nel periodo rivoluzionario', in B. Plongeron (ed.), *Pratiques religieuses dans l'Europe révolutionnaire (1770–1820)* (Paris, 1988), pp. 95–104.

133 Blackbourn, *Marpingen*, p. 364.

134 Russo, 'Religosità', p. 143.

135 Rosa, 'Italian Churches', pp. 75 6.

136 Smith, *German Nationalism*, p. 47.

137 Gramsci, 'I popolari', *L'Ordine Nuovo*, 1 September 1919, in *Religione*, p. 96.

138 M. Clark, *Modern Italy, 1871–1982* (Harlow, 1984), pp. 86–7. Leveroni, *Cicagna*, pp. 208ff. for a local example of the depopulation of the Ligurian periphery and the impact of economic dislocation on a centre of popular piety, in the course of the late nineteenth century.

139 Clark, *Modern Italy*, p. 86.

140 Zaghi, *Potere*, pp. 87–8.

141 Ibid., pp. 87–9.

142 M. Cuaz, *Le Nuove di Francia. L'immagine della rivoluzione francese nella stampa periodica italiana (1787–1795)* (Turin, 1990), pp. 188–94.

143 Blackbourn, 'Progress and Piety'. Sperber, *Popular Catholicism*, pp. 207–29. Smith, *German Nationalism*, pp. 42–4.

144 ANP F7 7018 (Rome) Bulletin, 2 August 1811.

145 ANP F1bII (Rome, 1810–13) Roederer to Min. Interior, 30 April 1810.

146 ANP F7 8826 (Gênes) 'Rapport administratif et politique de la ville de Gênes', January 1811.

147 ANP F7 6530 Instruction of 22 May 1808.

Chapter 7: The war against God

1 The thesis of Prosperi, *Tribunali*.

2 Brizzi, *Formazzione*, pp. 236–48.

3 Chadwick, *Popes*, p. 95.
4 Blackbourn, *Marpingen*, pp. 361–3.
5 Blackbourn, 'Populists and Patricians', p. 144.
6 For a regional example, based on the northern province of Sonora in the 1860s, which led to the later revolt in the 1890s: P. Vanderwood, *The Power of God against the Guns of the Government. Religious Upheaval in Mexico at the turn of the Twentieth Century* (Stanford, 1998), pp. 49–59.
7 Gibson, *Social History*, pp. 139–40.
8 Sperber, *Popular Catholicism*, p. 13.
9 Ibid., pp. 24–31.
10 Gibson, *Social History*, p. 140. On the estrangement between the restored Church and sections of the laity: M. Lyons, 'Fires of expiation: Book-burnings and Catholic Missions in Restoration France', *French History*, 10 (1996), pp. 240–66.
11 Sperber, *Popular Catholicism*, p. 21.
12 Chadwick, *Popes*, pp. 25, 36.
13 Ibid., pp. 36–7.
14 Sperber, *Popular Catholicism*, pp. 35–6.
15 AST Segretaria Interna, Serie V (Miscellanea), Registro Lettere, Buon Governo e Polizia, 1814–20, Pres., Buon Governo, to Pres. of Police, Genoa, 18 September 1816.
16 Sperber also notes of the Rhineland that the Napoleonic legislation abolishing the confraternities had been resisted and imperfectly imposed, thus allowing many of them to re-form after 1815: Sperber, *Popular Catholicism*, p. 30.
17 Ibid., pp. 29–30.
18 Ibid., p. 278.
19 A.J. Reinermann, 'The Failure of Counter-revolution in Risorgimento Italy: The Case of the Centurions, 1831–1847', *Historical Journal*, 34 (1991), pp. 21–41. On the changing religious ethos among the Piedmontese elite: Bona, *Amicizie, passim*.
20 A. Jemolo, *Chiesa e Stato in Italia negli ultimi centi anni* (Turin, 1952), p. 15.
21 Bona, *L'Amicizie*, pp. 307–71 for Piedmont; pp. 371–464 for Italy. Candeloro, *Storia*, vol. 2, pp. 52–64: This reliance was as true, if not as intense, in the progressive states of Tuscany and Parma, as for the reactionary regimes in Piedmont and Modena.
22 On the persistence of 'social observance' in the north into the late nineteenth century: M. Bendiscioli, *Chiesa e Religiosità in Italia dopo l'Unità* (2 vols; Milan, 1973), vol. 2, p. 175.
23 Gramsci, 'I cattolici italianni', *Avanti!*, 22 December 1918, p. 22. Cited in *Religione*, pp. 36–7.
24 The importance of which even the Prussian regime came to appreciate in the Rhineland by the 1850s: Sperber, *Popular Catholicism*, pp. 279–82.
25 Gramsci, 'I cattolici italianni', in *Religione*, pp. 36–7.
26 Jemolo, *Chiesa e Stato*, p. 20.
27 Gramsci, 'I cattolici italianni', in *Religione*, p. 36.
28 Gibson, *Social History, passim*. Harris, *Lourdes*, Part II, *passim*, for this process at work in the transformation of Lourdes.
29 Taylor, *Magistrates*, p. 451.
30 Blackbourn, 'Progress and Piety', p. 148.
31 M. Agulhon, *The French Republic, 1879–1992*, trans. A. Nevill (Oxford, 1993), pp. 102–3.
32 Smith, *German Nationalism*, pp. 42–3.
33 Agulhon, *French Republic*, p. 110.

34 Ibid., p. 101.
35 Blackbourn, 'Progress and Piety', p. 156. See also Ross, 'Enforcing the Kulturkampf'.
36 Blackbourn, *Marpingen*, p. 371.
37 Ibid., p. 370.
38 Vanderwood, *Power*, pp. 61–4.
39 Smith, *German Nationalism*, pp. 44, 47.
40 Ibid., p. 44.
41 Agulhon, *French Republic*, p. 104.
42 Smith, *German Nationalism*, p. 46.
43 R. Rémond, *L'anticléricalisme en France de 1815 à nos jours* (Paris, 1999), pp. 172, 220.
44 The central thesis of Smith, *German Nationalism*.
45 Blackbourn, 'Progress and Piety', pp. 148–52.
46 ANP F7 7018 (Rome) Norvins to Savary, 26 October 1813.
47 Blackbourn, 'Progress and Piety', p. 145.
48 M. Agulhon, *The Republic in the Village*, trans. J. Lloyd (Cambridge, 1982). J. Merriman, *The Agony of the Republic: The Repression of the Left in Revolutionary France 1848–1851* (Kingston, 1984). P. Vigier, *La Seconde République dans la région alpine* (2 vols; Paris, 1963). T. Margadant, *French Peasants in Revolt: The Insurrection of 1851* (Princeton, 1979). For the critique: T. Judt, *Socialism in Provence, 1871–1914: a study in the origins of the modern French left* (Cambridge, 1979).
49 R. Dupuy, *De la Révolution à la Chouannerie. Paysans en Bretagne, 1788–1794* (Paris, 1988), p. 329.
50 Ibid., pp. 331–2.
51 D.M. Sutherland, *The Chouans. The Social Origins of Popular Counter-Revolution in Brittany, 1770–1796* (Oxford, 1982), pp. 309, 311, 312.
52 R.J. Rath, 'The Carbonary: their origins, initiation rites and aims', *American Historical Review*, 69 (1964), pp. 353–70. J.M. Roberts, *The Mythology of the Secret Societies* (St Albans, 1974).
53 For an excellent, wide-ranging overview: Blackbourn, *Marpingen*, pp. 22–7.
54 The distinction between the two was first developed in: C.M. Lucas, 'Résistances populaires à la Révolution dans le Sud-Est', in J. Nicolas (ed.), *Mouvements populaires et Conscience sociale (XVIᵉ–XIXᵉ siècles)* (Paris, 1985), pp. 473–88. Dupuy, *De la Révolution, passim*.
55 Smith, *German Nationalism*, pp. 42–4. On Mexico: Meyer, 'The *Cristada* peasant war'.
56 Smith, *German Nationalism*, p. 42.
57 Clark, *Modern Italy*, p. v.
58 Stendhal, *The Charterhouse of Parma*, trans. C.K. Scott Moncrieff (London, 1992), ch. 1.

BIBLIOGRAPHY

Unpublished primary sources

I have listed here only those sources cited directly in the text, although a larger number of series and boxes were consulted in the course of my research.

1 Archives Nationales de Paris (ANP)

The Archives Nationales remain, indisputably, the greatest and truly indispensable source for the study of Napoleonic Italy. Their remarkable character resides in not only the territorial breadth they offer, nor even the insights into high policy they provide, but the wealth of local detail found in sub-series F7 and F19. These series, especially, are essential to the study of Italian local history in this period.

Série: Archives Privées

Archives Privées, Fondes Roederer AP29 15–16 (Correspondance de Antoine Roederer, Préfet du dépt du Trasimène, 1810–14)

SOUS-SÉRIE: AFIV SECRÉTAIRERIE D'ÉTAT IMPÉRIALE

AFIV 909 (Journaux du Cabinet)
AFIV 945 (Journaux du Cabinet)
AFIV 1045–8 (Cultes)
AFIV 1303 (Journaux du Cabinet)
AFIV 1317 (Conseil d'État: Cultes)

Série: F Administration Générale

SOUS-SÉRIE F1bII (PERSONNEL)

F1bII (Rome, 1810–13)

SOUS-SÉRIE F1E (PAYS RÉUNIS ET ANNEXÉS)

F1E 74–80, Piémont (1801–5)
F1E 81–84, Ligurie (1805–6)
F1E 85–88, Parme, Plaisance et Guastelle (1805–8)
F1E 89–92, Toscane (1807–9)
F1E 93–175, États romains (1809–14)

SOUS-SÉRIE F7: POLICE-GÉNÉRALE

F7 4308 (Correspondance rélative au Piemont ans ix–xi, affaires politiques)
F7 6523A (Toscane, Rapports des Directeurs-Généraux de Police)
F7 6529 (Plaques 1–5, Clergé Romain)
F7 6530 (Clergé Romain)
F7 6531 (Cardinaux Romains)
F7 7016 (Correspondance et Bulletins de Police, Directeurs-Généraux de Police, Florence)
F7 7017 (Plaque I: Correspondance et rapports du Commissaire-Générale de Police, Gênes)
F7 7018 (Correspondance et Bulletins de Police, Directeurs-Généraux de Police, Rome)

F7 8791–8797, Dépt Apennines
F7 8798–8810, Dépt Arne
F7 8818–8834, Dépt Gênes
F7 8836–8841, Dépt Marengo
F7 8861–8865, Dépt Montenotte
F7 8866–8873, Dépt Ombronne
F7 8887–8907, Dépt Rome
F7 8488, Dépt Sesia
F7 8911–8925, Dépt Sture
F7 8926–8933, Dépt Taro
F7 8934–8938, Dépt Trasimène

SOUS-SÉRIE F19: CULTES / POLICE DES CULTES

F19 355–6–7, Dépts Italiens
F19 397, Cultes, Italie
F19 596, Cultes, Italie (Confréries-biens)
F19 703, Cultes, Organisation, Piémont, an xi–1813
F19 704, Cultes
F19 709A, Cultes (Circonscription des paroisses, Diocèse de Gênes)
F19 894, Cultes (Nominations aux cinq siéges vacants de la 27ème Division Militaire)

F19 900, Cultes (Dossier A: Tîtres Ecclésisastiques; États des personnes: Evêquès)
F19 901B, Police des Cultes (Italie)
F19 902, Police des Cultes (Italie)
F19 903, Cultes
F19 1019, Cultes, Parme (prêtres romains)
F19 1020, Cultes, Pinrole (prêtres romains)
F19 1021, Cultes, Bologne (prêtres romains)
F19 1022, Cultes, Plaisance (prêtres romains)
F19 1072A, Police des Cultes (Italie)
F19 1072B, Police des Cultes
F19 1075–1082, Police des Cultes (Italie)
F19 1925, Cultes (Concile Nationale, 1811)

SOUS-SÉRIE F20: STATISTIQUE

F20 102, Statistique, Dépt Rome

Série BB: Justice

SOUS-SÉRIE BB18 (AFFAIRES CRIMINELLES)

BB18 700–702, Affaires Criminelles, Cour Impériale, Rome

2 Archivio di Stato di Bologna (ASB)

Fondo: Legazione e Prefettura di Bologna (Dipartimento del Reno)

Titolo XX, Polizia: Rubrico 4 (Oziozi e Mendicanti); Rubrico 8 (Censura di libri stampe)
Titolo XXIV, Religione: Rubrico 6 (Ecclesiastici in genere); Rubrico 15 (Predicazioni e missioni); Rubrico 16 (Chiese ed Oratori); Rubrico 17 (Confraternite e Consorzi Secolari); Rubrico 19 (Frati e monache / Soppressione di Conventi)

3 Archivio di Stato di Cuneo (ASC)

Fondo: Epoca Francese

Mazzo 48 (Preti e Parrocchi)

223

4 *Archivo di Stato di Firenze (ASF)*

Fondo: Buon Governe

ARGOMENTO: CULTO

Filzie: 409 (1808)
            460 (1808)
            461 (1808)
            463 (1808)
            464 (1808)
            465 (1808)
            466 (1808)
            467 (1808)

Fondo: Prefettura dell'Arno

This series was not catalogued. I had to rely entirely on the expertise of the staff of the Archivio, for what they could find.

Amo 476
Amo 485

Fondo: Segretaria di Stato I

Filzia 810 (Affari, 1808)
Filzia 820 (Lettere e Rapporti, 1808–9)

5 *Archivio di Stato di Genova (ASG)*

Fondo: Prefettura Francese

ARGOMENTO: CULTO

Pacco 11, fasciolo 18 (Chiese e Parrocchi)
Pacco 12, fasciolo 19 (Oratorii)
Pacco 78, fasciolo 106 (Culto. Pratiche diverse)
Pacco 145, fasciolo 188 (Culto e Polizia)
Pacco 163, fasciolo 219 (Pratiche relative al Culto)
Pacco 231, fasciolo 8 (Lettere del Prefetto, Culto)

ARGOMENTO: POLIZIA

Pacco 170, fasciolo 230 (Police-Générale, 1808–13)

ARGOMENTO: CORRISPONDENZA DEL PREFETTO
Pacco 492 (Lettere relative al Culto)

6 *Archivio di Stato di Parma (ASP)*

Fondo: Dipartimento del Taro

Sezione II. Buste 69, fasciolo 104 (Preti Romani, 1810)

7 *Archivio di Stato di Torino (AST)*

Archivo della Corte

EPOCA FRANCESE
Governo Francese, Serie 1, Cart. 19 (Dossier Prov. Alba)

REGNO DI SARDEGNA (1814–49)
Serie Segretaria di Stato per Affari Esteri

Vescovi e Archivescovi. Correspondenza, Mazzo 1 (1814–21)
Lettere Ministri. Roma, Mazzo 312 (1814)

Serie Segretaria di Stato per Affari Interni, I, Protocolli 1140

Serie V (Miscellanea) Buon Governo e Polizia (1814–20)

Serie Materie Politiche

Lettere Ministri, Roma, Mazzo 405. Registro II

SEZZIONI RIUNITI
Intendenza di Pinerolo, Sezione IV (Correspondenza) Cat. 2 (Epoca Francese), Articolo 50 (1811)

8 *Archivio Comunale di Genova (ACG)*

Argomento: Impero Francese

Correspondenza, Filza 220 (1808)
Correspondenza, Registro 222 (1810–11)

Filza 328 (Commissarii di Polizia)

Argomento: Municipio Francese

Filzia 317 (Stabilimenti religiosi, 1806–14)

9 *Archives de la Guerre, Vincennes (AG)*

Serie C4–41 Correspondance du Maréchal Junot, Gouverneur-Général des
    États de Parme, Plaisance et Guastelle, janvier–juillet 1806

Published primary sources

D'Azeglio, M. (1966) *Things I Remember*, trans. E.R. Vincent, Oxford.
Moulard, J. (ed.) (1914) *Lettres inédites du comte Camille de Tournon, préfet
    de Rome, 1809–1814: 1re Partie: la politique et l'esprit public*, Paris.
Pacca, B. (1850) *Historical Memoirs of Cardinal Pacca*, trans. G. Head,
    London, 2 vols.
Spina, A. (ed.) (1985) *Diario della deportazione in Corsica del canonico di
    Albano G.B. Loberti (1810–1814)*, Albano.

Secondary sources

To list all the books and articles consulted in the course of the research for
this study would inflate its size unnecessarily. All those secondary sources I
have cited and used directly are cited in full on their first appearance in the
text.

INDEX

227